THE SKY IS RED

THE SKY IS RED

by

GEOFFREY T. BULL   1921 -

MOODY PRESS
CHICAGO

66 - 4124

CONTENTS

Part I

AUGUR OF TEMPEST

Chapter   *Page*

   I.   THE THRESHOLD OF THE DAY   9

  II.   POPPIES IN THE GRASS   19

  III.   EARLY ENCOUNTER   25

  IV.   THE REDDENING SKY   35

  V.   HORIZONS AFLAME   44

  VI.   GRAPPLING ON THE HEIGHTS   55

  VII.   FACING THE STORM   60

  VIII.   THE BATTLE IN THE CLOUDS   68

  IX.   RIFT OF BLUE   82

Part II

LIGHT ON THE MOUNTAIN

  X.   "COME AND DIE"   97

  XI.   "ONE OF YOU IS A DEVIL!"   106

  XII.   UP FROM THE SANDS   112

  XIII.   ON TO THE SUMMIT   118

  XIV.   THE MUSIC OF THE MOUNT   122

  XV.   THE NINTH NOTE   129

  XVI.   HIDDEN CONQUEST   135

  XVII.   NO NEST, NO REST   146

  XVIII.   NEW CLOTH, NEW WINE   155

CONTENTS

Part III

INTO THE MORNING

XIX.	THE WIND IN THE TREES	.	.	.	.	.	.	167
XX.	THE BREAK-OUT .	.	.	.	.	.	.	179
XXI.	THE NAME AND THE NAMES	.	.	.	.	.	188
XXII.	BACK TO THE SOURCE	.	.	.	.	.	.	193
XXIII.	WHERE FLOWS THE RIVER	.	.	.	.	.	202
XXIV.	THE MASTER BUILDER	.	.	.	.	.	.	207
XXV.	STREAM OF HIS POWER	.	.	.	.	.	.	225
XXVI.	SINEWS OF FELLOWSHIP	.	.	.	.	.	235
XXVII.	RED SKY AT DAWN	.	.	.	.	.	.	253

Part I

AUGUR OF TEMPEST

THE THRESHOLD OF THE DAY
POPPIES IN THE GRASS
EARLY ENCOUNTER
THE REDDENING SKY
HORIZONS AFLAME
GRAPPLING ON THE HEIGHTS
FACING THE STORM
THE BATTLE IN THE CLOUDS
RIFT OF BLUE

CHAPTER I

THE THRESHOLD OF THE DAY

"He shall be as the light of the morning,
    When the sun riseth, even a morning without clouds;
    As the tender grass springing out of the earth
    By clear shining after rain."   David

"On December the nineteenth, 1953, my guards and I were early at the Canton railway terminus, although the train did not leave until about nine. It was crammed to capacity and stopped at every station. The sun was very hot and the country was more tropical, with papia, pineapple plants and banana palms quite frequently to be seen. Station by station, I was moving towards the great moment. Year after year I had lived for this day. God knows all it had meant ..., I had been spiritually and psychologically bludgeoned, until I was dazed and broken in mind and spirit, but none had been able to pluck me from my Shepherd and His Father's hand. In the crisis, I had found my faith and love, at times, too weak to hold Him fast, but the final triumph was not to be in my hold of Him, but in His hold of me. His love would never let me go. He would keep that which I had committed unto Him. In His own time and way, He was determined and able to make me all the man that He had planned that I should be ...

"Just before two, the engine ground to a halt before the frontier. A somewhat officious uniformed person led us to the customs barrier. My paltry belongings were searched yet again. I asked for my passport. 'I have no passport for you,' the official said. It was their final deception. There was much over which I might have fretted. I had but a 'mildewy' fifteen and fivepence in money, which had remained with me my whole stay in China, unexchanged. It was totally inadequate for my immediate needs. For all that I had been told, Hong Kong would be bankrupt. I could count on no friends or missionaries being there, but I knew all things were in His hand. I somehow felt He would prove Himself again, as I stepped into liberty. I repacked my darned garments back into the grip. My name was scrawled on a piece of paper and sent through to the British authorities. I waited for the word to move forward. A distracted Chinese woman went past as I stood. It would seem that there was some irregularity in her papers, for she was weeping bitterly. I turned and the official beckoned me on. I stood now within six feet of the barbed wire barrier. I could see the spotlessly white office buildings of the British frontier post. Above them fluttered the Union Jack in brilliant sunshine. On the farther side I could see one or two people walking about, then suddenly a man came striding towards the narrow gap in the barbed wire. I was signalled through; People's China had yielded up her prey; but a few steps and all was over..." (See *When Iron Gates Yield*).

Today is December the twentieth, 1963; thus a whole decade now stands between that memorable moment of my release from Communist captivity, and this moment of fresh endeavour. This book, *The Sky is Red*, is the final volume to emerge from my prison years in Red China. The first in the series, entitled *When Iron Gates Yield*, told the story of what God meant to me behind the bars and beneath the "brainwashing". It has now been published on both sides of the Atlantic, being made available in five European languages, and also in Chinese. Although written in much weakness and on the brink of nervous collapse, God has nevertheless taken it up in an unexpected way, and letters have come over the years telling of His own blessing on its reading. Some years later *God Holds the Key* was penned. This was different. It comprised a record of meditations and reflections culled from the long, lonely days of solitary confinement. It included also many another thought of His matchless way and gave, I trust, at least some insight into His tender sequel of the great ordeal. This has also been published in Britain and America and has opened doors in distant places. For long now I have sensed that the final book of this prison series should be written. Again, I feel, it should be different. Whilst it will look back a little to earlier days yet I long for it to be a book pointing on to the Summit and the Ultimate Fellowship. Prior to my prison years God showed me His great Answer, as indeed He does to all who bring to Him the question of their lives. In the prisons of Red China He allowed me to prove that Answer. It may be in this book I shall have the opportunity, through His enabling, to declare it. Yet to me, every book attempted is at first an impossibility. How much more a book that sets out to give God's Answer to a world where men have come to feel there is no answer at all. Let us be under no misapprehension. It is beyond the reach of any of us to present the entire truth of God, or even to etch the real compass of the Gospel, but each of us is obliged to declare the Gospel in the measure it has become his own. It is only when Christ has become real to "someone" that He begins to be proclaimed to "everyone". When He becomes *my* Answer, then with conviction I will turn to you and say, "He can become *your* Answer"; and then facing the world together we shall say, "He is *the* Answer". In this way the Gospel of our God is proclaimed to the utmost horizons of humanity; and through all the scattered coasts of men there rings today that voice which will not be silenced; millions crying in the irresistible strength of the Spirit, "He *is* the Answer! He *is* the Answer! The Father sent the Son to be the Saviour of the world!"

Many, in actual fact, have set forth what has been termed "the Christian Answer to Communism" This has generally entailed an analysis of the essential, doctrinal confrontation of the two faiths. Without doubt, in this field there have been many helpful and informative contributions leading us on to a clearer understanding of the spiritual issues of the present era. A person who maintains that a Christian can be a Communist, or that a Communist can be a Christian, knows nothing of either faith. He is ignorant, both of the doctrine of God and the devices of Satan. We undoubtedly need clear statements of truth and error but it must be conceded that when all has been lucidly and systematically explained, the Pulse of the Answer may still not beat within our hearts and we may be far from realising our personal involvement in the conflict of spiritual forces behind "the powers that be". As one who has passed through the fire of battle in the Communist prisons of China, I believe it is inadequate merely to "take heed to the doctrine" of the Christian faith and show how it contradicts and refutes the sophistries of atheism. When Timothy faced the New Testament world of his day with its slave society, pagan philosophy and imperialist rule, Paul wrote to him and said, "Take heed to *thyself* and to the doctrine." There is no evidence that a point by point overthrow of heathen doctrine by Christian doctrine was to be the burden of Timothy's ministry. The Gospel was not just another school of thought entering the forums and arenas of Greece and Rome. It was not some new polemic of man but the original dynamic of God. No doubt on occasions Timothy dealt with some specific aspect of pagan teaching and effectively

refuted the gainsayer but he was not to consider himself as some detached
critic or reviewer of human affairs, proposing the corrective of Christian
doctrine where needed. He was part of the evil world to which he spoke.
The moral and spiritual cancer that gripped his age could point to roots
located in his own evil heart. "Take heed to thyself," says Paul, "and to
the doctrine", then you will preach it in saving worth.

Communism like any other spiritual and sociological evil is a symptom
of a diseased humanity. People frequently denunciate Communism as
being the cause of social upheaval. Actually it is not so much a cause but
an effect, being the outcome of a far more deeply seated cause found in the
heart of every individual. If, in a remote theological way, I state my
appraisal of a system like Communism, the danger is that I shall take up
the symptoms only, and fail to isolate the virus. If, however, I "take heed
to myself and to the doctrine", I shall find that it is not so easy to brand
the Communists as untouchables, for I then discover that I also have that
same inherent disease of sin. The Gospel of Christ does not deal with
matters superficially but fundamentally. It does not judge merely outward behaviour but recognises the basic nature of things. It brands me as
a specimen of my race. It does not allow me to analyse other people or
denounce other systems until its doctrine has been applied to my own heart.
The Christian is not allowed to be clever instead of being good. He is not
permitted to state the case for Christianity unless he "be an example of
the believers". In the end it is not cleverness that overcomes. Argument
can silence a man but only the goodness of God can transform a man
because it leads him to repentance. The Communist, like many a non-
Christian today, is not waiting for a more explicit statement of Christian
teaching but for a more dynamic presentation of Christian living. He is
not concerned so much with our doctrine in isolation, classified and docu-
mented, and set over against his doctrine. He has experts to cope with that
kind of situation, at least to his own satisfaction, if not to ours. It is when a
man has taken the Christ and His doctrine to himself and becomes that
kind of person which Communism has never been able to produce; it is
when men together take Christ and His doctrine, and become a community
that Communism has never been able to produce, that the Communist
perceives the death sentence of God upon his own system and belief. In
China "rice-Christians" and "rice-churches" presented no difficulty to
the new Communist regime. They were rapidly organised into propa-

ganda units for the People's Government. It was the living seed, men born of the incorruptible Word of God, that startled and dismayed them. These men, who had embraced the Truth until it had utterly remade them, were men and women who were prepared to fall into the ground and die. The fire of revolution scorched the Confucian earth of China to a veritable ideological cinder but this living seed proved absolutely indestructible. Today it is on the move. These men and women like their Lord are putting forth their roots in a dry ground and thriving on the unseen yet perennial springs of God.

What does Paul mean when he writes, "Take heed to thyself and to the doctrine"? He leaves us in no doubt. He says when writing to the Galatians, who were a people more concerned in discussing the truth than submitting to it, "I am crucified with Christ, nevertheless I live; yet not I, but Christ liveth in me". Here we see Paul and the doctrine side by side; more than that, Paul and the doctrine here are found to *coincide*. The death and resurrection of Jesus Christ were not only historical facts which formed the basis of Christian doctrine but historical facts in which Paul himself was irrevocably involved. Indeed, through faith, these very events had become spiritual facts in his personal experience.

There are some stories which leave an indelible mark upon the mind. One such is the last scene in *A Tale of Two Cities*, and it has become all the more real to me since I came face to face with execution in China. Carton has taken the place of Evrémonde in the condemned cell. He wears Evrémonde's clothes. He goes forward now to the guillotine to bear the consequences of Evrémonde's "guilt". It is the last morning and the innocent little seamstress is also led out to die. She clutches what she imagines is Evrémonde's hand, and Dickens writes:

"As the patient eyes were lifted to his face, he saw a sudden doubt in them, and then astonishment. He pressed the work-worn, hunger-worn young fingers, and touched his lips.

" 'Are you dying for him?' she whispered. 'And his wife and child?'

" 'Hush! Yes.'

" 'O you will let me hold your brave hand, stranger?'

" 'Hush! Yes, my poor sister; to the last' . . ."

So to the guillotine and the doing of "the far, far better thing". From the viewpoint of the revolutionary authorities in France, Evrémonde was dead, though it was Carton who had died. For ever in the experience of Evrémonde the events attending that execution morning would be written with an indelible pen. He could never be the same again. He could never live as if this had not happened.

"Peradventure," says Paul, "for a *good* man some would even dare to die but God commendeth His love toward us, in that, while we were yet *sinners*, Christ died for us." That is Christian doctrine. When Paul takes it to himself, then he says, "I am crucified with Christ, nevertheless I live, yet not I but Christ liveth in me, and the life that I now live, I live by the faith of the Son of God who loved me and gave Himself for me." As far as God is concerned, Saul of Tarsus is dead, judged and executed in Christ. By associating the doctrine with himself, Paul takes up God's view of Saul of Tarsus. God in the Cross put His great "No" upon the life, nature and works of Saul of Tarsus. In Christ's death Saul's guilt was expiated but, of course, all rights to himself were forfeited and now as dependent on the grace and bounty of God, all his life and activities find their spring and centre in Christ risen from the dead. The Cross and resurrection of Jesus Christ are thus irrevocably woven into his experience. He can never be the same again. He could never live as if this had not happened. Having taken God's view of himself, he now stands with God, and views the world and all its thought, activity and systems from God's standpoint. Thus not only is Paul crucified to the world, but the world is also crucified to him. God's "No" is equally upon that world of which he is a part. This is the man who can stand with spiritual poise and power against the devil, whether it be in the tyranny of Rome, the philosophy of Greece, or the bigotry of Judaism. He does not necessarily have to analyse their error, piece by piece, and fit an answer to every query they raise. As he himself was judged at the Cross so he sees the whole world and everything in it judged likewise at the Cross. "The axe is laid at the root of the tree." God's answer is a new seed, a new planting, a new creation. And the man in whom the Cross and resurrection of Christ are both historical and spiritual facts is the man who speaks for God. He is the man before whom the Communists and all other God-haters and God-deniers tremble. It is then that the materialist for the first time in his life is confronted with the Eternal God in the life of a fellow human-being.

It is not without significance that in the history of martyrdom a young believer is sometimes found going to the stake with greater resolution than a mature theologian. Better a grain of truth sown in the soft soil of the heart than a whole granary of truth stored in the dry chambers of the intellect. In the case of the young believer the little truth he knows is essentially his and the flames of persecution cannot divide him from it. In the case of the mature theologian much of what he holds may be untried, in which case, a wisp of smoke is sufficient to blurr his professed conviction. The well-known Bible teacher, Graham Scroggie, was once asked, "What do you believe?" He said, "I believe what I am prepared to die for." When Christ's word runs all the way through us like the watermark in a banknote, then the world is prepared to recognise us as valid currency in the realm of truth and this applies both to the individual child of God and also to the local church of God. It is true on the personal level and it is true on the corporate level; and inasmuch as these are the only two levels of human existence which the world knows, it is important that the Answer of God be declared in an authoritative and valid way as adequate for both the life of the individual and the life of the community, which is prepared to recognise the True God, revealed in Christ, as its only Lord.

Communism also professes to be concerned with the individual and the masses, but for different reasons. With it "the masses" come first and the individual is a mere corollary. For the Christian, each individual born into the world represents an act of God, derived from a decision of God which is rooted in the purposes of God, and in some measure, however clouded by the Fall, each individual reasserts the image of God. Therefore, whoever the person is, we cannot view him as just "anyone" because God has made him "someone". "The masses" for the Christian truly include every one, and when God says He loved the world, I am fully justified in saying, "The Son of God loved me, and gave Himself for me." Communists on the other hand are restrictive in the use of the words "man" and "the masses". They frequently qualify the noun "man" in the new regime in China by speaking of a person as "a man of the people"* "The people" or "the masses" are similarly terms of restrictive use. These terms refer to the revolutionary classes. When I was in their hands and viewed as "an enemy of the people" I was made to feel that I was "no one" until they made me "someone". I was less than a real man† that is,

---

* Chinese—"*i ko jen min*".

† The Chinese term of abuse, "*Ni pu shih jen*"—"You're not (a) man", was used to humiliate resisting political prisoners.

less than a rightly functioning social unit—until I could be constituted one of "the people". This privilege, they maintain, is in their power to grant or deny. "The masses" therefore represent to the Communist the sum total of all persons whom they acknowledge as authentic individuals in their regime. Communism professes to frame all its policies to the ultimate good of the masses. This is the great category. Illusive, nebulous and intangible, this sociological term, "the masses", and its vaunted "good" haunts society like some spectre-god. This is "the sacred name" in which all labour is hallowed, by which all morality is decreed, to which every human talent is sacrificially offered. To hinder the determined good, contradict the means adopted to reach that end, transgress state law (which for the Communists is but the instrument whereby the interests of the mystical masses are preserved) is punishable by social annihilation. That is not necessarily execution but the loss of "people's status". In other words you cease to be one of "the masses" and in that sense you cease to be "someone". You become estranged and divorced from your fellows. You are removed because you are "infectious" and kept until you are reformed, or alternatively, if you should prove unreformable then you are finally removed altogether. The interest of Communism in the individual is not then a question of seeking the good of any particular individual but of ensuring that all individuals will contribute to this constantly publicised and idolised "good" of the masses. His labour and cooperation, voluntary or enforced, is essential for the arriving at that goal. He is taught that there is no good for him now, independent of the total good then. He is urged to solve his inward emotional crises in this regard by casting in his lot with "the masses" and working for "the good" of all. To achieve this purpose the instruction of the individual never ceases. At work, at play, in education or entertainment, in culture or religion, he is made unceasingly aware that there is nothing worth living for, nothing worth dying for, nothing worth procreating for, other than the official good enunciated by the Communist Party as the ultimate and inevitable goal of an "evolving" human society. In this way real men and women are made the slaves of a phantom. Beneath the aurora of this fantastic surmisal the millions are nurtured, cajoled, indoctrinated, regulated and employed, yet already behind this phantom "good" and the mask of the party, we see the face of the devil. It is a strong delusion but many there are who still prefer to believe a lie.

The Answer of God comes therefore in Christ to satisfy the heart longings of a lost and darkened humanity on both the level of the individual and the masses; both on the personal level and on the corporate level; as men alone and as men together. He gives us the Answer as *individuals* by showing us the way of Christian discipleship, a way that leads us out of our personal shadows into the high noonday of God; a way that lifts us from the sands of our sordid lives to the summit of the hill of the Lord. He gives us the answer for *corporate living*, the Answer if you like for the *masses*, by showing us a way of fellowship that leads us out of our self-centredness into the great "togetherness" of His Church, the Body of Christ. God's Answer involved Himself. If *I* embrace that Answer it will involve myself. If *we* embrace that Answer it will involve ourselves. Individually or collectively it is impossible to know that Answer, or present that Answer, without facing that involvement.

God's Answer on both these levels comes to us simultaneously and is worked out concurrently. If I become a child of God through faith in the Lord Jesus Christ then I must recognise that I am a member of the Church of God, otherwise I shall become wrongly individualistic in my faith. When I talk it will always be my faith, my experience, my work or even my sin. This leads increasingly to feeling, living and working independently of other Christians, when in actual fact there are no independent Christians. On the other hand, it is possible to become too ecclesiastically minded. We then tend to move only with "the masses" of our group and talk about "our Church", or what the Church does, and what the Church says, until the Church becomes our conscience and the Church's authority something in our minds which God never meant it to be. This leads to a discounting of the genuine individual witness of others who are serving sincerely in the Name of Christ. God's answer to each of us alone, and to all of us together, is not a divided answer. The individuals in the Gospels called to be disciples, are ultimately in the Acts, fused by the baptism of the Spirit, into the one fellowship of the Church.

Communism is also a belief with an eschatology. It points on to a culmination of "ultimate bliss" without God. There is not one shred of evidence that man left to himself in Time has ever been happy or ever will be. On the contrary we have sound reasons for believing from what we see in Time, that man left to himself in Eternity, will experience only the hell of the Bible. The Christian Answer shows that men and women all down history have proved God under every possible circumstance to be all that Christ revealed Him to be. Their testimony shows that it is possible to know "God with us" now, and to look forward with certainty to being with God for ever then. In this faith and in this fellowship both the child of God and the Church of God march on through the years to their final goal.

This book will consequently be in three parts. The first part will be a symposium of incidents drawn from earlier years. These have been specially selected to reveal some of the challenging and formative experiences leading up to my full-scale battle with Communism during my prison days in China. The second part will deal with the call of Christ to the pathway of discipleship, wherein we find His Answer for the individual. The third part will deal with His corporate Answer which the disciples ultimately found in the fellowship of the Church, the Body of Christ.

When the whole is penned, the book may well point to but the first steps in the Way, utter but a fragment of the Truth and exhibit just a glimpse of the great Life we are called to share, but of this I am sure, that outside of Christ there is no other Way; that outside of Christ there is no other Truth; and that outside of Christ there is no other Life. The word of Christ remains unchanged, "No man cometh to the Father but by Me".

Once this Star has risen in our hearts, we shall find ourselves on the threshold of His day.

CHAPTER II

POPPIES IN THE GRASS

"And the dragon stood before the woman which was ready to be delivered for to devour her child as soon as it was born".

Revelation 12

"Then Herod slew all the children . . . from two years old and under."

Matthew 2

"Unto us a Child is born . . . and the government shall be upon His shoulder."

Isaiah 9

IT was the dawn of an era in the affairs of Northumbria. Rumour was rife amongst the people and the king was conscious of the growing resentment of the druid priesthood at the intrusion of an alien faith. Feeling he must take the initiative, he called for an evening assemblage of his counsellors. In the long chamber the torches flickered, and on the great hearth the huge logs burned to a flame, as one by one men of influence and authority took their place. Outside the sun had long since sunk below the hills and the cold chill of the night struck through the glassless windows. Suddenly a cry rang through the hall. The low mumble of voices was immediately hushed to silence. It was the herald of the king. A few moments passed and His Majesty entered. All present rose, and walking through them he took his place upon the throne at the end of the council chamber . . .

Hour by hour the discussion dragged on. The druids were inflexible. False teachers could not be tolerated. What would they add to the ancient druid faith? What anyway was this "Jesus doctrine"? Such impudence would be paid for in blood. The king was uneasy. Who were these emissaries professing to bring a Gospel? Who was their God? Could they afford to abuse these men? Dare they murder them? At the precise moment of the king's dilemma a strange thing happened. A bird flew in out of the darkness and was caught for a moment in the light of the pinewood flares. Almost as quickly, it was away, out through the farther window, gone again into the night. The king paused for a moment then rose to address his gathered courtiers and priests. "The life of man" he said, "is like the flight of a bird across a firelit room . . . out of the Great Deep . . . into the Great Deep . . . ! If these men can tell us from whence we come and whither we go should we not receive them?" No voice dare speak, for God Himself had spoken; and in a little while, the Christian Gospel was proclaimed through all the kingdom of Northumbria.

God is the God of hope and He alone it is who brings us hope from the Eternal Deep. Down all the centuries men have probed and searched the depths of the inner space of their own personality and the outer space of their cosmic environment, but they have not found Him, for "who by searching can find out God?" They have returned from their quest disillusioned and dismayed. They have verified consciously or unconsciously the Biblical definition of hopelessness, which is to be "without God in the world". Men have looked to men, to the knowledgeable and venerable of science, philosophy and religion, yet few are the wise that find Him, save by the light of Heaven's Star. Then, and only then, do they see that in the Babe of Bethlehem the fulness of the Godhead dwells. Here Reason falters but Faith begins to understand.

God's hope is not in the adult, however mature he may appear, but in the child; not in the grown-up world but in the world that is yet to grow; not in the gnarled old oak but in the acorn fresh and green. God's hope is not in our endings but in His beginnings. Not in the old men but in the new men. Not in the full bloom of the fragrant flower but in the seed it sows. Not in the years that are spent but in the years that are yet to be. Not in what I have become but in what I can yet become if God be with me. God's hope is not in Adam, a man complete yet doomed to fall. God's hope is in the Babe, the virgin's seed. No other god has come from the Deep to take up manhood. No other god has taken manhood out and upward into the Deep as God. The Christian faith is the only word in history concerning our origin and destiny. It has therefore the exclusive authority to interpret that mystic interval between.

In the child all the purposes of God lie latent. In the man they know fulfilment. God's hope for a babe is that once a man, the man's heart shall be after God's heart; that the promise in the gift of life might be realised in the destiny of life. God stakes His all in the child. He came to us as a child and He has decreed that we must come to Him as a child. There was no other way for Him to come. Only then could we take Him in our arms and say, "My Salvation". There is no other way for us to come. Only then can He hold us in His arms and say, "My son, give me thine heart." The child is ever the choice of God for the achievement of His purposes. "When Israel was a child," God says, "I loved him."

Turning the pages of His timeless Book one finds as time unfolds, that

—the child is God's chosen means for the continuance of the race (Genesis 1, v. 28);
—the child is God's chosen vessel for the advent of the King (Isaiah 9, v. 6);
—the child is God's chosen lesson for the entrance of the Kingdom (Matthew 18, v. 4);
—the child is God's chosen allegory for the teaching of the Covenants (Galatians 4, v. 23);
—the child is God's chosen object for electing grace (Romans 9, v. 11);
—the child is God's chosen emblem of millennial concord (Isaiah 11, v. 6).

We can say the very counsels of God are sown on earth in the birth of a child. Isaiah in an age of despair grasped this revelation and with the supreme confidence of faith announced to all, "Unto us a child is born, unto us a son is given: and the government shall be upon His shoulder." The hopes of God in Heaven above and on earth beneath are vested wholly in the Child of His choice.

> "The hopes and fears of all the years
> Are met in Thee tonight."

This being so we are bound to believe that the God who sets His whole hope in *the* Child must surely have a hope for *every* child. This is certain for He appoints to each an angel. If He holds a sparrow as it dies, does He not cradle an infant, as it is born? He tells us without qualification, "It is not the will of your Father that one of these little ones perish." Again He affirms, "of such is the Kingdom of Heaven". There is not a single child consigned to hell. God has greater hopes for every little one. It is only as grown in unbelief that man can come to judgement. Consequently every child becomes a battlefield. We may run our fingers through his hair and lovingly caress his rosy cheeks, but let us remember, though poppies danced in Flanders fields, it was a battlefield for all that. The sweetness of the spring was churned into the blood and mud of war. Thus Satan contends for the child. The State clutches at the child. The religionist indoctrinates the child. In the fertile mind of the child the wheat of God and the tares of the devil are sown. Only God knows what the harvest will be.

The genealogy of the Christ is a certain proof of the importance Satan attaches to the Child. For Satan every child is an unknown quantity and down the centuries Satan feared nothing more than the advent of the Messiah, for the Christ-Child was that Seed whose life the devil would never be able to extinguish. Even though He fall into the ground and die yet in resurrection His triumph and His Seed were sure. He was declared "the Seed of David", the One in whom the Throne of God would be established in the earth. He was declared "the Seed of Abraham", the One in whom all the nations of the earth would be blessed. He was declared "the Seed of the woman", the One who should bruise the serpent's head. In the long line of succession culminating in the Babe born King, time and again Satan sought to strike a mortal blow, and every time it was against the children that he fought. Kill the child! Destroy the Seed! Only thus did he imagine he could break the interlock of destiny. So it was Pharaoh destroyed the baby boys of Israel; Athaliah murdered the seed royal; and Herod slew the innocents. Satan would devour the Man-Child if He could. "I will," said God, addressing the devil, "put enmity between thee and the woman, and between thy seed and her seed; it shall bruise thy head, and thou shalt bruise his heel."

As Satan sought to conquer and subdue *the* Child, so he seeks to conquer and subdue *every* child, for God begets a purpose in all the children whom He brings to birth. God rebukes His worshippers for idle words. It is not possible that He should engage in idle deeds. God's hopes are never generalisations. They are always specific. He never creates without reason. There is no being born, independent of the Divine intention. Paul, deeply conscious of His destiny, sees his birth as an act of God, just as his new birth was an act of God. The whole course from the womb to the tomb is for him to be related by faith to the very pleasure of his Creator. "It pleased God," he says, "who separated me from my mother's womb, and called me by His grace, to reveal His son in me, that I might preach Him amongst the heathen." Satan's hostility to such acts of God in the realm of procreation are evidenced in striking ways in the Scripture. Not only does he seek to slay children but he seeks also to forestall their conception.

In this connection it is noteworthy that all the Nazarite children mentioned in the Bible were born of barren women. They are Samson, Samuel and John the Baptist. The destiny of each in their particular period of history was so great, that God had to perform a miracle to break through the satanic dearth instilled in lifeless wombs. Each of these children prior to birth involved God in a committal of Himself to His people. Each was a subject of prophecy and of promise. We cannot over-estimate the spiritual warfare that wages about the birth of a child. It is little wonder that, once born, the conflict proceeds with such intensity. Many a man spends his whole live striving to achieve a postponement of death, and for fear of it is ever in a state of bondage. It would be good sometimes if instead o thinking always of our death we would ponder the circumstances of our birth. Then would we be more ready to fulfil the longings of the One who gave us life . . .

Somewhere in the early nineteen hundreds, there lived in a terrace-house in South-East London, a young hard-working housewife called Eleanor Taylor. At that time she would be about thirty years of age. Her husband was employed as an engineer and her two little girls had not long started school. Although she came from a religious family there now seemed so much to do, that she could hardly bring herself to think about the intricacies of spiritual matters or become too involved with churches and ministers. It did so happen, however, on one occasion that an evangelical preacher visited the district and managed to get a hearing somewhere up in the High Street about a mile away from where the Taylors lived. Whether it was just curiosity on their part, or a Higher Hand at work, who can tell, but one night Mr. and Mrs. Taylor allowed themselves to be taken to hear the evangelist. When they returned nothing passed between them, and it seemed that the evening had been largely a waste of time.

It was the next morning when it happened. Mrs. Taylor was down on her knees as usual, brush in hand, blackleading the big old-fashioned grate for all she was worth, when all at once she was conscious of the Presence of God. She was not really used to praying, but she knew almost instinctively what she should do. She was suddenly conscious of being a sinful woman with a heart as black as the grate before her, and whilst still on her knees she cried out to God for His forgiveness and asked the Lord Jesus Christ, who died for her, to be her Saviour. Later in the day her husband returned from work and she immediately told him that she had been converted. He looked at her, and felt ashamed. "I was afraid to tell," he said quietly, "but I have been converted too." It was not long before the two little girls noticed a difference in their parents. "I've got a new mummy," said Ethel, the little one, and so she had. After just a short while Mrs. Taylor introduced Ethel also to her new-found Lord and the young girl grew up to marry a fellow-Christian and bring up her own family in the fear of God. When their firstborn son came along it was thus understandable that they should bring him to God and say in His Presence, in the words of Hannah, "I have lent him to the Lord; as long as he lives he shall be lent to the Lord". This was 1921, and as I think on the background and circumstances of my birth, Paul's words take on for me a special significance. "I call to remembrance the unfeigned faith that is in thee, which dwelt first in thy grandmother Lois, and thy mother Eunice and I am persuaded that in thee also." My grandmother lived to see me converted to God, baptised, and later go out as a missionary to China and Tibet. She also lived to see her prayers answered in my return from Communist captivity. From the moment of her first encounter with Jesus Christ there on the hearth, she never looked back; and over half a century later, when she uttered her last audible words on earth, she cried, "O how I love Him! O how I love Him!" So, steadfast to the end, she passed to her reward . . . Such was the faith that dwelt first in my grandmother . . .

In 1921 another event took place many thousands of miles away from London. Strangely enough, it was the birth of the Communist Party in China. Nearly thirty years later they and I were to arrive on the remote frontiers of Tibet at precisely the same time; their intention being to bring Tibet to the feet of Marx and mine to bring Tibet to the feet of Jesus Christ. Some may call this an accident of birth but Solomon's words still tell their wisdom. "There is a time to be born . . . a time for every purpose under heaven."

CHAPTER III

EARLY ENCOUNTER

"Time would fail me to tell of . . . David . . . who through faith . . .
turned to flight the armies of the aliens."   Hebrews 11
"David prevailed over the Philistine with a sling and with a stone."
                                                  1 Samuel 17

I MUST have been little more than eight years of age when one evening, walking home from an evangelistic service conducted by the well-known missionary Harold Wildish, I made a startling announcement to my parents. We were just crossing the bridge over the underground railway at Burnt Oak when I turned to them and said, "I have been converted tonight." Looking back over the years it is hard to assess the spiritual impressions and experiences of one's childhood, but it seems that from then on I began to have some inkling of my future.

The time came at school, as it often does, when the teacher asked me, "And what are you going to be when you grow up?" Unhesitatingly I answered, "A missionary". One of my school friends, about nine years of age, also ventured such an enquiry on one occasion. "I'm going to be an engineer," he told me; "what about you?" "Oh, I'm going to be a missionary," was the unexpected reply. He was undoubtedly impressed . . . After a few moments' reflection he began to murmur his approval, "Yes," he said, "you will get about twenty pounds a week!" I must say, I had hardly thought of that; and twenty pounds was a lot of money in 1930!

When I was ten we had a holiday in the Isle of Wight at the popular seaside resort of Sandown. There a fresh pointer towards the future task was given. We had gone for a walk on the promenade one Sunday evening after tea, and had eventually been drawn to the edge of a large crowd standing on the waterfront. "For a long while that evening the old white-haired man had stood on the granite steps of the war memorial. He had preached with an impassioned love to the holiday crowds and now as his voice died away, they slowly dispersed. As darkness began to fall, the air grew fresher and we were left standing, looking towards the rough stone cross silhouetted against the evening sky. Away behind, the English Channel stretched into the twilight and the soft wash of the waves blew up gently on to the footworn shore. It was a moving experience, for during the evening the old preacher seemed to catch sight of someone, then, silently but deliberately, he threaded his way through the listeners until he astonished us by coming exactly to where we stood. A few words passed and then he looked down at me. Very tenderly he put his hand upon my shoulder and spoke to me. "God has a great work for you my boy— see that you do it." He had only met us in the morning. He knew nothing about us as a family. It seemed a strange thing to say to a child. In a few moments he was gone, lost to view among the people until he reappeared at the foot of the memorial. Being on holiday we never saw him together again . . .*

In spite of all this, however, I proved to be a poor frightened Christian at school and frequently hid my light under a bushel of silence. Soon after enrolling at Christ's College, a big school in Finchley, I felt out of my depth. I made no witness, quickly lost ground in class, and found out that compared with other boys, I was no good at games. Thus I had few real friends. I took the London matric the first time, and failing in English, groaned under another year of "swotting", finally managing to achieve a pass the next year in the unreal atmosphere of *A Midsummer Night's Dream* and *The Rape of the Lock*. I longed for the moment when I could be done with it all. When I was in the fifth form the English master arranged a debate one evening in the school library. The subject for discussion was 'Christianity versus Communism'. I felt vaguely attracted by the subject and went along. The library was packed with fifth and sixth formers. One of the "brains" of the school stated the case for Communism. I was utterly amazed. To me it was a brilliant performance by a boy who could only have been eighteen months older than myself and probably no more than seventeen-and-a-half. I cannot even remember the other boy, who formally took up the case for Christianity. It looked as if the young Communist and his second would carry the floor. Just before the debate was due to close a young fellow stood up and asked if he might say a few words. As far as the school was concerned he was a nondescript. My

* See *God Holds the Key*.

interest immediately quickened, for in a way he was rather like myself, a boy attending the school, of whom nobody took any particular notice. He started off almost apologetically. "I know you may not feel I am a very good Christian," he said, "but I want you to know, I do believe on the Lord Jesus Christ as my Saviour." He gave what might be termed a brief testimony as to how real Jesus Christ was to him and then sat down. The master decided as usual to put the issue to the vote. In spite of the scintil-lating presentation of the Communist case, Christianity carried the floor. Anyone teaching boys will know that most of them are not particularly emotional and I doubt if many in the library that night had come with a serious ideological interest; yet the reality of the Lord Jesus Christ in the experience of one of their school friends rang true, whilst the able colla-tion of data by the sixth-form boy, outstanding though it was, left them cold. As a secret Christian I went home feeling uncomfortable. That boy had spoken out for Christ yet I had kept silent.

In the Easter of that year something happened which completely liberated my personality. Having nothing to do in the holidays I attended a series of outings, games and meetings arranged by one of the local evangelical churches. In some way or other I allowed myself to become involved in a young people's prayer meeting. Normally I would have kept clear of anything like this, but there it was, I was in it now and had to sit it through. Then suddenly to my blank astonishment the leader, a young man hoping to engage in the work of the ministry, said, "Now we are all going to pray." This was not just a formal intimation at the commencement of the meeting. He really meant it and pointing to the youngster at the end of the row he said in a matter-of-fact way, "Now we'll begin with you." Whether or not this was the Scriptural procedure for prayer meetings caused him no qualms. As far as he was concerned he had chosen his own procedure and we had to obey. To my dismay and confusion the young person stood up and without demur prayed simply and sincerely with no apparent effort or nervousness. Then the next youngster stood, and then the next. I was dumbfounded. The panic in my heart reduced me to a state where I would have trembled all over had I not been so busy tensing myself for the awful moment. How could I ever do it? Yet how could I not do it? Not knowing what I did I was suddenly on my feet. "It" had come to me. I have not the faintest recol-lection of what I said but I did say something and then sat down. It had been an appalling experience. Yet once it was over an unexpected joy began rising within me. After a Sunday evening service a little while later on, I found myself longing to speak to a friend about Christ. In the old days this would have been impossible but now when the opportunity arose I just did it. As the words came I realised that everything was different. Somehow the Lord I secretly trusted was setting me free. The days that followed were very wonderful to me. That Light of Life of which Jesus spoke had come into my soul.

One night I arrived late at a meeting and because the speaker had commenced his talk I felt I could not go in. It was a cold night and snow was falling. I stood waiting on the steps of the meeting room, wondering what to do. Then I was joined by another late-comer, a young fellow about my own age. We chatted together and I soon found out that he did not know Christ as his Saviour. As the meeting proceeded inside, I told him outside there on the steps what it meant to be saved. As the time went by I said to him, "You realise you can be saved don't you?" "Yes," he said. "Well, do you want to be saved!" "I do," he replied. Finally I put the question, "Then are you willing to be saved?" To my great joy he answered, "I am willing," and there as we sheltered from the snow, we bowed our heads and he received Christ into his heart. Looking back now, I feel this was the very first soul I ever led to the feet of my Lord. In bringing His good news to others the purpose of God for my life was beginning to unfold before my eyes.

When I was about eighteen, I began to help in mission-work in the slums of Islington. This was a far cry from the prim little suburb where I had been brought up. Whilst my father and mother were not wealthy and had to plan carefully when my sister and I were small, yet I had never been conscious of poverty and had freely enjoyed all the comforts of life. Now I was confronted by another kind of society altogether. The wild antics and sheer disrespect of the boys at the Bible Class made me uneasy and awkward. I did not know what to say to them. Their language and dress were so different. In fact I felt they were just impossible; and they probably thought the same about me. The back alleys and the sinister looking tenements were like some dark forest which I had no real desire to enter for fear of what was lurking there! In my growing youthful zeal I nevertheless took part in this work and in various other evangelical efforts in the greater London area. One young fellow I contacted at an open-air meeting put the situation in a nutshell. He abruptly said, "I'm on the other side of the fence from you fellows." Many may feel it is their duty in society to remove the *fences* but they go deeper than we know, for they represent in reality our own social *defences* forged in fires of selfishness ever burning in our hearts. It was hard to submit to the idea that I and my message must be dismissed as unacceptable merely because of some unseen fence. Why should I be written off by other young people of my age? I did not speak with an Oxford accent. I was not a member of the upper classes. It had never occurred to me that class distinction works both ways, upwards as well as downwards. What really is class? Is it something objective or subjective? Is it something outside of me or something inside me? Where are the fences in actual fact? In the church to which I belonged there were both rich and poor, yet we worked together as one big family. People said that one of our members was a millionaire yet it never made any difference for that particular Christian was one of the humblest and most conscientious of us all. What most of us have failed to learn is that on whatever side of the proverbial social fence we may be, fences have far more to do with what we are than with what we have; but in those early days this was something I had not even begun to analyse.

About this time I had my first public dealings with the self-styled champions of the working class. Orange Hill Road was a pleasant street that ran between Woodcroft Hall, where we Christians gathered, up to the community centre about half a mile away. On either side of the road, neat little blocks of houses, set in their own gardens and enhanced by numerous greens and their surrounding footpaths, made this London County Council Estate look already well established. In its day it had been an ambitious scheme. Some years earlier, hundreds of families had been brought out to this suburb of Burnt Oak from the slums of the city. For them it was a new way of living and whilst at first the coal tended to be stored in the bath and old habits died hard, yet gradually ideas changed and many of the houses became fine little homes. As a church in the district we had a great outreach to the people. Over a thousand children attended our Sunday School, large numbers of local folk attended the services and Bible Classes, and a good measure of practical relief found its way into the homes wherever tragedy, unemployment or drunkenness had brought its sorrows. Such was the original social background, however, of the people at that time, that the Communist Party did not find it difficult to gain a foothold, thus it had its following too. In fact I should imagine for many a year the church meeting at Woodcroft Hall, the Salvation Army and the Communist Party were the only groups who convened regular open-air meetings to proclaim their teaching to the neighbourhood. Now it so happened that the organisers of the local community centre, a purely secular body, decided to convene a public meeting for young people in which a spokesman from each of the various youth organisations in the district would give a paper on "The Ideals of Youth". The invitation had been received by the young people's leader of our church and after some thought he approached me to see whether I would be willing to be their spokesman. For one who until comparatively recently had been ashamed to speak openly for Christ, it was a big assignment. But God was enabling me to open my mouth in witness as never before and I took up the challenge with real enthusiasm. On the appointed evening a contingent of some twenty or thirty of our own young people came along to give their support and soon the meeting was under way. A number of young men between eighteen and twenty-three spoke on behalf of the various youth groups. The Young Communist League had been sent an invitation but for some reason or other had declined to send a representative. Now my turn had come. "What had Christ to offer? What was His programme?" I asked, using these rhetorical questions in an attempt to sound contemporary. In the next ten minutes I outlined what I believed the Bible taught were the ideals of youth and then I closed by saying, "Listen to what He says", and opening my Bible at Luke, chapter four, I began to recite the Messianic prophecy which Christ read in the synagogue at Nazareth. Surely this was His manifesto . . . "The Spirit of the Lord is upon me, because He hath anointed me to preach the Gospel to the poor . . ." but then I faltered. I wanted to go on to His other great words, "He hath sent me to heal the brokenhearted, to preach deliverance to the captives, and recovering of sight to the blind and to set at liberty them that are bruised . . ." but I could hardly proceed further. As soon as I uttered the words "to preach the Gospel to the poor", jeering and laughter broke out from a block of young people in the middle of the audience. The Young Communist League was there after all. I could almost hear the members saying, "That's fine . . . on you go—preach the Gospel to the poor . . . A fat lot of good that will do them when they're starving." As their voices quietened I read on to the end of the passage, feeling nervously limp and spiritually crumpled. The archaic English of the authorised version so full of beauty and strength to me had been publicly derided, but what was worse, the very message of Christ had been laughed to scorn. Perhaps I had not expressed myself very well, yet I knew I believed every word I read and every word I said. As I sat down, my young friends from the church clapped me to the echo. It was kind of them, of course, although I realised only too well there was no spiritual elation to be found in that. What smarted and what remained was the laughter of that hidden group. Perhaps I had failed to realise just how spiritual the nature of the conflict was. This was not a question of young people airing their views. This was "a fight to the death" but none of us knew it yet. I have forgotten every one of the other groups represented at that meeting. For me there was only one group to contend with, the group that never sent a spokesman but was there just the same. Its members meant business and so did I. Little did we realise we would fight it out in the blood-drenched arena of red China in years to come. Its comrades would have guns and prison bars, iron chains and handcuffs then. They would bring to bear upon me all the dread equipment of their thought reform machine. Yet the word of my Lord would still defeat them and in the face of all their tyranny he still would set the prisoner free.

Meanwhile there were other battles to be won on a less spectacular front. It is one thing to preach, but God is concerned first of all with character. Soon I began to pride myself on being a keen Christian. I could take part in public prayer; I could give my testimony; I could speak at meetings. In the morning I would read my Bible before I went to work. To me in those days this was real Christianity.

At my place of employment, in a London bank, I was a junior clerk. Every morning I passed through those large doors, over the marble floor and into those mysterious precincts of polished mahogany, where cheques, ledgers and sometimes empty coffee cups lay in seeming confusion. Many were the escapades of those early days in earning my own living. I started with the modest wage of twenty-seven-and-six a week and although I had now matriculated and even passed the competitive bank examination, I found that my first job was writing the figures "1937-1938" at the head of each page of a large ledger. It was all very humiliating though no doubt very good for me. I prided myself on my mathematics—in fact it was the one subject in which I did obtain some distinction before leaving school—yet try as I might, I could hardly ever make the long columns of figures agree at my first attempt. I was better at making the coffee than doing arithmetic. Being confronted now with men rather than schoolboys, the first impact of the outside adult world began to make itself felt. My first manager was a freemason. As a Christian I disapproved strongly even then of anyone being a freemason but I soon found I was not the only one. The accountant, a likeable fellow, but one of those men who drenched every sentence he spoke with bloodcurling adjectives, really let his feelings be known. The manager had been given a better post in town, yet this accountant was not appointed our new manager. "If you've got to be a freemason," he said, "to get on, then I'll *never* be a freemason!" The bitterness with which he spoke remains with me to this day; and I became convinced that here was a serpent of the business world and an accursed thing to be avoided at all costs. The ledger clerk was rather Bohemian in outlook. Although unmarried, he shared a bungalow in the country with another fellow and two girls on certain weekends. As I viewed the a all, in spite of my general inefficiency at my job, I nevertheless felt I was their moral superior and as I had opportunity, tried to convey to them that I belonged to Christ. God, however, has His own way of showing us to ourselves. Amongst the many books that were daily trollied out of the subterranean strong-room was a copy of the bank regulatios. This irksome volume governed the activities of the staff and decreed the way in which the work of the bank was to be performed. It was, to say the least of it, uninteresting reading, but more than that, it made one feel that little was done in the bank which was really done quite as th ook prescribed. The ledger clerk was careful to explain to me that one   the inspectors would come and they would be bound to ask me whe   ne escorted me to the post when the day's mail was dispatched.   us was a "must" according to the book but a "never" according   staff practice. Sure enough it was not long before the bank inspector were on our doorstep and then for weeks they were poking in and ou of everything, asking the usual awkward questions. What should I say. Suddenly I was caught and before I knew where I was I had done the thing I could never have believed I would do. I had lied. The whole thing was accomplished so easily and the inspector seemed immediately satisfied that all was being carried out in accordance with the regulations. My conscience was now in a tumult. I had even lied successfully. Where was my moral superiority now? It may be, for all his cursing and swearing, that the accountant had spoken more truthfully to the inspectors than I had done. I had begun to preach the Truth at meetings, but I had now found out I could not even tell the truth at work. Broken and dismayed I could only seek some quiet place and cast myself at the feet of my Lord. These, I knew, were the kind of things that nailed Him to the tree; and they were the things that only His blood could cleanse. It was only after confessing my sin in deep contrition and facing the issue squarely in another branch to which I was later transferred, that at long last His peace returned again.

It is typical of the God of grace that not so very long after this downfall He should speak to me from His Word more clearly than ever before. Through this new experience He called me into His Service in a specific way and disclosed the nature of my future work with Him. "I had an old Bible bound in red Morocco leather. It had been given me on my first birthday and as I had grown up, it had become especially mine. How many times I had turned its crispy leaves of India paper I cannot say, but somehow, this particular morning it was different. The rather solid print seemed to leap up towards me, and I was grasped by just part of a sentence in the first chapter of Galatians . . . 'called by His Grace to reveal His Son in me'. The acclimatisation to business had been hard and hazardous. I was still only a junior and could hardly be viewed more insignificantly than I was, yet these words brought me now into a fresh understanding of what it meant to be a Christian. Could it be possible that God Himself should choose just a stumbling youth in an office, and make him a vessel in which the glories of His own Eternal Son should be displayed? He had done this for Paul, leading him from birth to new birth, flooding his heart with light and then shining through him to the world at large. I began to believe that God really intended to do this with me also. The following days found my heart singing at the sense of this vocation. Such was the joy that I decided a short while afterwards to return to the same passage and see what further light lay hidden there for me. I found the words I had so gladly embraced were in the middle of a sentence and now I followed on down into the next phrase which I had completely forgotten. Slowly I read it. 'Called by His grace to reveal His Son in me, that I might preach Him among the heathen'. The latter words could not be divorced from those that preceded them. Was this also for me? What did it mean? God stilled my heart. He had brought me to this moment. I could only accept the challenge and enter as God might lead me into the obedience of His call. I began to believe for the first time in my life that my vocation really was to take the Gospel to the nations. Indications of earlier years were thus confirmed. I believed my destiny was now revealed and I could never really do what I wanted again."*

* See *God Holds The Key.*

CHAPTER IV

THE REDDENING SKY

"Ye say in the morning, It will be foul weather today, for the sky is red and lowring. O ye hypocrites, ye can discern the face of the sky; but can ye not discern the signs of the times?"   Matthew 16
"Now the God of hope fill you with all joy and peace in believing, that ye may abound in hope, through the power of the Holy Ghost."
Romans 15

SWEET the paths to me of the "old gold common" for through all my boyhood years I knew it as my dream place lying on the fringes of the grown-up world. How immense it seemed in those far-off days, a vast leafy wilderness that swallowed up the last assault of an expanding suburbia and brought me to the great unknown beyond. To roam at will amongst those endless woods, play hide and seek amongst the ferns and dam the little streams down in the lower dells were well nigh heaven itself to me. Glad summer says with sunshine twinkling through the trees, blue sky above and the soft coolness in the glades—such are my youthful memories of our expeditions to the much loved Stanmore Common. Sometimes the village green, immaculately cut, and dotted with those white-clad figures crouching round the wickets, would claim my gaze and lying on the grass with legs a-dangle I would fall beneath the spell and drama of the game.

Yet now the years had passed. I was already twenty. The golden hours of childhood had quickly sped away and now I stood on the threshold of manhood. Young people have little time for memories. Their charter is to see visions and to venture forward to the far horizons. It is the old men that dream dreams. Thus that afternoon when Charles and I walked up through the bridle paths of the common to the brow of Brockley Hill, there was no nostalgia for those earlier days. All life was beckoning. There were so many problems to solve that our forbears had failed to solve before us. Little wonder that we burned the midnight oil, drank cocoa into the night, and stood for hours under lamp-posts deep in discussion when other folk were in their beds. This day our fellowship was much the same. Jesus Christ was Lord and the world was lost without Him. This was our business and we had no other interest but His Kingdom.

As the trees began to thin out and the foliage gave way to the quickly darkening sky, I was suddenly conscious of a red glow ominously mingling with the last faint rays of the departed sun. We moved on a little further until we looked out from the height of the hill across the vast expanse of London slowly merging with the twilight. Twelve miles away great ragged flames were tearing into the night sky. The docks were a laze. The blitz of 1941 had begun.

I was eighteen the year war broke out, but being young, the shock of that Sunday morning, when our morning worship was broken up with the first wailing siren, soon passed. The long lull of the "phoney war" made me feel those hundred thousand shrouds that Londoners talked about would not be needed after all. As a school boy I had seen something of Nazi Germany whilst visiting that country on a student exchange. I had viewed with mild amusement and disdain the exchange of "*Heil Hitlers*" in the shops, the adulation of the leaders, and the regimentation of the "Hitler Jugend" boys. Yet I enjoyed my time there both in the towns and in the countryside. I even attended the Olympic Games in Berlin. The only tricky moment was in Hamburg, when I was taken to see the launching of a liner. It was called the *Windhoek* after the town in one of Germany's former African colonies. The fact that after the first great war it had become a British protectorate was completely ignored. As the boat glided gracefully down the slipway into the waters of the Elbe, the vast crowd raised their hands like one man in the Nazi salute, and sang with fervour "*Deutchland, Deutchland über alles, über alles in der Welt*". Defiantly I kept both hands at my side. They would have no salute from me. A person next to me gave me a queer side glance, but my German friend was fair enough with me afterwards. He said, "You were right, you wouldn't have meant it if you had." He, himself, was an ardent young Nazi. When staying in England with us, we had invited him to a church service. It was the only time he ever spoke to us rudely. "I don't want your God!" he said. "My greatest ambition is to lay down my life for my Führer." As a Christian I do not think I had yet realised that an absolute claim once asserted calls forth an absolute devotion if once acknowledged. It is true enough that only what a man is prepared to die for, does he really find worth living for. When the devil usurps God's place *in* a life, then he follows it by making God's claims *on* that life. Dictatorship is nothing but a human imposture in the realms of Divine prerogatives. Communism and Nazism, Stalin and Hitler, these were the names that darkened the sky of my youth and already the blood they had shed on the earth was reflected in the reddening sky.

Have you registered yet? This was a question amongst the young people in the early days of the war. For many, national service was an escape from boredom and the restraints of "civvy-street", thus they signed on light-heartedly enough; but for me it was a critical event. On that day I had to decide whether to kill or not to kill; whether to surrender my conscience to the Government or retain it for God. Some may say the issues involved were nothing of the kind. All I can say is that these *were* the issues for me. I could not argue it through. I could not quote or marshal all the Scriptures for and against military service. I was too young. My knowledge was too meagre and my mind too bewildered. All I could do was to kneel before my God in my bedroom and seek to be honest to the light I knew. One hing I did know, that irrespective of circumstance, I could not as a Christian *promise* to kill anyone. The one Scripture that kept running through my mind was this, "If My Kingdom were of this world then would My servants fight, but now is it not from hence." The voice of conscience that forbade me to salute Hitler was the same voice that forbade me to take up arms against him. The date of the tribunal came and I made my way alone to Fulham Court. I could not countenance anyone speaking on my behalf as I knew I must stand or fall on my own personal testimony. Having some time to spare before my hearing, I walked along the pavement looking rather pensively in the shop windows. I came to a stationer's and there amongst the various books for sale was a Bible. It lay open at the Psalms. I was near enough to read it. These were the words that met my gaze, "Out of the mouths of babes and sucklings hast Thou ordained strength." I believed it was God's Word to me and I went in to face the Tribunal, strengthened beyond measure. I was only about three minutes before the panel of judges, who quickly conceded the genuineness of my conscientious objection and granted me "non combatant" duties with the corps bearing that name . . .

Now it was February 1942. The farewells were over and as the train ploughed its way through the desolate wintry fields, blinding snow filled the landscape. I was moving toward another world, known to us all in those war-torn days as "the Forces". A few hours and I was passing, with many others, through the barbed wire entrance of a requisitioned housing estate. It was my first taste of a military encampment. As we huddled about the rooms of the cheerless, unfurnished houses, we talked. What a cross-section of conviction. Christians and atheists, theosophists and socialists, Trotskyists and exclusive brethren, Roman Catholics and evangelicals, intellectuals and the mentally deficient, professors and painters, authors and artisans, bankers and bookworms. Nearly five years in this kind of company, working, eating and sleeping together, sharing the rough life and the hard labour, and daily discussing the momentous issues confronting humanity, meant that when my turn came to fight, I was not exactly unprepared. God has His own kind of schools in which to equip His men for His specific appointments . . . But now we were drafted. With over a hundred others I was billeted in a big empty mansion in a fashionable suburb of Liverpool. At night we firewatched on the docks and wandered through the slums. Near the billet lived an elderly lady. Her house was palatial with large rooms and beautiful furnishings. She placed a little study at my disposal and there I could withdraw when I wished from the hurly-burly of hobnail boots and strident voices. One day she showed me into the large cellar beneath the house. I was astonished. Here was a treasure trove of carpets, ornaments, furniture and many other precious things. "A foreign relative bequeathed it to us; it was brought here when she died," she said. In addition to all this, the mansion with its three or four stories towered above us, room after room, furnished with an aristocratic elegance. Her kindness to me in those first difficult days was unstinted. Some might say, "But she had need of nothing." Yes, in a way . . . except a cure for her boy. His eyes were strangely set; his eyebrows heavy and overpowering, He was nearly into manhood but an epileptic. He had not very long to live . . .

Effingham Street on the other hand was a drain and that was all; just a dark narrow slit a hundred feet deep amidst the sullen brick and mortar of bomb-blasted Bootle. We stood in dishevelled rows hunchbacked under our heavy greatcoats, rolls of blankets and gas masks. The cobbles beneath our feet were slimy with the refuse and dirt from the warehouses. Ominous notices pasted on certain doorways warned us, "Beware of poison gas." Fumigation of vermin had begun. Once the sergeant had given his orders we clambered up the spiral stone staircases, checked the fire-fighting equipment on the top floors and prepared for the worst. Rats! I have never seen such rats. We slept in the warehouses and so did they! What rat would be adverse to a warm bunk? On one occasion we saw a rat bloated like a football gorging itself with grain. One of the fellows took a running kick. It made no attempt to escape and went sailing through the air, a penalty, I suppose, in more ways than one . . . A feeling of revulsion came over me though it raised a sickening laugh at the time. All along the main road were huge piles of rubble and the stench of the dead. We wondered whether corpses still lay unretrieved from earlier raids . . . Through the ruins there were houses still standing. Some of us, who were Christians, held open-air services for the amazing number of children that still lived in the area. We taught them to sing choruses, told them Bible stories and even took them out into the country when we could. In this way we had an entrance into their homes. I remember McNally's place. He was a drunkard. It was always difficult to get hold of him and when you did he would hardly be sober. I spent tense sad moments in his little living-room. Do men drink because they are poor, or are they just poor because they drink? He loved his wife and children I do believe, and his young daughter of about eight with her sweet clean little face was such a contrast when one looked at his ugly bloated features. She was like a daisy growing on a rubbish heap. If ever a drunkard bore an angel, McNally did . . .

Then came a move to Derbyshire . . . and another wilderness of snow . . . Over our heads the stars were twinkling like an array of diamonds in black velvet. Eastwards the rounded hills, crouching low in the half-light, were suggestive of a slumbering giant, slow to emerge from his long white quilt. Because of the blackout there was not one friendly eye of light from the cottage windows but just the shadowy sense of drifts against the dykes and the far sweep of the frozen snow filling the pastures. At that early hour the whole scene was like a dull grey negative awaiting development. It would need the sunlight to bring to focus its inherent splendour. The only sound that fell upon our ears in all that arctic silence was the steady burr of the wheels spinning out two threads of ice dust on the hard-packed road. They belonged to an open truck and we were its contents. My companions sat motionless, voiceless humps huddling together under greatcoats and gas-capes. It was bitterly cold and we were numbed to the bone. Sitting on the steel sheeting, I conjured up a blazing fire within my mind and centred all my thought upon it. The burning coals were red with pulsating heat. I came close to it. I was right up against it. I was almost part of it. A sense of warmth came over me but a moment's mental relaxation and the embers would die out. Is there anything in it? Is mind the master of matter or is matter the master of the mind? For the moment it mattered nothing to me, nor did I mind, if only my limbs could be maintained above zero . . . One day, however, I was to find that it mattered immensely, for the mind must have its answer in the end . . . Near Doveholes, a high village in the Peak district where the wind always seemed to blow, the lorry crunched to a standstill and disentangling ourselves we finally assembled on the roadway. A brief order and we were filing through the ghostly slagheaps to the quarry face. Prior to the blizzard, fresh rock had been blasted and now it lay around us like giant-sized lumps of sugar. We took up our heavy hammers and brushing the thick snow from the boulders looked for a place to strike. Our bodies thawed, loosened up and began to glow. It was rugged labour and the limestone could be cruel on the hands but there was something great about it and a satisfaction which was hard to find with just a pen in hand at the bank. My doctor had said it would either kill or cure me. Crippled with asthma as a boy, God used this experience to put me on my feet physically. Only He knew what privation I was yet to bear when this war was done and the war of the spirit still went on. As the months went by I was drafted from quarry to quarry, spending a week on the face here, a day in the smithy there, or perhaps a month on the kilns somewhere else. On wet days we would cluster around the fire with the local quarrymen in one of the ramshackle shelters. It was rollicking hard-swearing company, but for all that hard-working too and down to earth. We would put our "bread-piece" or a split bap on the hot metal edge of the stove till it was scorched an ashen brown, then bite deeply into it. We were always ravenous, working in the hills. This kind of employment was all so new to me. Perhaps I had really crossed to the other side of the fence now, although I still felt a stranger in a strange land, a kind of visitor instead of one of the family. My hands were too clean and my background too tidy for these people, but if my heart would grow big enough to take them in, may be I would discover they were big enough to take me in. These labourers did not seem afraid of life or men. I did not disturb them as they disturbed me. They were strangely at home in their world of toil. I did not meet any Communists amongst them. I believe quite a few were Roman Catholics, being imported labour from Ireland, but to these hearty proletariats I suppose I was just one of the petty bourgeoisie; but for my own part, I felt more petty than bourgeois. I found somehow a secret admiration rising within me as I watched them work. These men could break up and load over twenty ton of stone a day. I could do only seven. They would slog on to achieve this output between seven in the morning and two in the afternoon and then go home to run their small-holding. I felt they deserved all they got. The question we asked too late was, "Do such men always get what they deserve?" Notwithstanding, in the setting of war, we needed to remember that there were thousands giving their lives at the front that we might enjoy the right of working at home; that we might be allowed to say what we believed. When I thought of it I began to feel I was a man who had no rights at all . . .

It was midnight and the corporals came staggering in. Taking a mirror from the wall, one of them, a big sallow-skinned fellow, slammed it viciously to the floor, smashing it to a thousand pieces. They began to overturn the first bed. They were blind drunk . . . Lights out in the barrack room and the filth began. A big tall ape-like fellow with long loose hands was on the prowl. I lay in bed in the dark. I could hear but I could not see. Perhaps it was as well. What should I do? Minutes ticked by and suddenly I could bear it no longer. With one dreadful shout I shattered the air. It was like a bucket of cold water on a whole room of hysteria. There was a sudden silence, and no one spoke for a long time. It was the long silence after sin . . . One of the rough diamonds came in when all was in blackness. He managed to find his bed then almost fell over. At first he didn't realise what it was but as his eyes became accustomed to the darkness, he found there was a man on the floor, and that he was on his knees. It was one of the Christians praying. "Sorry, John," he said . . . There was no cursing. The Lord was winning . . . One day I sat with one of the men in a quiet place. He must have been nearly forty. There were furrowed lines in his cheeks and his eyes were wet with tears. "I wish I were like you Christians," he said. "I used to be different." This always made me feel a hypocrite but together we slipped into the little chapel on the parade ground. God met us there and I sought to tell him there was a way back to God from

the dark paths of sin . . . a way paved for us by the very blood of Christ
. . . Well might we ask, "Has man any problems outside himself?"

So passed the years for me of the last great war. In addition to the fire-
watching and the quarrying of limestone, I dug in the road, loaded wagons,
humped food supplies, worked in the railyards, painted girders, stacked
sleepers, sorted letters and helped demobilise the troops. It was little
enough in so great a national crisis. Behind all this activity, however,
there was always one thing before me. God had shown me unmistakably,
even before I was conscripted, that my missionary labours would be first
in the Orient and that I was to go to the land of Tibet with His Gospel.
All my spare time in the Non-Combatant Corps was devoted to equipping
myself to this end. If I were a billet orderly, then once my duties were
done I would be down to my New Testament Greek. If there was a spare
moment, then I would bring my Bible out fron my "denim" pocket. I
would find all manner of little sanctuaries from the open fields to the
secluded pew of some city church; somewhere, just to be alone, just to
sense the voice of God; somewhere to let the rebuke of life sink deeper
into the heart in the light of His Word. I had correspondence with missionaries abroad and cultivated the fellowship of men of God, and as
opportunity arose continued to preach in public and seek opportunities of
personally conveying to those near me the knowledge of Christ. There
were moments of elation and moments of weeping. It seemed impossible
that out of the web of all those war circumstances I should one day stand
within the frontiers of Tibet. Towards the end of the war period, through
a mutual missionary friend on the Indo-Tibetan frontier, I was led into
contact with George Patterson. Together we began to share the burden
of Tibet and Central Asia. On one of my last leaves we met at his lodgings
in London, where he was taking a brief course of medical studies. Together we scrutinised a large map of Tibet spread out on the bed. When
and where would we enter? From the Indian side or from the China side?
Missionaries were not allowed in Tibet, but our God was the God of the
impossible and we believed He could take us in. Kneeling before the Lord
we poured out our hearts to Him for that great land and sought His grace
to tread His pathway to it. Thus began a friendship that has continued
through all vicissitudes to this day, a friendship which has never ceased to
stimulate to a greater faith in God and a greater obedience to His will . . .

In November 1946 I stood with my big cardboard box full of clothes waiting for the south-bound Pullman from York. The war was over and national service was behind me. Others were now laying their weapons down but as I looked into the future I longed to venture with my God in the high places of the field, there to prove in an even greater theatre of war the power of those weapons which are not carnal, but mighty to the pulling down of strongholds.

CHAPTER V

HORIZONS AFLAME

"Thou shalt be visited of the Lord of hosts with thunder, and with earthquake, and great noise, with storm and tempest, and the flame of devouring fire."
                                                                    Isaiah 29

LITTLE did I realise when I arrived in Shanghai with George Patterson in the spring of 1947, that these were "the last days of Pompeii". The fact that the currency had just bounced from twelve thousand up to thirty-nine thousand dollars to the pound, was perhaps more a matter of general interest than an omen of doom. Within just over a year I was writing a cheque for three hundred million dollars, though it was no more than seventy-five pounds, and in another month or two, people could even light their fires with bank notes. As we landed on Chinese soil, admittedly there was a bit of talk about fighting in the north. One day the Communists were winning, another day the Kuomintang, but Manchuria was half a continent from Shanghai and the daily haggle for the price of things was far more important to the average Chinese in the streets. To me the skies of China seemed promising enough although my spirit was numbed at China's sorrows, especially when little babies, bundled in rags, were thrown out on the streets of Shanghai. In those days I viewed the great land of China, for all its festering need, more as my highway to Tibet than a place of service. I felt I had a mandate for the far west and must soon pass on to the regions beyond. This day of arrival I considered was the dawning of my life work; and the realisation of my calling. As in most cases with young workers, I think "going out to be a missionary" meant more to *me* than the people to whom I had been sent. It was to discover that only when our going means more to *them* than it does to us, does the real work begin. I was living in an unreal world. If I could have seen through the years to 1951 I would have glimpsed myself a prisoner' in a very small room facing several Communist officials. "Why did you come to China?" one asked. "To help the Chinese," I replied. "We don't want your help!" he snapped. I do not think most of us had the faintest inkling as to how we "benefactors" appeared in the eyes of the ordinary people. We may call ourselves ambassadors for Christ and "stewards of the Lord's substance" but as we arrive in foreign lands accompanied with our bag and baggage, the native people have other thoughts; and when the Communist's arrive and call us "agents of Imperialism" it is not hard for them to believe it so.

Gliding slowly up the Whangpoo to the wharfside at Shanghai the first thing one sees is the imposing waterfront. In almost all places where the imperial influence of the west has been most powerful, one finds these magnificent waterfronts. Large grandiose buildings, all set for a thousand years of rule by foreign overlords. Behind the great façade of the waterfronts were the rabbit warrens of the Chinese populace. It was like looking at a film set of a city street. There was just the facing and then the disillusionment of the barren fields beyond. The difficulty for missionaries, of course, was how to get their western Christianity, western equipment and western culture from the waterfront into the rabbit warren. The generally accepted solution over many years was to build one's own "waterfront" inland, to create an oasis of Anglo-Saxon law and order in the interior, from which suitable spiritual operations could be launched. Undoubtedly in this way the benefits of education and medical attention *were* carried to thousands in the great hinterland, but spiritually it proved disastrous. This was the era of the mission stations and the mission compounds. In many places they were most imposing, but as to the Church life that revolved around them, too often it comprised largely the missionaries' meetings and behind the scenes were "dead men's bones". Too few were the men and women who would dare suggest, much less carry out, the radical procedure of going forward with nothing but the Gospel, and refuse to be just an outreach of the western way of life in an eastern land. There were good men in corrupt Jerusalem when Nebuchadnezzar invaded Israel, but the city of God was sacked and pillaged just the same. So in China there were amongst the many those men and women of God who gave their all that the true testimony might continue, but the flames of the Communist conflagration devoured the land notwithstanding. Ten men of God's stamp in Sodom and the fire and brimstone would have passed it by. May be it was just like that with China. Too much salt had lost its savour, too many lights had grown dim, too many opportunities had been cast away, and the hand of judgement was not stayed . . . These were things I did not know as yet and although on arrival I was made conscious that the skies to the north were reddening, I never realised that the whole horizon before me was aflame.

.   .   .

It was still dark when I was awakened by the voice of brother Jordan. "Do you want to see a fire?" he said. I staggered out of bed and upstairs until I stood by his side on the verandah of the big mission house. Peering through the darkness across the spacious and deserted grounds of the compound we looked beyond its wall to the city of Nanchang with its dense population. It was a large town honeycombed with streets and passageways and composed chiefly of little dwellings of bamboo and timber. We were so dumbfounded with horror, that we could hardly speak. The spectacle was appalling. A great area of the city was ablaze, and we could see the billowing smoke and the frantic flames leaping above the rooftops. Driven by a strong wind the fire was devouring all in its path. I dare hardly think of the terror and confusion as thousands of people jammed the little alleyways in a mad attempt to escape the fury of such an inferno. Once the daylight came there was disclosed to view a coarse black scar slashed right through the heart of the city where the fire had blazed its trail. In the providence of God we ourselves had escaped, owing to the particular direction of the wind, but how desperate now, the plight of the homeless multitudes. A little later I walked down through the town. There before me lay acre upon acre of devastation. At the scene of the fire, men and women were rescuing such idols as could be found from the charred remains of their homes. Pitifully they carried the blackened hulks one by one and stood them by the roadside. Ironically enough it was now a feast day and because of their fear of the already enraged gods many of these destitute people were refused accommodation by their neighbours lest new offence be given to these local deities. Meanwhile in nearly every remaining hovel you could see that fresh incense sticks were silently burning before the family altars. Whilst walking in a populated area in the vicinity of the tragedy there was suddenly a false alarm of a further outbreak. Immediately a sense of hysteria filled the narrow streets. It was very unnerving and I was glad to get away before a fresh stampede began. This was my first venture into the very heart of "the rabbit warren" of an inland China city and it remains one of those experiences I can never forget . . .

Yet what of the other fire? Like a prairie conflagration it was now creeping southward towards the Yangtse. In but a little while Nanchang, capital of Kiangsi, would know again the hot red breath of the Communist revolution. In former years the fires of insurrection had burst into flame in this very city and during the early nineteen thirties the scourge of Mao Tse Tung's social and military experiments had afflicted the province as he fought for the existence of Communism in China on this very soil. He was little known then, as were also Chu Te and Chou En Lai, but they were eventually to emerge as the brilliant, albeit implacable triumvirate of the Chinese People's Republic, becoming the human masters of China's six hundred million souls. For years battles raged, and even when the Kuomintang forces finally dislodged them in 1935 it was not to see the Communist cause extinguished but rather to see them take the notorious "Long March" west and northward, spreading the revolutionary fire wherever they came. These scattered sparks along the way, in the post-war period, would eventually grow to a veritable furnace, destined to engulf the whole nation. Later on when in prison at the No. 1 Penitentiary for Counter Revolutionaries in Chungking, I met a Lieutenant-Colonel of Chiang Kai Shek's army, an intelligence officer confined in one of the cells. He had done a certain amount of criminal investigation in Nanchang in his time and it was interesting to learn from him some of the details of these past events. His case was serious and he was liable to be sentenced to death for his activities. I remember him as a man of outstanding intellect, fighting cleverly in the thought reform, for his reprieve.

. . . Later that day brother Jordan asked me if I would accompany him on a journey through the extreme northwest of the Province to a place called Suishui. It would be through open country much of the way and along roads little frequented by foreigners. He already had thirty years' experience in China and I was delighted at the chance of getting away from the compound and my textbooks, into the real China beyond. There I could see the people at close quarters and exercise my newly acquired Chinese to my heart's content.

The main dirt track out of Nanchang ran northward toward Kiukiang some hundred and twenty miles distant. Obtaining a lift in a lorry, we travelled halfway, engaged a man with a big wooden wheelbarrow, then headed westwards into the country across the paddy fields. That afternoon we reached Peh Tsa, a large village flanking the north bank of a river. Our entry was quickly detected by the people, who gathered about us. We sat down at a little table in an open shop-front. It proved to be some kind of an inn but in actual fact was more like a delapidated outhouse on an English farm. We would have ventured to eat there and then but the curiosity of the people was so great that brother Jordan rose and in fluent Chinese spoke to them of the purpose of our coming. It was a fine opportunity and although tired after the journey the old man preached the Gospel with all his heart. After we had been duly scrutinised, our doctrine heard, and finally had our eating habits freely discussed, the crowd dispersed and by evening time we were able to take a quiet walk along the wide stretch of the dry river-bed before retiring. Returning to the village we were suddenly arrested by the sight of some burning straw outside a bamboo hut. It would have died away in a few moments and we would have thought no more of it, but down the street we could now see people running in a state of great excitement. Then we saw a man amongst them carrying a grotesque, crudely painted image upon his shoulder. Hurrying past us, he rushed into the hut outside of which the straw was burning, and placed it upon a table immediately inside the doorway. In the fast fading light we could just make out two priestlike persons in the shadows of the hut. Coming nearer we discerned their faces lit up by the flickering, eerie light of a solitary candle flame. One priest was dressed in a long Chinese gown, the other was stripped to the waist. This latter person seemed strangely sinister and was probably a medium. Both took their places now in front of the idol. The man in the gown bowed to and fro from time to time, whilst the other man in a demented, if not demon-possessed condition, began to perform various movements with a bowl of water, bowing down and reeling about in an alarming fashion. Brother Jordan in a courageous disregard of what to me seemed a menacing situation, walked into the hut and through to a small room behind the idol where we found a man severely ill with a high fever. The rites being conducted on the other side of the partition were apparently on his behalf. Brother Jordan spoke to him in the Name of the Lord Jesus Christ and after a little while we withdrew. As we came out the half-naked man was vomiting violently in front of the idol . . . Now I was beginning to understand why God had sent me . . . We returned to the inn, slept on boards in the loft and then with the first streak of dawn were up and on our way. There were other places to visit and a twenty-mile walk ahead before the next village was reached.

Every few miles we would come across some rough dwellings where travellers and coolies were resting, drinking tea, smoking, or just talking. The Nanchang fire was news and gave us an opening to demonstrate the folly of idolatry. Quite directly brother Jordan would sometimes ask, "Do you know who Jesus is?" Generally a silence would follow. "He did not come to us from a foreign kingdom," he would add, "nor was He from the Central Kingdom."* Someone would ask, "Then who is He and where did He come from?" "He came from the Heavenly Kingdom." In this way the interest of these peasant folk was aroused and they listened, some of them perhaps for the very first time, to how God loved men enough to send His Son to save them. The close of the day found us at Joh Ch'i. We made our rest for the night in very similar circumstances as the previous evening, only this time we actually slept *in* the shop. My bed was the counter. Before we could retire, however, there was much to do. We received an invitation from an English-speaking teacher of the local school, to address the older students. After supper we went over to what proved to be a barn-like building with no glass in the windows. This apparently was their school house and I spoke to them by interpretation. On the blackboard they had written in English, "Welcome to our kind friends." Within a year it would be replaced by "Down with the Imperialists". For those who could read it, the writing was already on the wall . . . The following day dawned fine and we managed another twenty miles on foot without too much discomfort. This stretch gave me a good picture of Chinese country life in the Kiangsi Province. The crops were now more varied. There were hemp, cotton, indigo, and maize as well as the usual rice being cultivated. We glimpsed occasional palm trees and encountered frequent patches of high pampas grass and groves of young bamboo. At times it took all three of us to heave the wheelbarrow over a rise but even so we made good time and soon the gate of old Wuning hove in sight. Although so much seemed to be grown in the fields and the maize in this area was excellent, the people remained for the most part poverty-stricken. This was because of the iniquitous

* China—The characters used by the Chinese for their own country are "Chung" (Central)-"Kuo" (Kingdom).

system in many areas, whereby the landlord took a large proportion of the crop into his own granaries and left the bulk of his tenants on the brink of starvation. In addition to this, under the Kuomintang the landlord remained untaxed whereas the peasant was taxed. This perpetuation in principle of the already three-thousand-year-old feudal system rendered the peasantry particularly susceptible to the Communists' appeal for land reform. With military success in such an area, it was comparatively easy to arouse the peasants to what they call "political consciousness", gather accusation material against local landlords, and then bring them to public trial. Large numbers were summarily executed up and down the countryside as a result of such meetings in this bitter struggle . . . In Wuning it was a heart-warming experience to be welcomed by a church of Chinese believers who were not under the patronage of a resident missionary. We were accommodated in the inner recesses of a Chinese house which seemed to extend a great distance in off the road through a series of courtyards. Far from being inaccessible, however, crowds of people streamed in to greet us and there was every opportunity of making Christ known . . . It was Lord's Day evening and already late when suddenly two policemen appeared in the gloom of the dimly lit interior of the house. They told us that the mayor of the city wished to see us. One of the aged believers accompanied us. Through the dark and empty streets we were escorted, until we entered a large courtyard. We were allowed past the sentries and were then taken into a room which was well-nigh pitch dark. We were sat down at a large table and presently a small oil lamp with a diminutive flame was brought in. Various other officials now gathered. After some considerable time the mayor arrived. He was fairly short of stature, seemed well dressed, at least in the poor light, and had his hair brushed back. He sat down and leaned across the table. He had a well-defined face with somewhat tense features and penetrating eyes. He spoke falteringly, but deliberately, in English. "My people are very sick . . ." are the words I recall most clearly. "Could a missionary or doctor come to heal them?" "We would provide the necessary facilities," he said. There was somehow a pathos in it all that words can barely capture. New workers would soon be on their way, we told him, but we could not promise a doctor. We could give hope, but no guarantee that help would be forthcoming . . . At length the interview was concluded. We presented him with an English New Testament and with profuse thanks he withdrew into the darkness of his official residence and we walked out into the night. It was a sombre conversation, held in the shadows. We were too late and too few and the greatest blackout China had ever known was soon to descend . . .

So on through the succeeding days across the great expanse of country contacting Christians in the different villages and preaching as we went. It was all so new to me, the unfolding of an unimagined world before my eyes. At Suishui I met brother Vines and his family, another valiant man reaching out to many in that remote part of the world. It was a town that could make you weep with its sin and pitiful isolation. Brother Vines had gone in after the war. Communications were cut, the road in disrepair, but he nevertheless had got through. The church was weak not so much numerically but through several cases of unjudged adultery and his ministry had been up hill all the way. Medically the work was overwhelming. Even while I was there I saw sufficient to sicken the heart. One day a man fell from a tree and landed astride another object desperately injuring himself. He was brought to the Fu Yin Tang* but little or nothing could be done for him and his relatives carried him back to his home. Two or three days later we went to enquire as to his condition. We went in off a courtyard and entered a sheer hovel of a place, that was little more than a dark cupboard. Although it was daytime yet it was necessary to have a lamp burning. Its light, though, was so feeble and the entrance of daylight so meagre, that it took some time to discern the man in the gloom. There he was. He was still alive stretched out on some boards but with no hope of proper medical attention, waiting to die in those appalling surroundings. The whole town was without a doctor and the nearest hospital at Nanchang . . .

Quickly the days slipped by and we decided to return. News came that there had been an unexpected victory for the Kuomintang in the north and brother Jordan planned to go back there if at all possible. This hope ultimately proved short lived, but it occasioned our taking the mountain road back towards Nanchang. It had been reported that bandits were active on the trail but we paid little attention to these stories and made the summit of the pass without incident. There we met a group of carriers and they confirmed that recently there had been several armed robberies on the stretch of road that now lay before us. They said there were six

* "Good News Hall", i.e. Gospel Hall.

men in the robber band four of whom carried firearms, and that they had been active but a short distance from the pass the day before. We took stock of the situation, put our trust in God and tramped on. As we descended the pass the vegetation became almost tropical with high grasses bordering the path so that we could see little more than the trail itself. As we rounded a bend, right there in front of us were six men in ordinary peasant dress, and to our consternation, four of them had rifles. It certainly looked as if we were in for trouble this time. We were walking one behind the other with Jordan leading. I wondered whatever was going to happen but my older companion never faltered or slowed his speed. He slipped a quiet word to me behind. "Pray up brother," he whispered, and continued to move straight for the men who seemed to be waiting for us. As we came abreast of them they stood mute at the roadside. "Out shooting for game?" asked brother Jordan cheerily. Not a word passed their lips. As we went gingerly by, brother Jordan added whimsically, "You're not out to shoot men are you?" Stony silence was all we got from this group of very doubtful-looking characters. Their eyes followed us as we continued on our way. So far so good, but our baggage such as it was had still to come after us. A few more yards and then we saw a little further on another six men similarly clothed and similarly armed. My immediate thought was, "This is an ambush. They now have us between them." On brother Jordan walked never flinching. Closer and closer we came to the men but they did not molest us and in the goodness of God we passed quietly by. After walking some further distance we came to a Chinese house and decided to take shelter, make enquiries, and await our carriers coming through. As we sat there quite a number of uniformed soldiers came into the clearing in front of the house. They were out on patrol to suppress the banditry that had been reported. Imagine our surprise when the men we had feared also came into the clearing. Apparently they were local militia organised to supplement regular forces in the clearing of the robbers from the road. We could only laugh at ourselves and give thanks to God, although the situation had been serious enough. The word given to me at the time was "I will surely deliver thee and thou shalt not fall by the sword, but thy life shall be for a prey unto thee . . . because thou hast put thy trust in Me, saith the Lord." It gave me a fresh insight into the Scripture which says of Barnabas and Paul, they were men who had hazarded their lives for the Name of our Lord Jesus Christ. The hazards of later years were hid from my eyes but God was preparing me, and tempering faith to meet a brigandage on a greater scale by far . . .

Eventually we entered the town of Wuning once again, renewed our contact with the Christians there and then made arrangements with some boatmen to take us several days down the river in their little sampan until we could get on to the Nanchang road. The boat itself was very small, being only twenty feet long and at the most five feet wide. It was made of wood and in the centre of it were a few planks covered by a matted bamboo roof. Under this covering we slept and ate together with the two boatmen who not only navigated the vessel but also cooked the daily rice which we ate with boiled turnip, red pepper and cabbage . . . For three days we moved slowly down the river, quickening course as we were jostled through the foaming waters of the rapids and losing time whenever we lodged on a sand bank . . . The boat had been gliding slowly downstream all day, when sometime before sundown the boatmen swung us out of one of the rapids, in towards the shore. After some while we tied up for the night with about six other boats. We were close to the river bank and we took the opportunity of stretching our legs and taking a walk along the beach. The weather was fine although the clouds hung low over the mountains. Standing in the stern of our boat we were able to look over into the vessels behind us and once we were noticed, the people in them, who were surprisingly numerous, came out to see the foreigners. Suddenly a young man stepped forward from the crowd and greeted brother Jordan. He proved to be the son of one of the elders of a church in the north-west of the Province. He and Mr. Jordan had met years before and this was one of those wholly unexpected reunions. After we had "eaten rice" we stepped over on to one of the other boats and went along the decks of the different vessels which were all moored side by side, to visit this young Christian and his wife. By this time it was dark but the little oil lamps shining out from the covered-in deck space of the boats was adequate for us to pick our way. After some conversation together, we all emerged and stood on the stern of our vessel. Then brother Jordan began to preach to the boat people who listened with interest and fascination. I shall always remember that evening on the river, with the cool night air, the clear ring of the voice as the Word was proclaimed, the dim lamplight in the encircling darkness, and the soft flow of the water beneath. It was the Lord's Day evening. I wondered what everyone was doing back in England. Christians would be worshipping around that same Lord, our great Emmanuel; "God with us, and God with them". One weird-looking old boatman who had remained seated in the dark interior of his boat now emerged into the lamplight. His hair was not cut but was tied in a large bun on the crown of his head. He had taken a vegetarian vow and was a great frequenter of temples. I sought to say a little to him about the Gospel of Christ. Afterwards brother Jordan and the young Christian couple came along and spoke to him quite a while. So the evening passed and we retired to our own boat. Far into the night we could hear the voices of these river people. They were talking, talking . . . talking about the Lord Jesus Christ . . . The sun had barely risen over the ridges when the pole was lifted and we began to draw away down stream. "*Tsai Chien! Tsai Chien!*" the voices rang across the widening stretch of water. "See you again! See you again!" So our ships passed in the night but doubtless some of them we *shall* meet again in the morning!

I had now had my first insight into the conditions prevailing in inland China with its backward communications, poverty, toil, exploitation, disease, and tragedy with no hope of medical relief: the primitive education, banditry and violence, and above all its abysmal superstition, immorality and debased idolatry. The words of the mayor of Wuning come back, "My people are sick . . ." A people in such a condition were bound to seek a cure, and if they did not embrace Christ, then they would embrace Communism.

On our return to Nanchang we received the startling news that the Communist forces in a brilliant advance had reached a point only a hundred and fifty miles north of the Yangtse—China's life-line was almost in their grasp. A few days and reports came through that some of their units had penetrated in places even to the river bank. Over the months, we had received abundant evidence both in outstanding signs and in special provision that we should take our journey to Tibet. In the beginning of November 1947 we knew the hour had come, and George and I, packing our bags, turned our faces to the west. The great venture into Central Asia was on.

CHAPTER VI

GRAPPLING ON THE HEIGHTS

"Zebulun and Naphthali were a people that jeoparded their lives unto death in the high places of the field . . . they fought from heaven; the stars in their courses fought against Sisera."   Deborah

THE next thirty months of my life were to be some of the most eventful I had ever known. First there was to be the long journey up the Yangtse through the stupendous gorges to Chungking. Then the establishing of God-given contacts with Christians in West China. The flight to Chengtu in an old army transport plane. Fellowship with simple New Testament groups of believers in Szechuan—young churches unallied to foreign missions. The proving of God's ability to supply all things, though I be down to the last few dollars in my pocket. The breath-taking trek into the plateau to Kangting, the gateway town of Central Asia. The learning of Tibetan and the pioneering of contacts amongst a broad cross-section of the Tibetan community, touching the extremes of both nobility and beggary. Witnessing the collapse of two currencies and learning to trade with gold-dust, bales of tea, silver dollars, silk and brocade. Making initial itineraries into the bandit country beyond, riding the grasslands at fifteen thousand feet and scaling the passes two or three thousand feet above that. Learning to speak of Christ to Buddhists in their white-walled monasteries and sipping buttered tea with nomads in the open hills. Learning to ride a fierce mountain pony, to handle a bear-like Tibetan hound and to keep my temper at high altitudes. Learning to sleep out under the stars and to show no fear when bullets are shot over one's head at nightfall. Learning to endure the extremes of scorching sun and biting frost. Learning not to lag behind at the pass where the brigands lurk, but to take first risk before the heathen. Watching the curtain fall on the Kuomintang regime, and seeing intrigue for Tibetan independence grow to action. Stitching a wound for the first time in my life and extricating a bullet from a man's leg with no real surgical training. Seeking to study, and read, and pray in a life of intrusion, travel and excitement. Experiencing my own nomad teacher murdered in cold blood by his enemies . . . In those tumultuous days, George and I lived with an ever increasing sense of spiritual conflict within and without. We were open to criticism, for in the face of Consular warning and every advice, and with other missionaries evacuating the area, we proceeded into the heart of Central Asia, not because we were braver, wiser, or superior in any way, but simply that we believed with all our heart God had said, "Go", and the Biblical concept of a soldier and a servant is somebody who does what he is told. This was high adventure in the realm of faith and as far as we were concerned this was the realisation of our destiny. We were come to the frontiers of Tibet for such a time as this. For many a century, Tibetan life had continued in its present Buddhist mould. Dalai Lama had succeeded Dalai Lama but now even Buddhist prognostication maintained this one would be the last. The Communists had taken almost all China and were poised for attack on the great frontier region of Tibet with the fullest intention of possessing the whole. Many missionaries over the years had yearned to see the land open to the Gospel, but now with our contacts both inside and outside Tibet we had, I suppose, greater prospects than any before us. Yet at this particular juncture the most militant, and avowedly atheistic, force in history arrives at the gates of Tibet and at precisely the same moment disputes this conquest. Surely this was God's moment, and if it were God's was it not ours as His servants? Retreat was inconceivable. By God's grace we would go through with Him, and trust Him in His own inscrutable way to bring forth a testimony to the world.

Looking through an old file of letters written from the Tibetan border at that time, I have recently come across some of my correspondence which was brought out by traders and Lhasa Government runners to the frontiers of India. They throw light on the way my mind and conviction were working in those days so shortly before the final Communist onslaught was made. A meditation from the beginning of my last prayer letter sent from that region becomes strangely significant in the light of later developments. It runs like this . . .

"Prayers and an Iron Gate! Like one of his early offspring, Satan is a 'forger of every cutting instrument of brass and iron' (Gen. 4 : 22). Yet Satan's iron, wrought through the centuries by deceit and lust in souls of men, with all its seeming permanence is found reduced to crumbling rust before the water and wind of the Spirit of the Almighty. Satan failing immediate conquest, aimed at eternal resistance, counting the iron of his perverted will, and hardened rebel-angel hosts as strength enough, but the God of all strength doomed him to defeat in Time. All the imposing girder work upholding the vast fabric of his kingdom wilts before our God in all His consuming and eternal fire. It is reduced to tiny twisted scrap, ready for the 'deep'. Meanwhile all down the ages God's children have felt and faced the devil's iron. From the devil's anvil came 'iron fetters' for Joseph (Psa. 107 : 8), and in turn, for Israel, Egypt became an 'iron furnace' (Deut. 4 : 20). In the land they faced the hostility of 'iron chariots' and from the giant Philistine the menace of a spear's head weighing six hundred shekels of iron. Later their enemies fought against them as with 'threshing instruments of iron' (Amos 1:3) and then under the discipline of God, as giving place to the evil one, Jerusalem was encompassed with an 'iron wall' (Ezek. v:3) and heaven above became to them an 'iron heaven' (Lev. 26:19) wrought in separating sin. Yet through grace, 'to such as sit in darkness and in the shadow of death, bound in affliction and iron', God is the One who 'hath broken the gates of brass and cut the bars of iron in sunder' . . . Since Jesus pierced the heavens, Satan's iron work seems to have specialised much in gates, gates of iron. Iron gates to shut saints up. Iron gates to shut sinners out. Iron gates wrought for all manner of frustration of the march of Grace. But a pierced heaven means an open Heaven, and praying children of God time and again bring forth the Hand of God upon the door to open or shut as may prove His sovereign will. So today there is prayer and an iron gate. 'Prayer without ceasing' and many gathering and today the iron gate swings!" This was written in May 1949.

In October of that year George and I, in the company of a great cavalcade of Tibetans, crossed the mountains and high grasslands of Kham, covering between three and four hundred miles in some three weeks, to establish an advanced base deep in Tibetan inhabited territory; a "striking point", from which we could enter Lhasa territory itself. There we set up in a little log cabin in the valley of Pangdatsang one of the leading Tibetan nationalists. From there George made his hazardous journey to India through unmapped terrain never to return; and from there I crossed over the river of Golden Sand into Tibet itself. In my first book of this series, *When Iron Gates Yield*, I record a significant event that occurred one day in our log cabin prior to my entering Tibet. I record it again here, as it represents my first real personal encounter with the Chinese Communists and it is part of this present narrative which is concerned with the factors leading up to our major clash in their brainwashing prisons. Whilst still there in the village of Bo, an advanced unit of the People's Liberation Army came through on reconnaissance to contact the Pangdatsang brothers whom they had reason to believe were the lynchpin in the whole strategy of overcoming resistance in Kham—and indeed in Lhasa-controlled territory itself. One day, in my little Gospel room in the log cabin, one of the Communist officers came to see me. On the whole he was quite affable. We talked about the civil war in China and I spoke directly with him, as I felt no reason to do otherwise. I said, I thought it a great pity that after the second world war China could not settle her domestic problems peaceably, for then her position and prestige were very high and she could have taken a leading part in Asian affairs. The throwing away of such a golden opportunity and the resorting to such a terrible civil war, I thought, was most regrettable and indeed shameful. This put him somewhat on the defensive and he went to great pains to try and prove that all the blame was on the head of 'bandit' Chiang Kai Shek. From this, I spoke of man's real condemnation. This was in the rejection of God's light. Taking down a Chinese John's Gospel, I turned to chapter three, showing him the words, "This is the condemnation, that light is come into the world and men love darkness rather than light because their deeds were evil." This trend in the conversation was not to his liking, so he turned on me and said, "All you preachers are deceivers of the people." "As to who is a deceiver, three to five years hence, your own regime will reveal. If you do not fulfil what you have promised the people, would it not be right to say you are a deceiver?" "O yes!" he said glibly, "but we shall do what we promise without the slightest doubt." He cast an accusing eye at a number of suspicious looking cases below the medicine cupboard, "Is that a wireless transmitter?" he rudely questioned. "No," I replied, "It is a box of surgical instruments and the other box you see is a typewriter." He was unconvinced. I watched him as he talked. He was sitting, as it happened, with his back to the big wooden cross in the poster on the wall. How unconsciously and with what strange coincidence was his attitude portrayed. There had been some candid speaking on both sides, but he nevertheless took with him a copy of each of the Gospels when he finally left me. I watched him go across Pa Shamba's roof, a soul for whom Christ died. Later I found a portion of one of the Gospels I had given him, torn up amongst the stones in the open-air toilet outside the big house where they were staying. In our first encounter the heart of my antagonist had been revealed. "For we wrestle not against flesh and blood, but against principalities, against powers, against the rulers of darkness of this world, against spiritual wickedness in high places." Beyond men's faces are their masters and beyond the gates of nations are the gods of the gates, but for me Christ's promise remained, "the gates of hell shall not prevail".

Before the spiritual conflict fully began, however, I was to see something of the conflict on the physical and military level. In the autumn of 1950 after only two-and-a-half months inside Tibet proper, I witnessed the defeat of the Tibetan army. These were days of bitter disillusionment for many of the Tibetan peasantry. I was the unexpected eyewitness at the death-bed of a nation. Corruption, immorality, devilry and treason, all played their part in the debacle, and in October, the Prince of Dege, Commander-in-Chief of all South-East Tibet, capitulated to the advancing armies. From the outback of the Chinese countryside, from the villages and fields of Kiangsi, the Chinese Communists had conquered. Peking, Nanking, Canton, Chungking all were theirs, and now the road lay open to Lhasa and who would stop them?

I was yet to learn that in the overall strategy of the Almighty, the immediate objectives before the servants of God are not to be confused with the ultimate ends of God Himself.

CHAPTER VII

FACING THE STORM

Jesus said: "They that are whole need not a physician but they that are sick. I came not to call the righteous but sinners to repentance."
Isaiah said: "Ah sinful nation, a people laden with iniquity, a seed of evil doers, children that are corrupters; they have forsaken the Lord . . . the whole head is sick, and the whole heart faint. From the sole of the foot even unto the head there is no soundness in it; but wounds, and bruises, and putrifying sores; they have not been closed, neither bound up, neither mollified with ointment."

ON October the seventh, 1950, the Chinese People's Liberation Army unbeknown to the outside world, began shelling the Tibetan strongpoints on the farther bank of the Golden Sand River, the name given to the upper reaches of the Yangtse as it pours down the mighty chasms that cleave Eastern Tibet from north to south. There had been some crossfire prior to this date, as the Chinese moved up supplies of men, arms, food and equipment to the east bank of the river, but the barrage at dawn proved to be the curtain rising on the long planned full-scale invasion of Tibet. Over the succeeding days by clever strategy, superior forces and better arms, the Chinese poured up the valleys and over the passes to occupy the villages and straggling townships of Tibet. An initial advance of eighty miles in the south saw the fall of Markham Gartok and in the north brought Chamdo to her knees. By the time all this had been accomplished and a vast bridgehead of Communist penetration into Tibet fully secured, I was already a prisoner, having been arrested in Markam Gartok as a suspected British spy. I was brought down over several days to their rear headquarters on the east side of the river at Batang. I entered my first prison cell, a dark dirty room under the central buildings of the big fort at Batang, on October the twenty-second, about a week after I had been officially apprehended. On October the twenty-fifth, Peking made its first announcement to the world declaring that the "liberation" of Tibet had begun. Before there could be any protest internationally it had made sure that the occupation of the whole of Eastern Tibet was a *fait accompli*. The narrative of my personal experience during those hectic and dangerous days and what befell me later is chronologically recorded in my earlier book, *When Iron Gates Yield*. There I describe the brain-washing as I encountered it and the all-sufficient power of Christ to meet it. Altogether I was three years, two months and a few days in their hands, only being finally released by the will of God, in answer to prayer, on December the nineteenth, 1953. Now after ten years of freedom, further study and frequent reflection I want to look at the experience and the teaching I was given then a little more analytically, although I hope not too academically. This is important for God gives us experiences of Himself in conflict with the devil, not that we might gloat over miraculous deliverances or exult in any sense of superior power, but that we might know Him better and enter into a greater understanding of His Grace and Truth. In other words, that we might become intelligent heirs of those things which He has prepared for them that love Him, thus bringing pleasure to Him in the worship we offer and the fellowship we enjoy. He wants us to be men of His counsel, true sons who share His confidence, a people who move with Him, serve with Him, and cooperate with Him, in the outworking of His Eternal purpose down the years.

For the first year of my imprisonment I was kept in solitary confinement and given almost daily personal instruction from a political angle. They did not at the beginning speak to me philosophically. They sought rather to lead me into a thorough criticism of the society into which I had been born and of which, as far as they were concerned, I was both a product and a representative. They did not as yet show me the place that the capitalist society of Britain had in their overall concept of history. This I presume was because they wanted me as an alien to tell them of things that I had said and done, and to make a straightforward and quick confession without getting at first too theoretically involved. On one occasion when they thought they had made some progress with me they said, "Now as soon as your question is settled then we will send you away to another place to 'learn'." When, however, they failed to extract the confession they required, and a renewed challenge on their part, after many months, only resulted in my restating my Christian convictions, then I was sent away to a more stringent reform institution. The so called "voluntary period" was thus soon concluded and the coercive period of my indoctrination began. It was in the early part if this second period that I began to get my first inklings of what they really meant by the word "reactionary" although it was still some time before I understood their reasons for such a strong insistance on the brainwashing.

One day the Governor of the prison addressed some of us "counter-revolutionary" prisoners in our cell and explained to us that we should regard the prison as a kind of hospital. We were the patients. Our trouble was that our minds had been poisoned by reactionary philosophies. If we could not be cured we would have to be destroyed. We would not be fit to live, or to share the common life of the people. In the prison, officials like himself were to be viewed as doctors, and the warders as nurses. They were doing all they could to save us from death. All sorts of "medicines" were prescribed—from special reading, "learning" classes, and meetings for "criticism and self-criticism". For "patients" with particularly "high temperatures" then, of course, more drastic means had to be adopted such as a dose of the chains and handcuffs. These were applied not as punitive but as curative measures. When "struggle meetings" were used, it meant that for hour upon hour the prisoner was psychologically bludgeoned with the shouting and raving of his fellow-prisoners who had already gone over to the Communist side. This was to bring the "prisoner patient" to his senses, that is, to a state of politcal consciousness before it was too late. A kind of "temperature chart" was kept in the office for each case in the prison, showing progress or decline in political health. When we were "well enough" and the poison in our thinking had been checked and largely dispersed, then we could go out to the "Reform through Labour" units and get really fit in our political outlook, shaking off, perhaps for ever, the infection of the lazy and exploiting capitalist, landlord classes.

This is not the imaginary, but essentially the true approach of the prison authorities, and the staff worked tirelessly to the ends they had in view. One of the chief interrogators said to me with evident satisfaction, "We managed to get twenty-five fit enough for release last year. This year we hope to increase that figure to fifty." The younger members of the staff were obviously enthusiastic in their assignments, working early and late to "pull through" the political patients in their care.

For anyone in the west hearing of these things for the first time, it is hard not to be sceptical. It all sounds so utterly incredible. "Whatever philosophy of life is this?" people will ask. Can men genuinely live and act like that? I believe the answer to these questions is vitally important, for whilst only certain people will be subjected to Communist brainwashing in quite the same way as I was, yet with the challenge of Communism reaching such global dimensions it is bound to confront most people sometime or other in this generation, and when it does, to be forewarned is to be in some measure forearmed.

Now as soon as we start talking about philosophy, people feel we are going to be academic and theoretical, but philosophy is not really an academic thing. Every man is a philosopher of one kind or another. Everyone of us has a philosophy of life. I suppose just about everyone in the world is convinced that there is something wrong with the world. This is the one thing we all agree about. We do live in a sick human society, and we are quick to acknowledge and criticise the disorder which characterises man's public affairs even though we often like to deceive ourselves that our own affairs are in order. What we disagree about is how to cope with a world that is so disagreeable and how to deal with a society that is so contrary to our ideals. The attitude and outlook that each man takes towards the outside world is really his philosophy. Ai Tze Chi, one of Red China's leading philosophers behind the scenes, explains this at some length in his work, *Ta Tsung Tze Hsioh.* I read this book, an introduction to dialectical materialism for the masses, whilst in the prison outside Chungking. In it he first of all outlines various kinds of people and their different outlooks on life.

Adapting it freely to our western minds, his approach, as far as I can remember, runs something like thus.

One kind of person says, "I'm out for a good time. I've got only one life to live and I'm going to enjoy it. Why should I put myself out and waste my time working. The more leisure and pleasure the better! Eat, drink and be merry, for tomorrow we die!" Philosophers call this kind of person a *hedonist.* Someone who reckons that pleasure is the chief good and squeezes every bit he can from life while he has the chance.

Then you get other folk who look at the world with rose-coloured spectacles. They will see beauty even in squalor and tenderness even in tyranny. A Hitler only has to caress the children and he is kind at heart after all. If their own youngsters break a neighbour's window, it is passed over with the remark, "Well, boys will be boys, they did not mean any harm." Royal occasions, emotional situations, news of high endeavour fill their eyes with tears or their heart with elation, so life goes by and the world to them is always something other than it really is. Thus they seek to escape the harsher impact of life in creating a world of their own. These people we call *sentimentalists*.

Akin to this class of people are those aggravating persons who say, "Oh, don't get upset! I can't understand what you are worrying about. Everything will come right in the end. Think of the last time. You nearly worried yourself to death, but things turned out fine. I always look on the bright side." This is the *optimist*, and this is his way of coping with the unpromising world around him. He is often admired as a "happy-go-lucky" type but he is far from a realist for all that.

On the opposite side you get the man who is quite convinced that there is no answer to the world problems at all. He will never say, "*If* the worse comes to the worst", but is always sure that the worse *will* come to the worst. Life is one long hopeless struggle against impossible odds. This kind of man is the *pessimist*. He always looks on the dark side of life. He seems to cope with the world and its ills by expecting the worst and then enjoying a brief respite when things do not turn out quite so badly after all.

A step further and we get another kind of person. His philosophy runs along slightly different lines. He says, "If it's going to happen it will happen." "If my name's on the bomb," he maintains, "then it will get me and I can't do anything about it." This is the *fatalist*. By the manipulation of this outlook he constantly avoids the burden of his own responsibility, absolving himself from helping others by saying that whatever you do nothing can be helped.

Then of course you get a large number of people of all types and of differing faiths who believe that everything in the world is at the whim of outside forces. They attend religious services, take religious vows and observe all manner of religious rituals. They count beads, say prayers, mumble incantations, go on pilgrimages and even do themselves physical injury, all the while hoping either to placate the demons or appease their gods. This type of person is a *religionist*. These differing philosophies are but the more common examples of the multitude of philosophies by which people seek to cope with the world in which they live.

But all these people, says Ai Tze Chi, are idealists. They fail to face up to the facts of the world outside themselves and try to solve their difficulties and problems by ideas conceived wholly within themselves. These ideas actually ignore the real world that confronts them. This is useless. There is another philosophy which he maintained was the right philosophy, that is, the philosophy of the materialist. What is a materialist? The Communists' concept of a materialist is a person who is prepared to deal only with the hard real material world round about him. He says, "I'm going to deal only in facts. I am going to admit of no other form of existence than that which can be tested in a laboratory. The world to me is material and nothing more. Being material, it can be analysed. I can investigate its laws and come to know them. Then I will apply them and work in accordance with them and not be so foolish as to disregard them or transgress them." He postulates, "If mankind can only grasp the laws inherent in material itself and cooperate with them, then he can be master of all things and move forward irresistibly to ever higher standards of living. To the idealist, he says, "It is no good letting your thoughts run away with you. Thought, mind, energy, spirit and emotion, have no existence independent of our grey matter. They are indissolubly linked with our material flesh and blood. Like the world around him, man is basically material and therefore his greatest good individually, and socially, is in living in harmony with his environment and putting it to correct use. In daily life, in national life, and in international life, there are therefore two camps," says the Communist. "You are either an idealist or a materialist. Whatever people like Kant and others have said in their writings, seeking to reconcile these two outlooks to constitute what has been called the 'Dualist' position, they are of no consequence. Capitalists and imperialists are all idealists. They live in a world of their own imagining, thinking the few can indefinitely exploit the many, for the benefit of themselves. This is no more than fantasy. All the time they are sowing the seed of their own destruction. It is not in accord with reality. History shows that this kind of thing can only go on so far and then there is an explosion in society, a revolution or some cataclysmic change." The Communist says that this process is identical in principle with the phenomenon we witness when water is heated. On reaching a certain temperature it suddenly changes into steam. This is not just an apt illustration. The materialist believes that the laws governing nature are not just similar to those governing society but are the same laws and that these laws must be respected and obeyed. This view then maintains the only way for humanity is to cooperate consciously and actively with the laws "existing in things". This means that materialists are not going to look to any God or gods, nor are they going to be afraid of demons, nor are they going to concede any life beyond this life. They are material men in a material world and therefore their salvation, in a material world full of senseless injustice, is in their own hands and in nobody else's. If the material resources or "means of production", that is, the mines, the factories, the land and all that produces wealth, is in the hands of people who do not understand the principles governing nature and society, and who are not using things for the good of all but for their own ends, then the materialists, championed by the Communist Party, will take them from them and according to their superior knowledge handle them for humanity as a whole. This is the only right course. Everything that will help this aim is therefore good. Everything that hinders it is therefore reactionary. It is retarding progress and therefore evil. Such is their conviction.

Let us pause and reflect on this concept of the universe. This teaching is nothing new but goes back to Marx and through him to men as far apart as Hegel and Plato for its varied sources, but when it strikes unexpectedly, it makes spectacular conquests. This was so in China. The mass of the intellectuals were born in an atmosphere of confused Confucian ethics mingled together with a traditional ancestral worship springing from the same root. Side by side with this, particularly in western China, was a corrupt idolatrous Buddhism. Even a smattering of western education in the minds of China's young people soon sowed a contempt for these superstitious practices. This smattering was largely received in mission schools where western culture, sad to say, so often outweighed the proclamation of the pure Christian Gospel. The result was that whilst this influence wrenched the youth of China from its old moorings, it anchored few in Christ. Into this fertile soil the seeds of revolution were extensively sown, and with Communist military success swiftly ensuing, a harvest of youthful cooperation was reaped for their new regime. Mao Tse Tung, soon after his control over the nation had been asserted, declared that the first task of the new republic was the "thought reform" of the intellectuals. The work in actual fact was already half done and with just a few weeks of concentrated campaigning in the schools, colleges and universities, the philosophy of Marxian materialism, backed now by the coercion of political authority, swept the mass of the student and much of the older educated section of the community, into the Communist fold. There was little resistance, and confessions, especially those of older lecturers, appeared with monotonous regularity and with consistent style in the press, acknowledging the reactionary and counter-revolutionary character of their past studies and teaching. This material in the daily papers was part of our reading in the prison to spur us on to a similar change of mind. Thus ironically, whilst China was throwing off western economic domination, she was submitting to an essentially western philosophy, the theory of which was laid down by Karl Marx in his many years of research in none other place than the British Museum! Britannia had nourished a viper in her bosom at the very time she ruled the waves. In 1848 Karl Marx published his notorious manifesto with its renowned clarion call to the proletariat. "You have nothing to lose but your chains. Proletariats of the world unite!" *Das Kapital* is Marx's cheif philosophical work and is still the basis in summarised form for all indoctrination in China. Mao Tse Tung, described to me by one of the officials as a Honan farmer, must not be dismissed as a country yokel with a gift for leadership who has risen to power on the crest of a revolutionary wave. He is a philosopher in his own right and in the Chinese tradition, who in his tumultuous lifetime has undertaken and achieved the monumental task of adapting Marxist principles to China's conditions. In China this continued statement of "theory and practice" is published volume after volume under the title of *Mao Tse Tung-Szu Hsiang*, which means "Mao Tse Tung's Thought". It is obviously the intention of the Chinese Communist leadership to do away with any suggestion that Communism is merely another western import. Mao's genius in this field makes the acceptance of Marxist teaching all the more plausible to the Chinese. It is being expounded in simple language and with historical illustrations that they can readily understand; and further it is being propagated as the guiding star for all the policies of the new regime. If the time comes in Britain we can be sure the devil will not be without his prophets, and the philosophy of Marx, whilst mildly discredited at present, will rise again with fresh national exposition, deceiving the many, and dumbfounding its critics. If the Christians of this country are not better grounded in the Word of God than were their Chinese brethren, they will fare no better before the devil's wiles.

CHAPTER VIII

THE BATTLE IN THE CLOUDS

"God hath chosen the foolish things . . . God hath chosen the weak
things . . . God hath chosen the base things . . . God hath chosen the
despised things . . . God hath chosen things which are not . . . that no
flesh should glory in His presence."   I Corinthians I

FOR the intellectual who can give time to specialised study, there are many
works already produced on the subject of "Christianity and Communism" but shorter material for the average busy person of sincere Christian
faith is still somewhat lacking. Before passing on to consider the positive
challenge of the call of Christ and the fellowship of the Church, I propose,
therefore, to take up some of the more obvious evils of Marxist teaching.
In the previous chapter I gave a brief outline of the philosophical position
of the Communist materialist. Here I state some of the fallacies inherent
in it; fallacies that I have had to deal with not merely as an item of research,
but in grim battle behind Communist bars and through Communist
courts.

I. The first fallacy is that matter is the only thing that really exists.
This kind of statement may have passed muster with the intellectuals of
1848, but in the latter part of the twentieth century with developments in
nuclear physics and other fields of scientific research exceeding anything
which Marx, Engels and Lenin might have imagined, it is altogether
different. The original Marxist-Leninist conception of material has now
been investigated to such a degree, and the relation between matter and
energy so explored, that it no longer makes scientific, much less theological
sense, to say blandly that matter is the only thing that exists. Communist
writings like to assert that energy is inseparably associated with matter,
and in such a way as to be no more independent of it, than the phosphor-
escent glow of a jelly fish is of its "jelly". Modern scientific research on
the other hand gives us every reason to believe that were it not for the
operation of immense forces of energy, matter and our concept of it would

not exist at all. Why is all this so important? It is important because if energy is just a property of material, then man makes his god in man's image. God becomes just a figment in the imagination of a piece of "thinking material", and that is precisely what the Communists say God is. On the other hand, if material is the product of energy then the statement in Genesis chapter one, "In the beginning God created the Heaven and the earth" is this fact expressed in its highest form. God is the source of all *creative energy*, the One before all things, and independent of all things, responsible for bringing into being the *material* universe. In this case it is not a question of man making his god in man's image, but of God making man in His image. This is exactly what the Bible says. Whilst science cannot go so far as to assert the personal nature of God when speaking of the Ultimate Source of creative energy, for this is the subject of revelation and given to faith alone, yet many scientists are beginning to speak of the universe today in terms which in principle accord with the opening narrative of Genesis. When Ezekiel was given his vision of God, an essential part of that vision was the concept, that the glory of God and the movements of God were associated in display with a concurrent circulatory system, described as "wheels within wheels". Two thousand five hundred years have passed and scientists have proved conclusively that from the whirling solar systems to the feverish might of the atom, this is the very hallmark of the universe. As planets revolve around the sun; as moons about their planets; as satellites steer their course and electrons circle their invisible neutron-proton nucleii, their intricate orbital systems are indeed "wheels within wheels". Without question, the very mark of the Maker is stamped through and through every article He has made. Whether a single grain of dust or a galaxy of flaming suns, each in all their detail proclaim Him, Lord of Heaven and earth. No wonder that David, musing as a shepherd beneath the starry skies, burst into song to tell us that His Name and glory are upon them all. Paul's words to the Romans take on therefore a very contemporary significance and put us all, the Communist included, into our "intellectual" place. For, he says, "*since the beginning of the world*, the invisible attributes of God, for example His eternal Power and Divinity, *have been plainly discernible through things which He has made* and which are commonly seen and known, thus leaving these men without a rag of excuse. They knew all the time that there is a God, yet they refused to acknowledge Him as such, or to thank Him for what

He is or does. Thus they became fatuous in their argumentations, and plunged their silly minds still further into the dark. Behind a façade of 'wisdom' they became just fools, fools who would exchange the glory of the Eternal God for an imitation image of a mortal man . . . They gave up God; therefore God gave them up . . ."*

The Christian says because God *is*, then consequently matter became a possibility. It was created and now we can believe that matter *is*. This is logical as a statement, for it sees the lesser derived from the Greater. Communism says, Material *is*; consequently man became a possibility and we believe that Man evolved and that Man now *is*, and God is not. This is illogical as a statement, for it sees the greater derived from the lesser and the Greatest of all denied existence on the sole ground that He has not been sighted. There are two means of discovery. One is physical and is concerned with the means of "*observation*". As Christians, we call this method "walking by sight". The other is spiritual and is concerned with the means of "*belief*". We call this "walking by faith". Observation takes in facts on one level only, the physical and the natural. Belief takes in facts on a higher level altogether, facts given by revelation from God and which are not discernible by the natural man through his natural approaches. Thus the writer to the Hebrews states, "He that cometh to God *must* believe that He *is* and that He is the Rewarder of them that diligently seek Him." The Russians having launched a space ship and brought it back to earth successfully, said, "We have been up there and we found no God there", thus seeking to emphasise their contention that God is neither here nor there, nor for that matter anywhere. This childish approach to spiritual things is rooted in the false idea that apart from material facts ascertainable by observation, there are no other kinds of facts. Yet even in our everyday living, we are conscious of facts other than physical. The Bible tells us God is spirit. This is not so unintelligible when we come to think of it, for although I am a man, I am a spiritual creature also. I am not the sum total of my physical organs nor just the ten shillings' worth of chemicals of which I am made. In my self-consciousness there is more than just a sense of taste and sight, smell, and touch, or hearing. There is elation and depression, intuition and aspiration, a love of the aesthetic, a moral judgement and a yearning for what we call satisfaction which is something quite other than physical. We, the lesser, have been

* Romans, chapter one, J. B. Philips' translation.

created by the infinitely Greater One. And when we believe that He *is*, and that the Creator has His will, mind and emotion and His infinite aspirations too, then we acknowledge that He must also have His will and purpose in beneficent design for us. To the man with this approach of faith, new facts, in a realm altogether other than the natural, are disclosed. This is revelation. When we trust Him, then it is He begins to trust us with this other knowledge, and lest this be thought mystical let it be said that thousands all over the world find this workable in the everyday affairs of their lives. If we say, as indeed the Communist does say, "Material *is*. Therefore God is not", we are like people in a dark cell. We feel the wall of our circumstance and groping around it we say, "This is the Universe; I must learn to recognise this wall and learn to live within this wall and my life here will be more tolerable." Yet all the time there is Light and the Great World beyond. During the year of my solitary confinement there were times when the loneliness seemed very, very terrible. If I had shouted myself hoarse, it is by no means certain that anyone would have heeded me unless it had been at meal-time or the hour of my interrogation. Yet what folly to say, because I shouted and no one came, that there was no authority in the prison, or that there were no persons there. Spiritually speaking, it is when we are willing to be readjusted to the Divine Authority outside our cell of circumstance that He then opens the door. It is at such a juncture His light shines in and our knowledge of Him turns our bondage into liberty, even if for a little while we must live our days within the confines of this visible universe. It is not just some first-century idea but an abiding spiritual law when the writer to the Hebrews states, "He that cometh to God *must* believe that He is and that He is the Rewarder of them that diligently seek Him."

It is this most vital experiment of all that the Communist materialist will not undertake. He will peer through a microscope, he will sit in a space capsule, but he will not dare to venture himself into the Arms of the Almighty. He refuses to believe that *He is*, and thus continues to grope in "his cell" alone. This refusal to accept the imperative of this spiritual law is interwoven with the whole make-up of the Communist individual. R. S. Osment and Douglas Hyde, both confirmed Communists who did finally dare to "believe", wrote after their conversion to God concerning those who are attracted to the Communist ranks, "They are mainly those already in revolt. It might be against religious or other restraints, which they know deep down to be right, but against which they had kicked, or wished to kick . . . How human to decide that, in revolt, the first person to be thrown out is God. Stripped of all the philosophical and political trappings this is still the fundamental revolt of all men." The fellowship of Communism is an unholy alliance of unbelieving men committed to the disregard and overthrow of all authority—God's included—by all means at their disposal, with the purpose of bringing the whole world under the heel of *their* concept of the Ultimate Good. You will search the writings of Communists in vain for a defined viewpoint of that good society. When the Communists destroy the ideals of others, people flock to them. When they try to construct and fulfil their own, the dictatorship they assert is so dreadful that multitudes flee their borders. The voice of Communism cries today, saying, "Let us break their bands asunder, let us cast away their cords from us." It is always easier to say, "Let us break" than "Let us make". Dictatorship, whether in Nazism, Communism, or anything else always says in the end, "I don't want your God". for a dictatorship is a claim to final authority and an insistence on having the last word, and that is something which belongs to God alone.

The stark tragedy of the Communist is that he believes there is no other centre for the universe outside of man himself. The ideal man is the Party man and the ideal realm, the State which he establishes. When he looks beyond that, he aspires to a "State-less" condition of humanity, where the State (which according to Lenin is that instrument whereby one class oppresses another) is no longer necessary, but all live communally in a classless society equally enjoying the common plenty. The naïveté of this outlook could hardly be further removed from reality. It is yet one more devilish hoax staged on a big enough scale to convince people that it must be true. The Communist may laugh at the idea of "heaven above", but the sheer folly of imagining that a world of self-opinionated, sin-stained and sin-ingrained men and women will some fine day produce a "heaven below", beggars description. If the Communists are the makers of their own "heaven" and Capitalist society is the equivalent of their "hell" then all that can be said is that people seem happier in "hell" than in "heaven". When man puts his whole trust in man then he turns in upon himself and all is darkness. In real terms this means that the Communist makes himself a child of no origin and a man of no goal. Life is to him but a juggling of "thinking things" and "thoughtless things" and though he gives it the

name of "law" yet revolution is no more than a jolt of the social kaleido-
scope bringing into being a new pattern that looks and feels better—
though the pieces are just the same. He makes the end of life the creating
of better conditions for living—but how can the goal of life be reduced to
the making of better facilities for living itself? Millionaires often commit
suicide—they have achieved an environment but failed to find a purpose.
If we could give all humanity a millionaire's social environment of pleasure
and plenty, then all humanity would be suicidal. We would be comfort-
able but causeless and we would find ourselves totally insupportable to
ourselves. When man has himself to himself and calls that heaven, then
he is treading the brink of hell.

When the Communist puts God out—what does this mean morally?
The essentially devilish characteristics of the system are again immediately
manifest. The moral consciousness of man is a divinely implanted sense
of obligation to his Creator. Once deny God's existence and you immediately tamper with the conscience. The Communist in his atheistic
approach to all problems thus foists upon man a concept of sheer expediency. He dares to maintain that all that furthers the revolution is good, all
that retards it is evil. This, says Lenin, is our morality. There is for them no
other criterion. They profess to be objective but nothing could be more
subjective than this. They first imagine a Utopia. Then with that in mind
they devise means to achieve it; but means on which they are never agreed
at any one time. Finally the word "morality" is attached to those means.
Thus to refute or transgress the Party line is an immoral act. If the policy
should be reversed, then your former "immorality" can become "moral".
This is nothing more than man alone on the high seas, without anchor,
without helm, without compass and with no star in the sky. When Paul
experienced these conditions in a real-life shipwreck, his comment was
"All hope that we should be saved was taken away". Then it was that
above the howling wind and the wrack of the storm Paul's voice was heard,
"I believe God, that it shall be even as it was told me"; and this is the only
answer.

With saddened heart I think back to the atheists and materialists of the
prison staff in Red China. Theirs is a dusty world. Dust they are and to
dust they shall return—but in their view, being only dust nothing but dust
can remain. What does the Scripture say of such? It tells us they are men
out of orbit. How contemporary the description in Jude of twentieth-

century atheists. They are "wandering stars, for whom is reserved the blackness of darkness for ever". This very hopelessness is reflected in the pathetic words of one of our present-day atheistic philosophers who writes in this vein, of man in a godless universe. "The life of man is a long march through the night surrounded by invisible foes, tortured by weariness and pain, toward a goal that few can hope to reach, and where none may tarry long." This is what it means to be deluded by the Communist fallacy that matter is the only thing in existence. It is to be without God, and this, says the Bible, is to be without hope in the world. The whole agony of unbelieving man down the ages has given to this Scriptural assessment its unquestionable confirmation.

2. The second fallacy, and we have already touched on it a little, is the idea that only what can be tested in a laboratory is real. It would be good to go into this somewhat further. If the laboratory were our only court of appeal regarding reality, then life would be a chimera indeed, for people were experiencing realities, demonstrating realities, and proclaiming realities long before the idea of a scientific laboratory was ever thought of. Can we as a generation profess to have a monopoly of reality because we now have, not only test-tubes and bunsen burners, but atomic reactors? The truth is that those realities in human life which provide us with the greatest challenges of our existence; those things which move us to the depths and bring out the very worst and best in us, are nothing to do with a laboratory at all. Take a few at random. Let us ask ourselves, "What has the laboratory really got to say about our appreciation of beauty, falling in love, the sense of guilt, grief at bereavement, the sense of destiny, the will to martyrdom or the desire to worship?" Yet these are the realities in the realm of experience which constitute the warp and woof of all the lives that make up history. Man has lived with reality since his shadow first darkened the earth. Reality in life is not something we have to set up a Research Institute in order to discover. It is with us every step of the way and meets us inexorably at every turn of the road. The biggest reality in ourselves, with which we have to contend, is something that the laboratory has shunned time and again, and that reality is sin. Man has more to deal with than his mere material environment. The Communist says he is only willing to face up to truth in the laboratory. His dilemma is that he has failed to face up to reality in himself. This is wholly allied with his refusal to acknowledge the facts of the spiritual realm, for

where there is no God, there is no law of God, and where there is no law
of God, then there is no transgression of that law and therefore no ac-
countability. He believes there must be another kind of explanation of
evil which the laboratory will reveal in due course. What fantasy! The
idea first put forward by the Communist was that evil in the world was
due to the ownership of private property, and that evil was really limited
to those classes owning the means of production. Destroy them and the
world would be free from their cancer. Administer the means of production
correctly and everybody would be happy. This is hard today, even for a
Communist to believe, for the history of the Communist Party itself is
one of purge upon purge. To say that those purged represented remnants
of bourgeois thinking begs the question for the very purist of Marxists
and many of the most ardent of Communists have been amongst those
purged by their fellows. The leadership itself is purged by bloodshed, much
less the rank and file, and yet we are asked to believe that these activities
are altruistic, and essentially for the good of the people. The straightforward truth of Scripture that man is sinful by nature, and that, being
born in sin, he grows up to practise sin, is the obvious reality. The sins of
Communists and the sins of capitalists are essentially the same. Whatever
a man's social class, he is liable to lose his temper or commit adultery. Is
it not transparently clear that his malady has to do not so much with what
is around him but with what is within him? In the confessions made by
prisoners in the No. 1 Penitentiary at Chungking, if they once began to
confess sins of immoral living, the authorities said, "Oh, we are not
interested in that kind of thing!" If, however, you had served in the Chiang
Kai Shek civil service, the chances were that you were iniquitous, and if
you had taught English in a Chinese school, then you had almost certainly
committed cultural aggression. The fact that you may have been an
adulterer and broken up the happiness of several families was inconse-
quential. The heart-breaking realities of life, the things with which we
are ultimately concerned on the deepest personal level are things which
the laboratory has not yet sifted, and it would seem also that they are
things about which the Communist regime does not really care. They are
things, however, that God cares about, and He cared so much that He
gave for us His own Son, that He might deliver us from this present evil
world and also from the wrath to come. Once you face the fact of God
the next fact He will show you is the fact of sin. I suppose that is the reason

why people are not anxious to learn about Him or acknowledge the facts of the spiritual realm. It would be too embarrassing. The difficulties are not so much intellectual as moral. The prodigal tried to forget the father and no doubt for years he succeeded. As soon as reality caught up with him, however, and his world of dreams was shattered to pieces, he was obliged to remember his father. The very next thing he then says is, "I have sinned against heaven and before thee." Once concede that God *is*, then the next reality, whether you work in a laboratory or not, is the inescapable fact of your own individual sin and rebellion against Him.

3. The third fallacy is that natural law inherent in material only has to be understood and obeyed and man automatically progresses socially. What are the facts? The plight of man at the present time is evidence of the very opposite. Man today is in fuller possession of the truth of the natural laws governing the universe than ever before. Furthermore, he has learned to obey, and also to cooperate with them on a scale greater and more world-wide than ever before, yet the past fifty years have seen more men die a violent death, more widespread tyranny and maltreatment of human beings, more extensive devastation wrought by man than all the activity of the human race has achieved in its entire past history. The Communist maintains that as the ape evolved into a man, so the man of today will evolve into a superman; that as society has changed and "advanced" over the years, so present-day society will give way to a higher form of society and that the evolution in nature which produced man, is now continuing in human society, leading us on by definite stages towards the Communist Utopia. First let it be stated that evolution as usually propounded from outdated textbooks and uninformed teachers in our day-schools today is something contrary both to the Bible and also to any self-respecting system of scientific thought. There is not one shred of evidence in either bone or stone to substantiate that one species of creature ever evolved from another. There is, of course, modification within a species by reason of environment so that you get pigmies in the forests, small Chinese on the plains, massive Tibetans in the mountains. In this sense environment can influence the physical and even the mental developments of people and animals, but that is a different thing entirely from asserting that a species is changed into something else altogether. The bringing of order out of chaos as described in Genesis chapter one is effected by God on the principle of division and fixture. He divides the

light and the darkness and thus fixes the concept of day and night. He divides the waters, and fixes the concept of an expanse above and an expanse below. He divides between liquid and solid and fixes the concept of land and sea. He divides one species of herb from another so that each brings forth after its own kind. He divides the day from the night by the appearance of ordained celestial bodies and divides season from season and year from year. He divides between one species of animal and another and each brings forth after its own kind. He makes man and divides between the sexes. And the record that began with God, and proceeded to the creation of an environment for man, closes with God and man together, in that environment. God has never precluded development within the fixed categories of his creation, but His judgement rests on any attempt, ideologically or in practice, to confuse those categories, for He is not a God of confusion but of order and of peace. The Communists in their Marxist adaption of the Darwinian theory maintain that all natural law is hinged to an inevitable evolutionary principle and that the universe being one, man's society is also governed by it. Mao Tse Tung's public boast is that the Communists are the only people who grasp this principle (delusion though it be) and that therefore in moving with it they are the vanguards of human betterment and move forward in an inevitable tide of victorious progress. Any setbacks can only be temporary. The final goal is sure. The ultimate good of which they dream is bound to come to pass. For them the certainty of "the millenium" is actually inherent in the out-working of natural law both in man and his evolving society. If you can jump on the 'band-wagon' of this law and even help it forward a little by correct procedures, then it will bring that goal all the sooner within man's grasp.

Nothing could be more fallacious than this. Obedience to natural law naturally issues in facility of action and we talk about knowing the way to do a thing, and of the best way to do a thing, but that does not mean it is the best thing to do. It does not automatically ensure morally sound actions. We can learn the laws of atomic energy and in obeying them and harness-ing them become possessed of enormous power; but the knowledge we have acquired does not tell us in what direction we are to use that power or for what purpose. That lies very much with the heart of man to decide. We certainly do not automatically use them for the social good. The Communist will say, "But we understand also the laws governing human progress and we are in a position to decide if this power should be used to generate kilowatts or kill a whole generation." What monstrous arrogance! That is precisely what Hitler said. It was good for the world to be ruled by the Germans; it was good for all of us not to have any Jews, so he murdered millions for the "good" of all. Capitalists are the real sinners, say the Communists, therefore they and their lackeys must be eliminated. Capitalist nations are the real aggressors, therefore they must be over-thrown and destroyed. The Communists are so self-confident in their analysis, so self-righteous in their assertion, that they assume the role of Deity and pronounce the final judgement. But are the world's ills confined to these persons, these classes, and these nations alone? The delusion which the Communists hold has the direct moral evil at the heart of it. A thoroughly disillusioned ex-Communist writes: "The Communist can bring himself to engage in or support activities which he knows will have the most appalling consequences in terms of human suffering, provided only that they serve the cause of Communism and the revolution"—in other words if these activities are in harmony with the object of assisting the law to achieve its "destined" end they are desirable. Writing after the last world war he says, "Today the Communist throughout the western democracies can work night and day to aggravate the difficulties of post-war economic reconstruction, can oppose Marshall Aid in the hope that it will precipitate an economic crisis with all that means in terms of un-employment, malnutrition and misery. By such means, they hope, will the Soviet Union citadel of Communism and its Eastern European satellites be assisted, and the cause of Communism everywhere advanced." I personally have met this outlook. One person of similar conviction said to me that he would not help any charitable work or assist anyone in material need because that would only bolster up the present system and make it easier for the capitalist to go on ruling over the masses of the people. In other words, better to spend your life making the lot of the average man more and more difficult, so that provoked to revolution, the collapse of the present capitalist society will be hastened and the opportunity given for the "law of inevitable progress" to make a big leap forward. This is what is meant by *understanding* the law of inevitable progress and applying it to present society. Lest any think this is exaggerated, let me quote authentic data. On December the tenth, 1948, the Universal Declaration of Human Rights adopted by the United Nations spoke of the "inherent dignity" and "inalienable rights of human beings". The *People's Daily*, one of the official organs of propaganda concerning policy in Red China, said that such concepts were "bourgeois individualistic ideas" and that "they must be made to thoroughly stink and must be thoroughly burned"! Why? The Communist answer is that sometimes human beings stand in the way of the onward march of the law of progress in which case it is morally right to liquidate them, for the future good of the generation to come. In other words the understanding and obeying of "natural law" means the killing of the living for the betterment of those as yet unborn. Are they serious about this? They certainly are. Po I Po, speaking as Peking's Minister of Finance, said in his speech entitled 'For Lasting Peace, For a People's Democracy': "In the past three years we have liquidated more than two million bandits." Mao Tse Tung in his speech of infamous deception in which he said, "Let a hundred flowers bloom", ostensibly inviting criticism of the regime, said, "The total number of those who were liquidated by security forces numbers 800,000 up to 1954." I restrict myself to their own reports. Why were these people removed? The context of the speeches leaves us in no doubt. They were hindering the free outworking of those "laws" inherent in nature and society which make for progress.

I have walked the narrow lanes and squalid terraces of the destitute refugee population of Hong Kong. I have been inside the pitiful shacks and witnessed the wretchedness in which these people live. With pathetic, yet tenacious ingenuity men and women struggle for their very existence. Old boards, lengths of corrugated iron, bamboo matting, dirty canvas, in fact any rubbish that can be scavenged and converted into a shelter, are being amassed and slung together in a frantic endeavour to protect their ailing and wasted bodies from the burning sun and the driving rain. One typhoon and all they have is blasted across the hillside. One disastrous fire (and there are many) leaves them once again under the open sky. Yet they would sooner live in freedom's squalor than eat their rice in silent fear those few short miles away in People's China. They would sooner entrust themselves to the "tender mercies" of a derided and reactionary imperialism than to the "brilliant", "progressive" exponents of natural law on the other side of the frontier. Even if you have no bread it is good to know which side you like it buttered. The refugees have made their choice and they are not mistaken. Are these cynical words? I trust not.

If they but awaken people to see that the sky is red and to realise the fallacies inherent in Communist teaching, it will be well that they were written.

.   .   .

Communism says the world is sick and that this sickness is in the
reactionary classes and their possession of the means of production. This is
the root of all our ills they say, as if our malady lies in what we have rather
than in what we are. They profess both to diagnose and to heal, yet it is
from their own perimeters that the pus of human suffering oozes out,
revealing the ulcerous condition beneath their own political skin.

The idea of adopting the parable of ill health to depict the condition
of an ailing humanity is not originally theirs. First Isaiah, then supremely
the Messiah, spoke of the human condition as a sickness. The Communist
is wrong both in his diagnosis and in his cure. In Tibet they put dung on
a festering wound. That is what the Communist does socially. On to the
festering wound of human society he binds a poultice of hate to foment the
abcess to heat and to breaking point. In this he not infrequently succeeds.
There is an outbreak and we see the running sore of revolution, but with it
all, there is fresh and more serious infection, for the virus of hate, once in
the blood stream of a society, can never be eradicated apart from the grace
of God.

Jesus Christ does not single out a class as sinners but speaks to us all
individually, as sinners. Man's deep-seated ill is in his sin still unrepented
of. Through sin man is cut off from his spiritual life-source and thus
as Isaiah says, "is putrid from the sole of his foot to the crown of his
head", that is in all his walk and in all his thought. Jesus Christ comes as
the only possible Physician for He is the only Man who is not infected with
sin. He comes not to give men a new start, but a new heart. Not to ask
for a new leaf but to impart a new life. Not to make man work for salvation but to receive it as a gift from God. He comes not to overturn
society, but to recreate the members of society. He takes up the real
problems, the very things that can never be solved in a laboratory. He
tells how guilt can be removed and sin cleansed through the blood of His
Cross. He tells how evil habits can be broken and purity maintained in
the power of His Spirit. He tells how we can know true freedom in
fellowship with Him who made us and in the fulfilling of the plan for
which He brought us to birth. He tells us the secret of love, not as a senti-

ment but as a dynamic. He tells us to love not just our friends but our enemies. He draws the sting of hate and pours in the balm of His own peace. He teaches us the right appreciation of that which is truly good and gives us hope for our tears and His own wondrous consolation in tragedy and death. He says, as time tapers away into eternity, "I will never leave thee nor forsake thee." He says to those who trust Him, "The darkness is past and the true light now shineth." He meets us on the level of our personal need. His word is not "revolution" but "regeneration". Communism may seek to destroy the old—but it is the Son of God who makes all things new. This is what Jesus does. Communism can take the bourgeoisie and throw them to the proletariat wolves, but our God can take beggars from the dunghill and set them among princes. Looking at time we can say, Marx may endure for a moment, but gazing on to Eternity, we can say, the Son abideth for evermore.

CHAPTER IX

RIFT OF BLUE

"Then were the disciples glad when they saw the Lord."   John 20
"A light shined . . . and his chains fell off."   Acts 12

IT was springtime, the first springtime since my release from Communist imprisonment, yet it was still the winter for me. Bulbs were pushing their leaves up through the softening earth into the warm bright sunshine. Sleeping seeds had wakened to life and on a massive scale were filling the earth with green in their strange irresistible power, yet I sat numbed and fatigued in spirit, broody and depressed. A few months previously, though spiritually battered, I was, by the grace of God, still facing them, even if it be for the three hundredth time. Now I was free and I was home. I was surrounded with kindness; I had all that I needed, yet I felt less able to face life than ever before. I was in a far-away world. No one seemed to understand. Physically exhausted and nervously distraught, I could settle to nothing. Convalescence had become a burden and in the home I was frayed and irritable . . . I suppose my real trouble was that God seemed more distant now than ever before. I had not read my Bible for years, for it had been taken from me. My prayer life had been broken under the harassing of my fellow-prisoners and I had been out of touch with other Christians for a long time, but I had everything back now, and yet somehow I was "not back", certainly not back to what I used to be . . . Amongst the Communist novels in the prison, one had told of a revolutionary war. A lad is going to the front full of youthful vigour and suddenly he meets a detachment returning from the battle. It is carrying one of the revolutionaries in a dying condition towards the rear. Blood streams from his wounds but his eyes catch sight of the keen young fighter. In the brief moment as the two men pass each other, the wounded man says very simply and yet so pathetically, "Comrade, I was like you just a few hours ago . . ." In any warfare I suppose these are the thoughts of the wounded . . . Now I could look on at the keen young Christians who seemed to have

no problems and to press on so cheerfully in their Christian witness on
the edge of London. Everybody seemed so on top attending the meetings,
talking about the Bible and expounding it to each other. They were
alive and well and their Christianity all so water-tight . . . but I was only
thirty-three and seemed to be finished . . . I could say, "I was like you a
few years ago . . ." but now, I felt I would never be the same again.

I had become an exhibit. I was an object of interest to reporters, news-
paper editors, acquaintances and friends; rather like a man I once met who
had fallen down a sewer and been swept out through the great subter
ranean channels until he was at last picked up in the sea. One lives to tell
the tale. In the minds of many, it is a nine days' wonder, and in the minds
of some even a triumph of the grace of God, but who can forget the darkness, the terror and the stench of the sewer. This is something that even
time cannot remove. The danger confronting all museum pieces is loss
of function. The steam engines of yesteryear may thrill the schoolboys as
relics of the past, but they no longer rattle down the rails. They continue
to exist; they have useful reference value but they do not do anything any
more. This was the kind of moment to which I had come. If ever I felt
like scrap it was during the first six months or so, after I came out of
China.

What people did not know and what I did not fully realise was that
there was a fearful legacy of unbelief cluttering my thinking from the
prison days. In the excitement of my release, mingling with Christians
again, reading my Bible again and on occasion even preaching again, I
had fondly imagined that I was back to my old self once more. I thought
I could just shrug my shoulders now whenever the Marxist teaching arose
in my mind; that with the oil of the Spirit upon me, I could just shake it off
like water from a duck's back, but I was terribly mistaken. My spiritual
injuries were greater than I knew. In the goodness of God I had emerged
from the ordeal still believing. I did not doubt the existence of God or that
I was a Christian. In fact, in facing the foe, my sense of Christian identity
had been confirmed. In this, God had kept me by His power. I had realised
fully how the Communists seek to banish God from Heaven. I had fought
them on that issue but there is somewhere else from which they seek to
banish Him and that is the course of history. As I reflected more and more
on my own melancholia, I was narrowed in my thinking to this one issue.
God showed me that under the Marxist materialistic indoctrination I had

allowed Himself to be reduced to a mere shadow in my thoughts of the history of man. That is why He seemed so far away. God was in Heaven but the Communists were now on earth. I had lived for years in such a Communist dominated environment, and had been confronted so continuously with their concept of history, that whilst I believed in God as the Lord of Heaven, the great truth that He is also Lord of earth, had been devitalised in my conviction. I had to learn afresh the meaning of the great words spoken by Daniel the prophet, in the face of a world domination as crushing to him as Communism was to me, that "the most High ruleth in the kingdoms of men and giveth it to whosoever He will, and setteth up over it the basest of men." It may be hard to the reader to see how important this matter was now to me. If the progress of history was due to the interplay and outworking of economic forces as the Communist said, then it seemed to leave little or no room for God in the affairs of men. If man and his universe were all interlocked in an iron system of natural law that precluded any idea of interference by external forces, then faith in God had no real relevance in history. If ideas were but appendages or excrescences of the economic conditions of society, and in this, world religions take their rise and fall, then where was God in history? If these matters were in doubt, then my whole life, calling and purpose of being were also brought into doubt. I do not consider that at any time I really believed the Communist theory of history in the basic sense, but the thought of it made inroads upon my conviction in such a way as to almost knock the breath of God out of it, leaving me winded and unable to continue in the race. Until this matter was fully settled I would be useless for Him.

To those readers who have never studied Christianity and Communism side by side there may seem something mysterious about all this. Perhaps I should therefore explain the matter in more detail so that the danger of this pernicious philosophy might be exposed and the answer that God gave me in such a marvellous and sovereign way might be the more appreciated.

The Communist view of history is what is called Historical Materialism. This is the Marxist teaching of Dialectical Materialism as applied to the development of human society down the centuries. The English word "dialectic" comes from the Greek verb "*dialego*" meaning "discussion". This takes us back to the times when Greek philosophers met together to pursue arguments that would lead them to a right understanding of truth. Their method was to put up a proposition, meet the contradictory evidence to it, then out of these considerations seek a conclusion that was nearer the truth. This idea of "progress" out of "contradiction" is the prime thought in the modern usage of the word "dialectic". The dialectic is thus the thought method, or mode of analysis used by the Marxist materialist. When applied to history it means that, given the basis of an utterly materialistic view of the universe, including within it human society itself, the cause of progress is seen to be in the resolving of contradictions existing in society at each stage of its development.

The Communist maintains first of all that man arose from amongst the apes in the evolutionary process, solely on account of his ability to use sticks and stones as tools. His view of man is essentially that he is a tool-using animal and that the species of ape which first began to use "tools" underwent consequently such a change physically and mentally as to eventually constitute a new species, namely, humanity. Thus he says that "Labour created Man". Communists then go a step further and say that "Labour created History" and finally that "Labour created the world about us." Why do they say that? This is because they view the increasing production of the labouring masses of the people as the basic explosive force in each era of human society. They do not believe that distinctive men and outstanding leaders, prophets, apostles, philosophers or even founders of religion, etc., have any lasting bearing on history. They believe that as the working masses produce more goods and their overlords exploit them more cruelly, then disparity between rich and poor, the "haves" and the "have-nots" becomes so accentuated that a sudden and drastic change is bound to take place. This they call qualitive as distinct from quantitive change. Out of the contradiction between exploiter and the exploited, there comes revolution, or some measure of social upheaval which brings into being a new relationship in society in the realm of production, and thus a society which is essentially different in all its parts. This is the dialectical view of history and when linked with an undiluted materialism means that the evolution of human society is but an extension and continuation of evolution in nature. In all this the Communist believes there are laws which must be both understood and acknowledged; and he believes he must cooperate with them if society is to be helped forward to that ultimate goal, when contradictions of this nature will all have been resolved. Putting this theory into concrete form the Communist says history is divided into five great epochs, Primitive Communism, the Slave Society, the Feudal Society, the Capitalist Society and the Socialist-Communist Society. When man first rose above the apes with his primitive tools in hand, he lived, they say, in groups. This form of society the present-day Communist describes as Primitive Communism. This was because the game it killed and the fish it caught were only adequate to support the people as living together. Things were so primitive that they had to hunt together, shelter together and there was only a bare subsistence level maintained. There was no possibility of private property. When, however, by their united labour and with better tools and with the introduction of cultivation, more was produced for the community, then gradually certain individuals took over the control of what was really group property, and making themselves property owners began to laud it over their fellows. This brought into being the Slave Society in which the means of production, the land, the early mines and quarries, the ploughs, the seed, the boats etc., were in the hands of the few, and the rest of the people were left with only their labour. This they rendered to the slave owners, getting in return nothing more than their "board and lodging" and in many cases hardly that. Out of the slave rebellions and kindred social upheavals, the Communists maintain that the Feudal Society evolved. In this society the lot of the exploited was less severe and the relationship in production was of feudal lord to serf. Here a greater, albeit still very small remuneration was given to the exploited, often in kind, and he was viewed as having a small measure of freedom, at least within the confines of his master's estate. As in the Slave Society, however, the labouring man was made to work so hard that not only did he make enough to keep himself alive but he made just that much extra. This surplus was "robbed" from him by his exploiting master for his own uses. Marx made much of this surplus as do the Chinese Communists today. Many a landlord has been shot in China because of what he has taken from the peasants of this surplus value. The time came, however, when the relation between serf and feudal lord could no longer be maintained, for with the increased wealth in society through improved production methods, there was more to go round and therefore the accentuated disparity could not be tolerated indefinitely. This brings us now to the Capitalist Society, where we have the relationship in production between worker and capitalist. Here the worker actually gets wages. It was in this era that Marx was born. Viewing with indignant anger the exploitation in the factories, he went to work on investigating the evil behind it all. He claimed to discover in the unfolding events of the centuries an inevitable law of evolutionary progress. He considered that the contradictions existing in a society were the factors leading to its dissolution and also the factors which caused a new society to emerge from the ruins of the old. With this conviction he called the workers, whom he termed proletariats, to unite, overthrow the capitalist or bourgeois class, and establish what was to be a proletariat dictatorship for the purpose of bringing in the Communist era. Actually we are told by the Communist that this final society will be ushered in historically by an initial stage, called Socialism. Socialism means the state ownership of the means of production and the remuneration of the worker on the basis of ability. When production has reached truly immense proportions then the ideal Communist society is to be inaugurated in which each person gives of his labour and each enjoys the fruits of the labour of the entire community according to his need, irrespective of whatever his ability may be. Thus they say the disparities between living in the country and living in the town will be past and the disparities between the intellectual and the artisan will be no more. Man, they say, will then move on to a different level of living altogether!

Of course, history has now left Marx far enough behind to show that his theory, for all its ingenuity, does not work, for in the very countries where capitalism was most advanced and the conflicts of factory owner and worker most pronounced, Communism has signally failed to establish a government. The countries which have become Communist in government have been more the feudal countries. Russia was mostly feudal when the 1917 revolution succeeded, and so was China. Other Communist countries are only in existence today through the aggressive external pressure of Russia and China. They did not come into being by any mysterious inevitable law of progress, not by the revolution of the workers. In capitalist countries, ironically enough, the worker is far better off than in Communist countries. The reason is, for the most part, that the class war has been modified by a definite introduction of a Christian ethic in the nation's history. This has affected the national conscience to such a degree, that it has smashed the Marxist idea of inevitability altogether.

Economic forces are therefore by no means the only force at work in history. Men have arisen time and again, and far from being the product of their age they have been quite different from their age and we have to reckon with the great Biblical concept "There was a man sent from God", and more than that, the great fact that the Father sent the Son to be the Saviour of the world.

In the prison, however, the shadows were very deep. The authorities sought to show in no uncertain terms that I was the product of my capitalist society, that I thought as I did and acted as I did, not because of any call of God but because it suited the capitalist and imperialist country of Britain to foster that kind of religion and disseminate it. Only thus did the British grant me a passport. If it did not assist their imperial expansion then how would they do it? They said in coming to China under these circumstances I was furthering western influences and "poisoning" the minds of Tibetans against them. I was hindering the course of the revolution in China headed by the oppressed workers and peasants. I was therefore their class enemy, a mere tool in the hands of the capitalist-controlled government of Britain. If I were not sent officially by them, I nevertheless fitted into their pattern and policy of expansion in my missionary work. As far as they were concerned, I was a wolf in sheep's clothing conducting what was essentially a political mission under the cloak of religion. This would not be permitted. I must be judged as a counter-revolutionary and make amends for my crime. To help me see the enormity of what I was doing I must have a "proper" view of history, thus in their books and the unceasing indoctrination classes the ideas of Historical Materialism were carefully expounded. Humanity was evolving socially and had now reached the decisive, indeed convulsive phase where the contradiction and conflict between the worker and the capitalist was so great, and capitalist's offspring, imperialism, had become so voracious, that open conflict was inevitable. "But things can change in Britain without bloodshed," I protested. "If they try to have a revolution in Britain without bloodshed then it will not be thorough," was their answer. In other words they were saying, "Without the shedding of blood there can be no purging of society." Let every reader of these words be fully assured that if Communism ever gained control of Britain, our left-wing neighbours, in the ensuing purges, would hound us to the gallows and the country reek with the blood from one end to the other. Co-existence is not an end achieved, it is simply a means adopted. It is just a tactic in their overall strategy to reach the Communist goal which has never been renounced, for to renounce that would be to throw away their entire concept of history as an inevitable march of progress towards the classless utopia of peace and plenty. When Russia and China disagree it is not that the "funeral" of the west has been cancelled but simply that the way the funeral is to be conducted has not yet been mutually decided. The constant return to, and reiteration of this historical emphasis was used to incalcate a sense of guilt in the prisoner. "You say you haven't done anything!" "You maintain you have said very little against the Communists!" "Do you realise that your activity is adversely influencing the welfare of future generations? You, together with the many like you, are responsible for increasing the misery of millions in delaying the dawn of a better world. You are trying to hold back history. Not that you will, of course, but that is what you are doing, siding with the reactionaries, the backward-looking elements of your generation, instead of throwing your lot in with the Communists who are the vanguard of all that is progressive. If you fail to see your error and do not repent of it then you will just be trampled under foot by the onward march of the masses. You will die cursed by the people. What a death! Cursed by all the peace-loving people of the world!" For three years in one form and another this was the doctrine and allegation that I faced. It influenced me in the end more than I ever realised . . .

Now I was in freedom, it was not something that argument could overthrow, although the marshalling of plain fact can, in a sense, overthrow it ideologically today. The struggle was not an intellectual one but a spiritual one. I was not really facing the Communists, as a child or representative of capitalism. I was not even interested in politics as such. The true character of the struggle was clear. Behind Communism stood the devil, who was no mere medieval imp but the highest order of being in the original creation of God and possessed of intelligence and power such as made the challenging of the Throne of God a feasibility in his mind. He had sought to usurp God in Heaven but failing this, he continually seeks to usurp God in human hearts on earth and all too frequently he succeeds, for man has also the capacity to choose. To usurp God in my heart was his purpose now and this dreaded philosophy was the instrument he had chosen. There is only One who can answer such a foe and that is God Himself;

God, who dealt with him in Heaven; who dealt with him on earth at the cross; and who will yet deal with him in the lake of fire.

As I grappled with these things during my first few months of freedom even the Scriptures seemed divested of their power. How could it be? Was there no rift in the clouds that could let me see again the blue of heaven? Suddenly one day when I was reading in Matthew's Gospel, the very light of God shone from the page. I do not know that I was even thinking of my problem at the time but it was one of those moments in my life when God acted decisively for me and yet altogether apart from myself. I do not think I was even praying. I was only floundering. I was not, as far as I can remember, particularly looking for truth but reading almost mechanically, when in a flash of God-given insight I knew I had God's Answer. In Matthew, chapter thirteen, there are seven parables, often referred to as the seven parables of the Kingdom. God only needed the first three, in this instance, to deal with the entire system of Historical Materialism propounded by Marx, and to smash it in my thinking so completely, that it has never been able to fasten on me again.

I read through the first parable. It was about the SEED. This, the passage told me, was the "Word of the Kingdom".

I read the second parable. It was again about the SEED. This, the passage told me, was the "Children of the Kingdom".

I read the third parable. It was once again about the SEED. This, the passage told me was indicative of the Kingdom itself.

Through my mind began to run the words, "The Seed . . . the Seed . . . the Seed . . . God's Answer was in the Seed . . . not in dead material but in living seed . . ."

What was the seed in the first parable? The living word of God brought to us in Christ. What was its result? It brought forth children of the Kingdom spoken of in the second parable, and these together, constituted the living unity of the Kingdom of God explained in the third parable. This was a progression, a development; something initially introduced from without, which once put into the ground mastered it, broke it up, transmuted it and finally grew to bring forth a further harvest of living seed.

All at once the sheer triumph of this development was upon me.

In the first parable the Word of the Kingdom was opposed. There were fowls to devour it. There were stones to hinder it. There was sun to scorch it. There were thorns to choke it; but God's triumph was with the

Seed. Some fell on good ground. Some brought forth a hundred-fold, sixty-fold, thirty-fold. Nothing could stop it. The harvest was sure. The very life of God was in the Seed. It began to look rather like something which had haunted me before; something very like a concept of "inevitability", but the wonder of it in this case was that the inevitability lay with God.

I looked at the second parable again. Was this principle there too? The Seed, which this time was the children of the Kingdom, was also opposed. There was the night when men slept, there was the stealth of the enemy, there was the sowing of the tares. There was the seeming total confusion of the crop, but the conquest of the seed is re-enacted. Irrespective of circumstance, the harvest is sure. The householder counts as an absolute certainty the day when every tare will be burnt and the wheat gathered into his barn. Nothing could stop this course of events. The end was sure. The inevitable triumph was with the Seed.

What of the third parable? I read it once more. Here too there was everything against the seed. It is the least of all seeds, says the Scriptures. *It is the least* . . . something despised and quite insignificant. BUT when it is grown, it is the greatest among herbs. *It is the greatest* . . . This is the nature of the triumph latent in the seed of the Kingdom. It begins as the least; it ends as the greatest. But the opposition is again formidable for as it grows to a tree it is marauded and befouled by innumerable birds which are not of it, yet take advantage of it; notwithstanding it survives, and when it is grown it is the greatest. The inevitability of life's victory is not with man, not with material, not with the world, certainly not with the Communists or the devil, but with God.

I felt like someone who had been shown a secret. In fact in Matthew thirteen the words of Isaiah are quoted "I will utter things which have been kept secret from the foundation of the world." This is what Jesus was doing. His light was coming in from without. Karl Marx was part of the material world which he sought to explain and as part of it he could never speak independently about it. He could never be truly objective concerning it. But here was God who had founded the world making *His* secret of inevitability known to me as one of His children in the world. This was objective truth. The purpose of the parables was to bring this truth to light and all unexpectedly that day in May 1954 God did something for me which chased all the intellectual clouds from my horizons.

Later I began to seek light from other Scriptures and I found that they confirmed what had been given to me.

Concerning the "Word of the Kingdom" I found, "Heaven and earth shall pass away but my words shall not pass away."

Concerning the "Children of the Kingdom" I found, "I give unto them eternal life and they shall never perish . . ."

Concerning the Kingdom itself, I found, "The God of Heaven shall set up a Kingdom which shall never be destroyed . . ."

That which is born of God is born of incorruptible and therefore indestructible Seed.

That which has affected history most profoundly and most fundamentally is not an imagined impersonal law operating in dead material, but the Spirit of the Living God entering into it through His Word, through His Christ, through His Children, through His Kingdom. Economic forces there may be, but in themselves they achieve nothing at all. Through the operation of such forces there is simply a reallocation of material but there is nothing redemptive or regenerative about them. If we boil water it may change to steam but it is unchanged in its molecular structure. A change of temperature may affect it but it will never turn it into wine. Such is man and his society. The social pot may "boil" at times as in revolution, or "freeze" as in China with its three thousand years of feudalism, but material things and the heart of man remain unchanged. Nothing less than the life of God introduced from without can make men new. Inevitability is with God and when the Word of God is truly received, an action is begun which transforms a son of man into a son of God. This is the product of *Life*. This is the basis of the new fellowship. It is the essence of the Divine Answer and in the aftermath of the storm it was His own glorious sunshine breaking on my soul.

"Man, earthy of the earth, an hungered feeds
    On earth's dark poison tree—
Wild gourds, and deadly roots, and bitter weeds:
    And as his food is he.
And hungry souls there are, that find and eat
    God's manna day by day—
And glad they are, their life is fresh and sweet,
    For as their food are they."

Tersteegen*

* Quoted from the *Hymns of Tersteegen and Others* translated by Frances Bevan and published by James Nisbet and Co. Ltd.

Part II

LIGHT ON THE MOUNTAIN

"COME AND DIE!"
"ONE OF YOU IS A DEVIL!"
UP FROM THE SANDS
ON TO THE SUMMIT
THE MUSIC OF THE MOUNT
THE NINTH NOTE
HIDDEN CONQUEST
NO NEST, NO REST
NEW CLOTH, NEW WINE

CHAPTER X

"COME AND DIE"

"Come . . . take my yoke . . ." Matthew 11
"Come . . . take up the cross . . ." Mark 8
"Master, I will follow Thee . . ." Matthew 8

An autograph book is one of those things I have never really possessed, yet when one comes to think of it, this mode of contact has become quite a social institution. For hunters it opens up an endless vista of "prey"; for the ambitious, a most convenient advertising medium of their association with the great; for the curious, a psychological picture gallery, and for the genuinely affectionate, a means of holding on to a memory when a friend has gone his way. If we are honest, most of us will confess to a strange sense of fascination as we peruse someone else's autograph book.

In such a hall of fame, unknown artists exhibit without shame, aspiring poets pipe their doggerel with pride; tired maxim once again holds Wisdom's stage and should sheer impudence intrude, forgiveness is benignly granted.

One day, however, whilst quietly browsing through such pages I was suddenly accosted by a harsh and rugged statement. What had begun as a carefree excursion into the minds of others suddenly ended with Someone coming into collision with my own. I no longer flicked back the leaves but stood staring at these startling words: "When Jesus Christ calls a man, He says, 'Come and die!'" In a moment the entertainment was concluded and the crisis of the Cross begun.

Yet for many would-be disciples the Christian life is no more than a glancing through an autograph book. Of course we favour Christian contacts, but on analysis, the people in our church amount to little more than a collection of signatures. They are simply individuals who, by being there, have registered their name as "Christian" in our experience. It may be we are very particular. We insist that their behaviour be morally legible and their spiritual intent spelt out with no mistake. Christians, we feel, should always be epistles known and read of all so if they smudge their words or blot our page, we feel censorious. We are annoyed if we find it hard to read their contribution. Without our realising it, our Christianity becomes a mere symposium of spiritual acquaintances and religious recollections. Our "faith" is not really Christ but rather a much-thumbed sequence of impressions we have gained. There are glimpses of persons, sidelights on character, snatches of sermons or fragments of Scripture. There are meetings, outings and even discussions. There are clubs and classes we may attend, even though at times we give little attention. Whilst not in "it" as some are in "it" yet we are not out of "it" as some are out of "it". We would not be bereft of Christian contacts and indeed if challenged we would maintain that we were Christians. After all, have not some of our happiest moments been with the "church" people? So we have our unseen book of religious memoirs. When it pleases us we open it, add a little, scan a little, then sharply close it when it palls. To be quite candid we have approached the Christian faith as peruser, collator, utiliser, and very barely as participator. It provides in its current social setting a desirable diversion and even a consolation. We cull what we will and forget what we want, but it seems good to have the spiritual autograph book inside us and to go over it when the whim is with us. In actual fact what is meant is this. We have a relaxed interest in religion but intense interests elsewhere. We enjoy a T.V. thriller on Saturday night but are not opposed to church on Sunday morning. We will indulge in Christ as an adjunct of our culture but fail to own Him as our sovereign Lord. We like generalisations about the "teaching of Jesus" but want nothing to do with "the blood of His cross". We like to talk about His life and ethics; but the Master is a Person with wounds in His hands and feet. "When Jesus Christ calls a man, He says, 'Come and die!' " To have these words written on our hearts is perhaps an embarrassment too great for most of us to bear.

In the sunlit hills beyond Kowloon, where the muddy little paddyfields begin to terrace the lower slopes of the mountains, there can be seen a huge boulder. Its appearance is unusual and its surface strangely smooth. No doubt it fell from a neighbouring crag some centuries ago and so today lies poised above a lonely valley that falls away to the coast of China. Near at hand is the home of some devoted Christians committed to the great task of winning Buddhist monks to Christ. Over the years they have come from the far corners of China seeking the true God. In the quietness of the hills they have been taught, painstakingly, the great lesson of Christ Himself, until this lesson has become their Master. After long months of earnestly considering the Lord Jesus and His claims, some will come to the point of decision. Their choice is to abandon and then to embrace, to put off the man-made robes of Buddhism and to put on the God-given robe of Christ, to let go their idols and to lay hold on the Redeemer, to see that what they yearned for in the Lotus is only furnished in the Cross. At such a moment as this, a monk will be led out to the great stone. In one flank of it, is a small aperture serving as a doorway, and through this narrow opening the monk now passes. As he enters into the very heart of the great boulder, he finds a room, hewn out of the solid rock. The tiny domed chamber is hushed and still. Through a solitary window a shaft of light streams in. There is no furniture but simply a place to kneel on the farther side. As the monk's eyes become accustomed to the twilight he sees upon the wall above him, the beckoning words, "Lay down thy burden." The letters are written on a piece of wood. They express the deepest longing of his heart, and so he kneels. He has come to Jesus. For the first time in his life he knows the wonder of forgiveness. It is the *total* committal of his life to Him who bought him with the *total* price of death. This for him is a crucifixion and a resurrection. As he kneels to Christ, he dies; as he rises in his faith, he lives again. The time slips by. At last he turns towards the doorway, and as he does so, he notices some other words above it. They are the words of his new-found Master. "Take up thy cross," they say, and as he steps into the sunshine they are branded on his soul.

Christian discipleship is the forsaking of all that we have and all that we are, to receive all that He has, and to be all that He desires. It involves a "taking up", not only a "laying down". A disciple is a man of one master; and a Christian disciple is a man of the one Christ. Would you follow Jesus? Behind the rough words of the autograph book are the words of *the* Book, words which He spoke when discounted as the mere carpenter of Nazareth and derided as a demented blasphemer. We must know that in the Gospels there is no Christ of the Christmas card, or of the stained-glass window. There are no "colour-slide" illustrations in the New Testament story, but only the workman from Galilee with no bed for the night; the village artisan who handled nails and wood for a living;

then was nailed by His hands, to wood, in His death. And thus He comes, as one of the poor "unknowns" of earth declaring the "Great Unknown" of Heaven. He offers no social advantage, holds out no hope of aggrandisement. There is no dividend for the faithful or a cash bonus for the apostles. Every time a man puts forth his foot to follow, the Nazarene puts a cross in his hand . . . On He trudges down the roads of Palestine till He comes to Calvary and still "there is no beauty in Him" that men should desire Him, yet paradoxically, men trusted Him, loved Him, worshipped Him and later, even died for Him. Ruthlessly He routed the imposters. His words "slaughtered" the hangers-on. Would some make Him king for a day, or a pin-up preacher for an hour? He becomes elusive. The fans are just fakes. He is calling men to martyrdom. This is no hotch-potch movement of the malcontents. This is the Heir returned. This is Messiah. Not a contestant for the throne but the Man born King. Not another passing prophet but the Eternal God in Person. To stand with Jesus was to stand with God. To confess the Christ was to confess Jehovah. To receive the Son was to receive the Father. For simply being what He claimed, the secular authority and religious powers savaged Him like wolves and hounded Him to Golgotha. They maligned Him, cursed Him, spat upon Him and publicly impeached Him. They scourged His back and pierced His hands. They spiked his feet and speared His side. They murdered the Saviour whom their God had sent. Their vicious verdict, like some crying spectre, haunts the centuries, "We will not have this man to reign over us." This is the conflict cleaving the heavens and dividing the earth. There is no neutral ground. God or Satan, Light or Darkness, Christ or anti-Christ. In the face of His coming and in the face of His Call, to cling to the world and the things of the world, to pride oneself on being someone and having something in a planet usurping every right of its Creator is spiritual treason. It is the flagrant denial of the only Potentate; the dastardly repudiation of the fundamentals of human destiny. He has come to us in His matchless incognito. He is known to faith alone. They looked for a Caesar-type conqueror and were confronted by this peasant-type carpenter. They stumbled at the offence of a suffering Messiah. He has chosen to found His Kingdom not in the wielding of His sceptre but in the bearing of His Cross. Only those that suffer with Him shall share the glory of His final Throne. How can we "reign as kings" in the world that crucified our Lord? How can we lift up ourselves upon an earth stained still with His own precious blood? Can we be accepted where our Master was refused? Are we greater than He? The logic of the Master's words becomes apparent.

"Whosoever doth not bear his cross and come after me, *cannot* be my disciple."

"Whosoever he be of you that forsaketh not all that he hath, he *cannot* be my disciple."

Until we accept this criterion of discipleship we cannot know in experience the reality of His Answer. Whilst we cling to ourselves and the things we have gathered around us, we continue cluttered with our problems. When all is relinquished and we launch out in faith then we are free. Then it is our feet are off the bottom and we are borne up on the mighty ocean of His love. "If it be Thou," cries Peter, "bid me to come to Thee upon the water." Then Jesus our Lord says "Come", and in that moment's trust we are into the impossible. The life of faith has begun and from the start it is all or nothing. We cannot have one foot in our boat and one in His. He has no boat. His way is in the sea and His footsteps are not known.

It is those world movements which ask for everything that get the most devoted allegiance. Without God man is left causeless. The cause of God requires the utter abandonment of man to God Himself but if God and His cause are curtained and screened behind a medieval and corrupted religious system then the next highest bidder for the heart of man will find that there are those who are prepared to pay the price. The devil is no fool in this regard. Determined to usurp God in every sphere through his fiendish devising of alien causes, he asks for nothing less than the highest and the costliest man can give.

In the east, men will measure their length in the dust, hundreds of miles, to a place of pilgrimage; they will allow iron hooks to be put through the skin of their back, and iron nails through their cheeks. They will shut up their wives for life, or walk barefooted through the fire; and all this in the name of religion. Politically the scene is even more bizarre. It is Communism that provides us with the most fantastic examples. Instead of going to Russia or China for an illustration, let us quote the words of a young American who was converted to Communism in Mexico. Here is a youth in the first love of his new-found faith. Communism asked him for everything and he did not think the cost too high. He writes to break off his engagement, seeking to give to his fiancée the political reasons lying behind his decision.

"We Communists have a high casualty rate. We're the ones who get shot and hung and lynched and tarred and feathered and jailed and slandered, and ridiculed and fired from our jobs and in every other way made as uncomfortable as possible. A certain percentage of us get killed or imprisoned. We live in virtual poverty. We turn back to the party every penny we make above what is absolutely necessary to keep us alive. We Communists don't have the time or the money for many movies or concerts, or T-bone steaks or decent homes and new cars. We've been described as fanatics. We are fanatics. Our lives are dominated by one great overshadowing factor, *the struggle for world communism*. We Communists have a philosophy of life which no amount of money could buy. We have a cause to fight for, a definite purpose in life. We subordinate our petty, personal selves into a great movement of humanity, and if our personal lives seem hard, or our egos appear to suffer through subordination to the party, then we are adequately compensated by the thought that each of us in his small way is contributing to something new and true and better for mankind. There is one thing in which I am dead earnest and that is the Communist cause. It is my life, my business, my religion, my hobby, my sweetheart, my wife and mistress, my bread and meat. I work at it in the daytime and dream of it at night. Its hold on me grows, not lessens, as time goes on. Therefore, I cannot carry on a friendship, a love affair, or even a conversation without relating it to this force which both drives and guides my life. I evaluate people, books, ideas and actions according to how they affect the Communist cause and by their attitude toward it. I have already been in jail because of my ideas and if necessary, I'm ready to go before a firing squad."

If in the place of "Communism" we had put "Hitler" then for my young German friend of earlier years this statement would have been equally true. The dictatorship of an "absolute idea", whether it be the racial superiority of Hitler or the inevitable triumph of "progress" inherent in the Communist ideology, calls for an absolute dedication. Satan knows that an "absolute claim" will never fail to capture at least part of humanity just as his "absolute claim" did not fail to capture a third part of the angelic host. All fully fledged human systems, being satanically

derived, exert the claim of an absolute idea; but the supreme claim of
the Christian faith is that it calls men to the allegiance of an Absolute
Person, God Himself, revealed in Jesus Christ. This Person is Absolute as
our only Creator and sole Redeemer. Once acknowledged, He declares
to us His absolute claims. He reveals to us, how that in all things we are
totally dependent upon Him, and therefore logically, can only find the
Answer to our being, in a total abandonment and dedication to Him.
Everything short of this makes the profession of the Christian faith a
mockery. When I first read C.T. Studd's biography, I was fired by his
spirit of dedication. I do not profess to have lived up to it or to have done
what he did, but his words are the only logical conclusion to the Absolute
and Divine claims of Jesus Christ. "If Jesus Christ be God and died for me,
then no sacrifice can be too great for me to make for Him." Every man
who has taken up his cross and gone after the Master in that spirit, has left
his footprints on the sands of time and pointed us onwards in the Great
Direction. Going back to the first century what do we read:

"As Christ's ambassadors we speak . . . as God's fellow-workers we
entreat . . . as God's servants we seek to commend ourselves in every way . . .
by great endurance, by afflictions, distresses, anguish; in floggings, im-
prisonments, tumults, by toil, sleeplessness, hunger and thirst; by purity,
knowledge, patience, kindness, by the Holy Spirit, by sincere love, by
truthful speech, by the power of God, by the weapons of righteousness in
right hand and left, through honour and ignominy, through calumny and
praise; regarded as imposters, and yet true men; as unknown, yet well
known; as dying and behold we are yet alive, as chastised, but not done to
death; as grieved, but always joyful; as poor, but enriching many; as
having nothing yet possessing everything . . . beaten with rods . . . stoned
. . . shipwrecked . . . in journeyings oft . . . amid dangers from rivers,
dangers from robbers, dangers from my own people . . . dangers in the
city . . . dangers in the desert . . . dangers by sea . . . dangers among false
brethren; in labour, in frequent fastings, in cold and lack of clothing . . .
We are handicapped on all sides, but we are never frustrated; we are
puzzled but not in despair. We are persecuted but we never have to stand
it alone; we may be knocked down but we are never knocked out! Every
day we experience something of the death of the Lord Jesus, so that we
may also know the power of the life of Jesus in these bodies of ours . . ."

"God hath appointed us unto death. We are fools for Christ's sake, we are weak . . . we are despised . . . we are naked and are buffeted and have no certain dwelling-place, . . . we are the offscouring of all things unto this day." Some protested but Paul answers, "What mean ye to weep and break my heart? for I am ready not to be bound only, but also to die . . . for the Name of the Lord Jesus . . . for to me to live is Christ and to die is gain."*

Let us come on to the fifteenth century. When I emerged from the prisons of Red China, one of the little books that greatly helped in my weakness was *The Imitation of Christ*. In it Thomas à Kempis wrote, "Why therefore fearest thou to take up the cross which leadeth thee to a Kingdom? In the Cross is salvation, in the Cross is life, in the Cross is protection against our enemies, in the Cross is infusion of heavenly sweetness, in the Cross is strength of mind, in the Cross is joy of spirit, in the Cross height of virtue, in the Cross the perfection of sanctity. There is no salvation of the soul, nor hope of everlasting life but in the Cross.

"Take up therefore thy cross and follow Jesus, and thou shalt go into life everlasting. He went before bearing His Cross, and died for thee on the Cross, that thou mayest also bear thy cross and desire to die on the Cross with Him. For if thou be dead with Him, thou shalt also live with Him.

"Go where thou wilt, seek whatsoever thou wilt, thou shalt not find a higher way above, nor a safer way below, than the way of the holy Cross."

These men have passed. Time has buried them but the Spirit of their Master still remains. Their blood is as seed springing up in fresh flowers of sacrifice. From the hot steamy jungles of the vast wilderness behind the Andes come posthumously, the words of the martyr, Jim Elliot. He is a man speaking to us in the very midst of the twentieth century.

"God, I pray Thee, light these idle sticks of my life and may I burn for Thee. Consume my life, my God, for it is Thine. I seek not a long life but a full one, like you Lord Jesus.

"Father, take my life, yea my blood if Thou wilt, and consume it with enveloping fire. I would not save it, for it is not mine to save. Have it Lord, have it all . . . Saturate me with the oil of the Spirit that I may be

---

* Culled from Paul's writings in various versions of the New Testament.

aflame. But flame is short-lived. Canst thou bear this my soul? Short life?
In me there dwells the spirit of the Great Short Lived, whose zeal for
God's House consumed Him. 'Make me Thy Fuel, Flame of God'."

Such was his prayer as he went to the Aucas and God took him at
his word.

Until we are prepared for this, all that we say about Jesus will count
but little in this world with its reddening sky.

CHAPTER XI

"ONE OF YOU IS A DEVIL!"

"Then Jesus turned and saw them following, and saith unto them, What seek ye?"   John 1

THE first character in the Primer was Rover, an affectionate example of the canine family, whose services had been solicited to enable my five-year-old son to learn to read. Then there was Baby, not forgetting the ball; and by the time that Rover, Baby and the ball had done all that a dog, a baby and a ball could do together, my five-year-old son could, in a stumbling kind of way, read a page or two of the English language. For me it was a learning to read all over again, and when I tried to correct him, it was disconcerting to find how ignorant I was when it came to Rover and the baby, not to speak of the ball. Of course he knew it and I didn't; fathers don't know anything about school books! In fact, compared with teachers they are rather uneducated! "Don't you think you should go over the first pages again?" I suggested tentatively. "But I've done that!" came back the impatient little voice. "Yes, but do you know it?" I asked. I might have saved my breath. Naturally he knew it. After all he had "done" it. "I've got up to page 26!" my little boy expostulated. "Look, the teacher's ticked it off." I gave up. My son was obviously a "genius". The advance was sure. It was only "poor old Dad" who didn't know what he was talking about.

Too many of us treat God like Santa Claus. We post a prayer up the long dark chimney and think of Him as some benign grandfatherly person esconced in heaven waiting to visit His children on occasion, to give them their hearts' delight. Actually He *is* a Father but He is a Father who will stand no nonsense; who expects His children to be like Him, who exhibits not only the love that feeds but the love that scourges. He expects us to do what we are told and to listen to what He says, with no answering back. Believers in the Lord Jesus Christ are not only sons in

God's family but scholars in God's school. That is to say we are Christ's disciples. This term speaks of the Christian in his character as "learner" and if anything shows our ignorance before God, it is when we claim to be spiritual know-alls. Time and again He will insist on our returning to first principles, but how we resent it! "I know that," we say. "I've heard that before", or "What's new about that?" Paul, who was constantly teaching the Word, knew this attitude. Notice how he pinpoints the delusion. He says, "If any man think that he knoweth anything, he knoweth nothing yet as he ought to know. But if any man love God, the same is known of Him." Love is the first lesson; the first word we are set to spell; love that obeys. Some of us may think we have gone far. We can talk theologically —but if we only listened to what our Father was saying, we would find that we have forgotten the first lesson altogether. We cannot spell out "love" practically. Thus what we write, and say, and do makes no sense. We are still spiritual illiterates. We try to write out our Christian character but we are all up hill and down dale and people are bound to say we are hypocrites, however much we try to tell them we are filled with the Spirit. Had we really learned our first lessons, we might have proved more stable and fruitful Christians in our later years.

"But Christianity is different from a language," someone might say, and anyway there is no such thing as a primer of discipleship. Actually Christianity is not so different from a language as we might think. In fact it is the only language that men of every tongue can understand without an interpreter. The love of God transcends all frontiers. It is the life of love that communicates to all nationalities. We read other people's lives, and should our own not be readable? Christ Himself, for instance, is known as "the Word" and to quote the apostle's challenge to the church at Corinth, "You are a letter written not with ink but with the Spirit of the Living God, written not on stone tablets but on the pages of the human heart." Our lives, therefore, in order to be legible to men and to carry the realities of God to their consciences must have at the back of them a clear and practical understanding of the ABC of Christian discipleship. As for the Primer we only have to open our New Testament at the first Gospel and we shall find one there, but before we do that let us make sure that we get the Biblical setting of the term "disciple" clear.

Now it is very easy to state in a brusque kind of way that a man is either a disciple of Christ or he is not, but a look at the Gospels will show that in those days, as indeed today, the reality of a disciple was not so readily discernible. Discipleship is really a state of teachableness. Many said they were disciples, claiming they were learners at the feet of Christ, but, of course, what we say we are, is sometimes quite different from what we truly are. The Master was not deceived. "He knew what was in man." Unlike us, He did not oversimplify. He placed His disciples in at least three categories.

1. There were those whom He called "disciples indeed". He described them like this. "Then said Jesus to those Jews which believed on Him, 'If ye continue in my word, then are ye my disciples indeed.' "

2. There were those whom He called the twelve. "Have not I chosen you twelve," He says, "and one of you is a devil." This acquaints us with the frightening fact that it is possible to have the name of a disciple and the heart of a devil.

3. Then there were those who at first "turned up", but who later on "turned coat," and who finally "turned tail". "From that time," the Word records, "many of His disciples went back, and walked no more with Him." It becomes obvious from this statement that whilst some may sit for a while in the classroom, it is not everyone who goes right through the school.

If in the Gospels the term disciple appears to be a more general description of Christ's followers, once we read the Acts we find that it becomes very particular. In the first chapter of that remarkable record we are told that the names of the disciples numbered about one hundred and twenty. Who are these faithful few remaining from the great multitudes that thronged the Master in the way? These are the "disciples indeed". These are the men and women who have followed Jesus to the farther side of the Cross. They are the witnesses of the resurrection. Their qualification for this is in their continuance. Peter refers to them as "these men which have companied with us all the time that the Lord Jesus went in and out amongst us". They had continued in His Word. They therefore were "disciples indeed", for true discipleship is verified not in the profession we make, but in the proving we endure. Like our Master we are to learn obedience by the things we suffer. There is a course set for our feet. All our living is a going out to die. Our Lord Jesus has no disciples without crosses. We must have the sentence of death in ourselves. The true disciple is the man, who in the light of what the Master says, is prepared to accept the full demands of the Cross and go right through with all its implications into the power of His resurrection.

This is a principle. Our God is a God who kills before He makes alive. He never reforms. He always replaces. If the first is corrupt or obsolete, then He takes away the first that He may establish the second. He does not change the old into the new. It is when old things have passed away that all things become new. *There is no evolution with God*; only crucifixion and resurrection. *Moses knew this* (Deut. 32:39). As a mighty impulsive Egyptian prince he must be blotted out; then as a meek and aged shepherd he can lead God's people. *Hannah knew this* (1 Sam. 2:6). The chafing, striving, sorrowful Hannah is unfruitful but the new Hannah, believing, resting and rejoicing in the Word of God, conceives and bears a Samuel. *Paul knew this* (Gal. 2:20). That proud audacious Pharisee, Saul of Tarsus, must die before the spirit-filled bondslave of Jesus Christ can emerge.

As we pass from the Acts of the Apostles we are startled to find that the word "disciple" cannot be traced in the Epistles. Whatever has happened? It is here we begin to discover the significance of this word "disciple". The Gospels and the Acts bring before us men and women who knew Christ personally on the earth; people who were in contact with Him here, in the days of His flesh. The Epistles bring before us teaching that unfolds to us the believer's connection with Christ above, and speaks of our heavenly calling, position, and ultimate destiny. In the Epistles the believers are mostly called "saints". "Saints" is a permanent word. Those "in Christ" will always be saints. It is not only a term for us whilst on earth but a term that describes us for ever in Heaven. The word "disciple", however, in its Biblical setting, is strictly confined to our relationship with Christ here. It is a learning from His life and teaching, lived out on earth in the harsh and hostile atmosphere of men. The fact that we are saints, linked with Christ in Heaven, gives us *the reason for holy living*; but once we recognise this reality that as "He is in the world so are we in this world" and again that we should "walk even as He walked", then His life on earth becomes for us *the way of holy living*. The *power* for this is the Spirit sent from above and the *pattern* for this is the walk of Christ below. Campbell Morgan in his very first book written as far back as 1897 puts it most succinctly. "The term disciple marks an individual relationship, and though it has largely fallen into disuse, it is of the utmost value still, in marking the relationship existing between Christ and a single soul, and suggesting our consequent position in all the varied circumstances of everyday living."

Discipleship, then, is concerned with my attitude to, and relationship with Christ, as associated with Him on the earth. It is a mistake to link the thought of discipleship too arbitrarily with heaven. Sometimes a preacher will say, "Become a disciple now and one day you will go to Heaven." Whilst only real disciples will be in Heaven, yet we do not earn heaven by becoming disciples. We are brought to Heaven by grace and not by any effort of our own. All our learning at the Saviour's feet could never make us fit for Heaven. Discipleship itself cannot merit everlasting bliss, no more than good behaviour can make a waif, a son in someone else's family. The right to enter the Kingdom of God is by a new birth. To be found in the Father's family we must be born into it. It is in *receiving* the Son that we receive the gift of life. In *learning* from Him we understand the likeness into which we ought to grow. Discipleship is not then a status before God but a disposition of our hearts towards the mind of Christ.

All this will search our motive. Jesus turned and saw them following and saith unto them, "What seek ye?" He wants to know what we are after. They said, "Master, where do you live?" He said, "Come and see." They wanted to be with Him where He was wont to be, and all their days with Him turned out to be just that; dwelling with the Master, listening to the Master, walking with the Master, until He led them to where He had always dwelt, in the bosom of the Father. As He called men after Himself, some knew not what they wanted, others thought they knew, but He always showed them what they needed. "What seek ye?" He says. Following Jesus means life in the soul and a cross on the back. He bore the Cross to give us life. If life is received then we must bear a cross for Him.

True discipleship is a way of no returning. I must leave all that I knew, all that I had, and all that I was, prior to the encounter, and follow Jesus for ever. We must not "follow" Christ for vain reasons. Can it be that I expect after all something "earthly" out of it? Was it for nothing Judas kept the bag? Have I an eye for business in my Christian connections? It can "pay", of course, to be in with the "church" people. Perhaps nothing so tawdry as that, but can it be that as the time passes I will develop a grudge-complex. Will I say like the disciples, "We have left all, what shall we have therefore?" It may well be that nothing is further from our thoughts, yet on the other hand we like to have a sense of influencing people or of instructing others. We may be a nobody in the world at large and yet be quite a somebody in the local church. Although most of us would repudiate such suggestions, yet we must ask ourselves, are we better than the apostles? Did not Peter, James and John argue who should be the greatest? Did they not like to have their say, and are we not the same today? They looked for seats at the Throne before they had learned to take their stand at the Cross. Little wonder the Master said, "What seek ye?" In the east the danger is "rice-Christians", in the west the danger is "nice Christians"; the suitability of a nominal church connection amongst the petty-bourgeoisie. This cuts no ice with the broad masses of the working class for they view hypocrisy in Christians as the unpardonable sin.

Discipleship is thus not an attaining to a spiritually superior position It is not a moral pedestal nor an apartheid concept of holiness. Nor is it an insurance policy against the rainy day of judgement. It is simply learning Christ. He is to be followed for His own sake. As one Christian who lived long ago once said, "Let all be loved for Jesus but Jesus for Himself."

If this much is clear, let us turn to the fly leaf of the Primer.

CHAPTER XII

UP FROM THE SANDS

"They were fishers . . . I will make you fishers of men." Matthew 3
"Thou art . . . thou shalt be . . . " John 1
(Reading: Matthew 4, vv. 17-22)

THE first mention of the word "disciple" in the New Testament is in Matthew, chapter five and verse one. By the time we reach chapter ten we find that many lessons, both of oral instruction and practical demonstration, have been given to these men called "disciples", by their supreme Master. Then quite suddenly twelve of these disciples are designated "apostles". A disciple is one who is taught, but an apostle is one who is sent to teach. Within the events of these five chapters, something very wonderful has happened, for under the divinely ordered training of our Lord Jesus Christ, mere learners have become entrusted teachers. It is an amazing advance. In the first place they were called *to* Him. Now they are sent *by* Him. First they heard His word, "Come after Me." Now they are told, "Go for Me." In the beginning it was the challenge of a "conscription". Now it is the honour of a "commission". Then they "freely received". Now they are to "freely give".

This progress does not mean that they know everything about discipleship. The Lord has much more to say later on. Nor does it mean that they were exempt from the possibility of failure, but it does mean that the fundamental lessons of discipleship have been vouchsafed to them. To use our illustration, they have completed the basic primer in discipleship. This being so they are given the opportunity to put into practice what they have learned and to build on the foundation that has been given them. Thus they are sent out with the message of the Kingdom to the lost sheep of the house of Israel.

Matthew's Gospel, chapters five to ten, are therefore a fundamental portion of the New Testament as far as our first steps in discipleship are concerned. We shall take them as *"our* primer", but like all primers it has an introduction, a sort of flyleaf, introducing us to the kind of persons being instructed.

We shall begin first, then, with the Master, as in chapter four He walks along the sands of far-off Galilee.

"From that time Jesus began to preach and to say, Repent; for the Kingdom of heaven is at hand."

Here is the Lord Jesus Christ, the Son of God, standing on the threshold of one of God's beginnings. This is His initial promulgation of the heavenly Kingdom. It declares that the rule of the Heavens, and the One who wields that righteous sceptre, are come to earth. This divine and august administration is no longer distant. Suddenly it has come to hand. Christ in fulfilment of the prophets has come unto His own, and being now presented to them, awaits their personal enthronement. Thus He begins His unprecedented ministry. This is God Himself at work, and what "the Mighty God" begins He unerringly completes. Satan may raise a cross to thwart it but by the Cross He will effect it. Rejected by the nation He will be received by individuals. He will establish His dominion there within each heart, and the good work once begun will be inevitably perfected in the day of Jesus Christ.

As Jesus steps forward into the multitudes, He finds Himself the only person in an ascending way. Everyone else is coming down hill, scarcely aware of Him, brushing past Him, stumbling and falling in the great descent to doom. He sees the nation of Israel, indeed all humanity, treading the broad way to destruction. This is the circumstance of the encounter and as He meets us He arrests us with His swift imperative. "Repent! Turn back!" He cries. "The Kingdom of Heaven is at hand." He calls on man to turn and face the Authority from which he flees. If rebels will but turn and bow the knee, then there is grace; but if in wilful unbelief they hold upon their downward way, it must be judgement at the last. Once we have met Him and he has spoken, our life can never be the same again. That one encounter crystallises our responsibility.

"And Jesus walking by the sea of Galilee, saw two brethren, Simon called Peter and Andrew his brother casting a net into the sea: for they were fishers."

Here He is walking and moving still in His great direction. This is no stroll along the beach. He is in transit. He is light striking through darkness. He is treading the path before ordained, the path of the just that leads through crucifixion and resurrection to the high noonday of the Throne.

"And He saith unto them, 'Follow Me'."

That is, come after Me in this great direction in which I move. He has found them at sea-level. It is the lowest plane of human existence, a physical fact pointing to the spiritual reality. Now they are to climb with Him. All life from now on will be an ascending into the hill of the Lord. He is going to lead them from the plane of life they know to a new and higher plane altogether. He is going to take them from the sands to the summit. From the standards of men on the shore to the standards of God on the Mount. They were fishers, but now He says, "I will make you fishers of men." *"Thou art* Simon," He emphasises, "but *thou shalt be* called Cephas, which means a stone." He finds them on the natural level but He will employ them on the spiritual level. Thus He introduces the fishermen of Galilee to that Kingdom which shall never pass away.

The call of Christ to discipleship, therefore, immediately confronts the individual with three vital issues.

1. A new attitude, for He says, "Repent!"

2. A new sovereignty, for He says, "The Kingdom of Heaven is at hand."

3. A new direction, for He says, "Follow Me." Inherent in this response is a fourth involvement. It is

4. A new dependence.

"And straightway they left their nets and followed Him. And going from thence, He saw two brethren, James the son of Zebedee, and John his brother, in a ship with Zebedee their father, mending their nets; and He called them. And immediately they left the ship and their father and followed Him."

— These fishermen depended for their livelihood on their "tools of production", in this case their nets; but nevertheless, "They left their nets."

— These fishermen depended for their livelihood on a specific employment. They had one trade. It was inseparably linked with their ship; but nevertheless, "They left the ship!"

— These fishermen depended for their livelihood on their family connection. Peter and Andrew were brothers. They comprised one "firm". James and John were both sons of Zebedee. They with their father represented another "firm". This connection was vital to them; but nevertheless, "They left their father."

That is to say they left without question and without apology the objects of their natural reliance to follow the Man Christ Jesus away along the beach, out and upward into the unknown future into which He was calling. When He said, "Follow Me", they did not as on another occasion say, "Where, Lord?" It was not a question of "where" but "Whom". *Here was Someone who in His very Presence and Person met all the clamant spiritual needs of their being.* If He could cater for them on that level, then He could cater for them on any level. He was their Answer and in one moment of revelation, they knew it. Their father, the ship and the nets were not wrong in themselves. These inferred wholesome and right relationships, but for the true disciple they are not the ground of dependence. When we trust ourselves to the Lord Jesus Christ, then He becomes our Source of supply in every department of life. All other persons and things are but the channels through which He ministers. Following Christ means contact with *the Source*. He will not allow us to confuse the means of livelihood with the ends of our existence. We do not work to live but live now to work the works of Him who calls and sends. Career is replaced by vocation, the concept of secular employment by a spiritual deployment under Higher orders. Without this initial forsaking, every profession of following is hypocritical. Except I leave how can I cleave? Except I unclasp how can I grasp? Except I reject how can I accept? Except I repent how can I believe?

"So likewise," says the Master, "whosoever he be of you that forsaketh not *all* that he hath, he *cannot* by my disciple."

For many the call to follow and the Divine appointment may find them still continuing in close proximity to the things of everyday. The family, the ship and the nets are still part and parcel of life's daily round. Once in the Way, however, these must cease to be the indispensable bulwarks of existence, nor must they be any longer the actual ends we seek to serve. Outside of Christ things and relationships can both use and abuse us. There is a tyranny in circumstance, but Christ in His call brings us to the new dependence. Our faith takes hold, in Him, of the Cause and End of all things. Those things on which we once relied become our servants. If we depend on "things" then they will chain us, fret us, drive us. In the new dependence Christ sets us free to do the will of God. We suddenly find that "all things work together for good to them that love God, to them who are called according to His purpose".

If we forsake our family for Christ's sake, we do them the highest service. We are then truly free to help them as being spiritually independent of them. As relying solely on Christ we cease from our demands upon them. They are no longer the object of our faith. We exert no rights, claim no preferences and introduce no pressures into our relationships. Should they abandon us we know that the Lord will take us up. We can be at liberty in their presence now. We can love them with a love that seeks no more its own. In serving them it will not be for duty's sake, nor for mere pity's sake but for Christ's sake. He loved them, He died for them, He longs to bless them. I owe my all to Him thus as cleaving to Him I am a debtor to them. If they fail me I dare not fail Him. It is therefore when I forsake my father for Christ's sake that I learn what real honour to my father means. There is more hope of realising my sonship, than ever before.

If we forsake "the ship" for Christ's sake, we do our employers the highest service. If I rely on them then I will quickly share their spirit, their earthly aims, and their go-getting concepts of enterprise. It may be I shall succumb to their dishonesty. Should the call of Christ still find me in a "firm's" employ then in it or out of it there must be the forsaking. My witness is to show with grace the existence of the Independent Authority and to reveal in humility my outside Source of supply. In quiet confidence I must show that I do not fear the loss of my post provided I am fulfilling my vocation. I am not a "yes-man" for the sake of advancement or the cause of expediency for I have said "Yes" to Jesus Christ. It will mean either dismissal or promotion but either way the light of God will pierce the haze of industry. The Kingdom of God will have come nigh the men who so often plan without Him.

If we forsake the "nets" for Christ's sake we set them in their right perspective. We dare not say, "These are my tools I cannot do without them." We dare not say, "I am trained to use them so this must be the work I do." We are disciples. Our business is to go where Jesus leads. We must not become enmeshed in our own training and ability. May be with trust, is mingled pride in our techniques. To preen ourselves in what *we* can do is so often to miss the task He calls us to do. If we say, "I have nets," so often it is equated with the idea that I do not need the Saviour. To be self-sufficient is spiritual suicide. The nets must go. How they fascinated Peter! Once he returned to them but Jesus met Him. The Lord must show him that for all he knew about nets he knew little about fish. We are not so clever as we think and the little we have can mean nothing to the Master till forsaken utterly. It is not His will that we should toil vainly in the night but walk and work with Him while it is called today.

Whether the call of Christ issues ultimately in the command, "Go forth", or in the word "Go home", in each case the forsaking must be complete or the following will falter. It is only when we are content to have nothing, that God entrusts us with everything. It is only when we are content to be no one, that He allows us to be someone. We must be weaned from all the world gives, if we are to give to the world the Christ it needs.

"Father, let me be weak that I might loose my clutch on everything temporal. My life, my reputation, my possessions, Lord, let me loose the tension of the grasping hand. Even Father, would I lose the love of fondling. How often I have released a grasp only to retain what I prized by 'harmless' longing, the fondling touch. Rather, open my hand to receive the nail of Calvary, as Christ's was opened—that I, releasing all, might be released, unleashed from all that binds me now."*

* Quoted from Jim Elliott's writings.

CHAPTER XIII

ON TO THE SUMMIT

"Ye have heard Him . . .
  Ye have been taught by Him . . .
    That ye put off the old man
    That ye put on the new man
  Which after God is created in righteousness and true holiness."
                                            Paul to the Ephesians
                    (Reading: Matthew 4, v. 23, to 5, v. 1)

GLORIOUS sunshine fills the bright blue sky, and grassy hills clamber lazily up from the road, and there, all along the dusty way, the wistful expectant crowds meander slowly after the amazing Man from Galilee. Will He speak? Will He heal? Where is He going now? If only at this very moment He would turn and do something. Is not this Jesus of Nazareth the carpenter that some have dared to call "the Christ"? Suddenly the Master does turn but not as expected. The way of the Spirit is unpredictable. In a moment He has moved away from the broad highway to take a narrow footpath that winds slowly and ever more steeply towards a summit of rock that seems to reach into Heaven itself. At the parting of the ways the crowd hesitates and falters. They had not counted on a climb, and certainly not on a climb like that! There is only a handful of people who pass through the little gate and follow up the mountain path where He has gone. Such are the circumstances in which the Sermon on the Mount begins. Such, too, are the circumstances in which it reaches to its close.

"There followed Him great *multitudes* of people . . . and seeing the *multitudes* He went up into a mountain" (Matt. 4:25; 5:1).

"When He was come down from the mountain great *multitudes* followed Him" (Matt. 8:1)

So there were few at the top but many at the bottom of the hill that day; many on the broad road to destruction but few in the narrow way of life, yet "when He was set His disciples came unto Him". These were the few who had ears to hear. To them He would speak the mysteries of the Kingdom of Heaven kept secret since the world began. It is one thing to see a miracle. It is another thing to perceive a mystery. This was one of the first tests of true discipleship. Were they prepared to climb? The incident in some respects is rather similar to the occasion when Moses went up into Mount Sinai to commune with God. The people stayed in the valley. The elders went part way up but Joshua went with his leader on towards the summit. I heard it described like this on one occasion. "Joshua? He was one of the 'out and outs'. The elders who went half-way up, they were the 'in and outs'. The people remaining at the foot, they were the 'down and outs'." It may sound colloquial but somehow rings out the truth. Whether in the Old Testament or in the New, we have the same thing. Few are the men who will climb the hill to listen to the words of God. It will cost everything to learn Christ. Christianity is not just an extra subject that we can pick up as we go along. Jesus may call us on the shore but He would teach us first upon the hill. The truth must be bought from the beginning. One step of faith will take us from the broad road into the narrow way but from then on it is the great ascent. An old poem echoes the question of our hearts:

> "Does the road wind uphill all the way?
> Yes to the very end.
> Does it last the live long day?
> From morn till night, my friend."

In considering the Mount, it is not without significance that we read of seven mountains in the Gospel of Matthew. In this Gospel Christ leads us from one peak of wisdom and authority to another. On the first peak He foiled the usurper (Matt. 4). Before the faultless Son of God, the fallen angel stretches all the kingdoms of the world and the glory of them. The devil says in effect, "You can be king over all, if you will own me God over all." He has said it many times since. "You can have the world if you will sell me your soul." With the rebuke of divine authority the appointed Heir of all things expels the tempter from His presence and with the sword thrust of the Divine wisdom reduces the evil one to impotence. "For it is written," He quotes, "thou shalt worship the Lord thy God and Him only shalt thou serve." Having repudiated every Satanic suggestion of treasonous short cuts to power, on this the second peak, our Lord now lays down the positive principles of the Kingdom of Heaven.

Jesus is seen here in a characteristic posture. David records the long viewpoint of Jehovah concerning Messiah and His Kingdom. He says, "Yet have I set my King upon my holy hill of Zion." Here in Matthew as He establishes the moral foundations of His reign, He is "set on a hill" (cf. ch. 5:14) and a glance through Matthew will show that the word "set", whilst a very simple one, is linked in a marked way with the authority of the Throne. Twice over, first in chapter nineteen and then in chapter twenty-five, we have the statement "the Son of man shall sit on the Throne of His Glory"; the word "sit" and "set", of course, being identical in the Greek text.

Here then is the great Teacher-King set upon the hill. The first teacher-king was Solomon, the son of David. Christ as great David's greater son fulfils all that was portended in Solomon.* As Teacher He is the "Wonderful Counsellor" and as King He is "Prince of Peace"; that is to say, He is Christ, the Wisdom of God, and Christ the Power of God, to everyone who believes. It will be recalled that as Matthew's Gospel opens, Jesus is introduced to us as the one "born King", whom wise men worship. As the Gospel closes He is seen as the one invested with all authority in Heaven and in earth sending His wisdom to the whole wide world. How great then is Christ, the ultimate Teacher-King. The Queen of Sheba, we are told, came from the uttermost parts of the earth to hear the wisdom of Solomon, but Christ sends His wisdom to the uttermost parts of the earth that both the masses and the monarchs might receive His Word. Our condemnation therefore is the greater if we heed not Christ Himself, Who is the source of all the wisdom Solomon once knew and all the power he ever wielded.

It should be noted also that whereas men will speak to Jesus on the shore; at the summit Jesus speaks alone. There is no discussion, no voicing of opinion, no alternative suggestion. No one dares to ask, "Can any good

---

* Solomon is mentioned three times in Matthew, but always in eclipse.
    —In Matthew 1 he is shadowed in his birth for he is "born of her that had been wife of Uriah."
    —In Matthew 6 he is shadowed in his glory for looking at the lilies Christ says, "Even Solomon in all His glory was not arrayed like one of these."
    —In Matthew 12 he is shadowed in his greatness, for we read, "a greater than Solomon is here". The Christ had come.

thing come out of Nazareth?" The Christ is set upon the hill and we can only come to Him and listen to the Word He speaks, a Word so final and so complete that when the heavens and earth dissolve it still shall stand. Such then is our Master. No wonder that His word so quickly shakes our puny thought to pieces. Yet His sure intention is to make us whole, and more than that, to make us worthy citizens of that glorious Kingdom which shall never fade.

So much then for the "Flyleaf". We have travelled now from the sands to the summit. Let us take our place with earnest desire at the Saviour's feet and be ready to learn the first lesson in what we have called the Primer of Discipleship.

CHAPTER XIV

THE MUSIC OF THE MOUNT

"A golden bell and a pomegranate, a golden bell and a pomegranate
upon the hem of the robe." Exodus 28
"A woman which was diseased came behind Him and touched the hem
of His garment." Matthew 9
"Making melody in your heart to the Lord." Ephesians 5
(Reading: Matthew 5, vv. 2-6)

WHEN I read the Sermon on the Mount it takes me back to those dis-
gruntled Saturday mornings when, at the age of seven, my play was
curtailed by the inevitable music lesson. My first tutor was a lady,
probably still in her twenties but to me quite an "aged" person. She taught
me what is called "English fingering". Then, for reasons which I have long
since forgotten, a new teacher was engaged, who turned out to be a
gentleman of a kindly but very firm disposition. He came to my home
each week and to my dismay insisted that I now be taught "Continental
fingering". There followed a period when fingers and thumbs became
hopelessly entangled. The old system and the new struggled desperately
together and the danger of discord was great, not only on the piano but
between myself and my teacher. It was like starting to learn all over again.

This is what staggers us once we listen to the Master at the summit.
All we ever learned along the shore is utterly discounted. There we built
on the sands but now we must build on the rock. There we did what we
liked. Now we must do what we are told. There we could say one thing
and think another. Now our very motive is brought to judgement. There
it was the survival of the fittest. Now it is the triumph of the meekest.
There it was what a thing looked like that mattered. Now only reality
will count. There life was geared to impress men. Now it must be governed to express God. There we said, "Let's get what we can while we can."
Now we are told about treasure in Heaven. There we struggled to make
ends meet. Now we must take no thought for tomorrow. There it was
blow for blow (and what fights there were). Now if a man strikes we

must let him strike again. Is this fantasy or philosophy? It is a different world from ours, and not one of us takes to it kindly. In actual fact this is neither fantasy nor philosophy. This is God reigning; the impact of the Kingdom of Heaven on earth-soiled men. Our reaction is immediate. "You can't win like that!" we blurt out. "The thing is impossible." But Jesus Christ did win like that and He will teach us how very possible it is.

Ter Tseegen, in a quaint translation of his German verse, sums it all up so suitably:

"To learn and yet to learn
Whilst life goes by;
So pass the student's days.
And thus be great
And do great things and die,
And lie embalmed with praise.
    My work is but to lose and to forget
    Thus small despised to be.
    All to unlearn, this task before me set,
    Unlearn all else but Thee."

The story is told how an old bell-tuner came to a village where all the neighbours were at sixes and sevens. He took up a small-holding and grazed his cow with all the others up on the hills. He was a kindly man and in return for little favours he purposely solicited from one and another, he got into people's homes and people's hearts and invariably ended up by tuning their cow bell. For a whole season he lived in the community until one by one all the bells were in tune with his own little bell which he kept in his cottage. One evening as twilight was deepening over the ridges and the children of the different homesteads came clambering up the hill to fetch their family cow, they were surprised at the sound of music. Following the tinkling harmony they suddenly came over a brow of the pastures to see all the cows together, their bells striking up an enchanting chorus as they continued to graze. Then all at once, they saw the old bell-tuner. "Wait a little while," he said, "and your parents will come for you." Darkness was falling and soon, one by one, fathers and mothers began coming up from the holdings and just like their children, they too were suddenly arrested by the hrmony of the bells. It was quiet on the hill and the sound of the music in the gloaming caught at the heart of these country people. Some of them had hardly spoken to each other for months.

There had been bitter quarrels but suddenly the spell of ill-will was broken. Softly one called to another and then another answered until together they herded their cattle down the slope to the village. It was only a little while afterwards that the old bell-tuner left. It was always a mystery why he moved away or even where he went, but deep down, there was the thought that he had come for a purpose and then had left as soon as his work was done. Little doubt, he was one of those men who had learned the music of the Master on the hill.

To the hearing ear, the words of Jesus on the Mount are music indeed. The eight Beatitudes, sounding note on note, form the central octave of the whole vast range of heavenly truth. From these eight notes all moral harmony is formed. Each note, struck with the touch of the Master's hand, sends a vibrant challenge ringing to the very core of our being. In sequence they form a majestic and ascending scale, lifting us to heights unknown. Beginning with the note of the Kingdom (v. 1) the divine scale of values mounts until on the ultimate level of blessedness the note of the Kingdom is heard again (v. 10). This is God's octave and all the songs His joy inspires can find their full expression here. Thus to the climax the Master moves; but listen—the last high note resounds again and though the pitch be still the same, the application now intensifies. Eight times Jesus affirms, "Blessed are they . . ." or "Blessed are the . . ." but the final blessedness, that of the persecuted for Christ's sake, is struck again and from the third person (v. 10) He changes arrestingly to the second (v. 11). The "Blessed are they . . ." becomes "Blessed are ye . . ." In this deft movement the full force of the whole scale of Divine values is sent peeling through our consciences; each Beatitude, a clear still bell of truth ringing out His blessing into our life's wild sky; ringing out the old life, and ringing in the new.

And now the first bell rings!

"Blessed are the poor in spirit for theirs is the Kingdom of Heaven."

The world says, "Blessed is the man who 'attains', and the man who 'obtains'. Happy is the man who can have what he wants and do what he wants." It has been well noted that true bliss is not so much in "having" or in "doing" but in "being". Here Christ is telling us that a man is blessed because of what he is; blessed because of the outcome to which his new condition leads. Real wealth lies in character. This is the first thing we have to learn; to be able to say without hypocrisy, "I am nothing, I have

nothing, and I can do nothing, but by the grace of God I am what I am."
This is the joy of His reign. This was Paul's testimony and God gave him the
Kingdom, till the world empire of Rome trembled beneath the final
force of his ministry. He was a man "having nothing" but "possessing
all things"; a solitary and despised figure in the world arena, yet a chosen
vessel mighty through God to the pulling down of strongholds. The
Kingdom that he served in poverty and weakness is the only Kingdom
that will remain. Though men laughed him to scorn he was undismayed
for as poor in spirit he knew the Kingdom was already his from God.
Rich is the pauper who has access to the King of kings; poor is the millionaire whose only resource is his gold; destitute indeed, the politician
left to his own devices in a ruined world. This however spells nonsense
to humanity at large. "You've got to stand on your own two feet", they
will say. "If you don't stick up for yourself, nobody else will. You've got
to fight your way through; show weakness and you're finished! You've
simply got to give to others as good as they give to you. Who are they
anyway? You're as good as they are!" This is the talk on the shore, but
we are come to the Summit and to Jesus, and we have to make our choice.
It is with the poor in spirit His blessedness begins; but let us not stop
there, even though we must start there. The scale ascends.

The second bell:

"Blessed are they that mourn, for they shall be comforted." What a
sombre sentiment! Is that what we feel about it? "Let's forget it!" says the
world. "It will be all the same in a thousand years. It's no good crying
over spilt milk. After all, that's life and what can you do about it? Have
a good time while you can. I admire the happy-go-lucky fellow. Nothing
worries him. Laugh and the world laughs with you; weep and you weep
alone. If you try to carry the world's cares on your shoulders you'll be a
nervous wreck before you are thirty! Come on let's have a night out! A
good drink and you'll feel better!" That is what they say at sea level but
we are on the Mount with Jesus now and He does not talk like that. He is
the Man of sorrows and acquainted with grief. "Verily, verily," He says,
"ye shall weep and lament, but the world shall rejoice; and ye shall be
sorrowful but your sorrow shall be turned into joy." Men may try to
make all life a comic strip or treat it as a variety programme but this
bespeaks a race without perspective. There will be no laughter when the
curtain falls. Think for a moment of the starvation, disease, illiteracy and

destitution of millions on the earth and then take stock of the selfishness in our own callous hearts. Is it not enough to make us weep? The Master who proclaims the blessedness of His Kingdom, but a few sentences later speaks of the possibility of hell. Is it not enough to snatch the smirk from our faces and sober us? In the Orient I have seen infants abandoned, lepers clothed in rags and despair, people sleeping on the streets, men and women rotting to pieces because of sin. I have seen idolaters sell their little ones to the devil, and hatred trample people in the dust.

As Jesus climbs Mount Calvary, He says, "Weep not for Me, but weep for yourselves, and for your children." This is the confirmation of the prophet Jeremiah's words, "Let tears run down like a river day and night: give thyself no rest . . . Arise, cry in the night: in the beginning of the watches pour out thine heart like water before the face of the Lord: lift up thy hands towards Him for the life of thy young children, that faint for hunger in the top of every street." Today is the generation of a wolf-eyed youth, and a bleary-eyed parentage. Few are the eyes that weep in prayer. Few are the men and women who mourn for their own sin and the iniquity of their generation. Few are those who care for the myriad moral casualties of our age. Yet Jesus says there is comfort for the mourner when the derision of the Almighty shall sweep iniquity from the earth. Laugh if you dare laugh, but do not be ashamed to cry. The riches of the mourning spirit are the tears in His eyes. They are counted as pearls in Heaven. They are priceless, because so rare. From the Tibetan borderland I pen again the words God gave me then:

> O Lord, I have not learned to cry,
> Perhaps I laugh too oft, for true conformity
> To Thee and Thy rough cross, or try
> To love Thee without sorrowing—
> Talk, but touch not, thus they heed not.
> What heart, O Lord, moved through the garden?
> I too have slept, but wake me Lord,
> E'en though it be to love with tears.

The third bell:

"Blessed are the meek; for they shall inherit the earth." Here is humility without hypocrisy, and the ability to endure humiliation without resentment. The meek dares to believe that "the Lord worketh for him who waiteth for him"; believes that men can be moved by prayer alone; is not afraid of missing now what God has promised at the last; will never snatch by force what must be obtained by faith, for it is faith and patience that inherit the promises. Meekness, surely, is one of the greatest adventures of all. The men to whom God ultimately entrusts the most stand out as great and blessed in meekness. Joseph waits in the dungeon. Moses waits in the wilderness. David waits for the moment of his Lord. "Kill him!" say his wordly-wise servants, looking down on the sleeping Saul. "I'll spear him to the very ground!" says Abishai some time later, but again David replies, "Destroy him not. As the Lord liveth, the Lord shall smite him; or his day shall come to die . . . the Lord forbid that I should stretch forth mine hand against the Lord's anointed." "How ridiculous!" the world would say, "Let your enemy go and miss a chance like that? Not likely! Strike whilst the going's good. All's fair in love and war! All this talk about not hitting a man when he's down. It's useless. He'll hit you all right when you're down, make no mistake!" This is sea-level behaviour. It is typical of the jungle warfare of business, of politics, and of nations today. Jesus does not talk like that. He is great David's greater Son. To Him pertain the Heaven and the earth. He is the man after God's own heart. To Him, the Father says, "Ask of Me and I shall give Thee the heathen for Thine inheritance and the uttermost part of the earth for Thy possession." Meekness dares to ask but never presumes to grasp. How great the last triumphant words from the Cross, "Father into Thy hands . . ." Thus does meekness inherit the earth. It counts on God for the culmination of His righteous purpose and casts aside as totally worthless the carnal and clumsy tools of violence, overthrow and annihilation. "I am meek," says the Master . . . "Come . . . learn of Me and ye shall find rest for your souls."

Fourth bell:

"Blessed are they which do hunger and thirst after righteousness for they shall be filled." The Lord Jesus Christ does not talk about being "thrilled" but about being "filled". That is the difference between His way and the world's way. The world sets out to thrill us. "It was a good film," men say, "a good programme." "It was a good show, a good game, or it was good fun." Perhaps it was and it thrilled you, but when all was finished it had not filled you. The prodigal had his thrill with the harlots and then tried his fill with the husks, but the fatted calf was all the time in the Father's house and he was never filled till he returned and feasted there. When we begin to hunger after righteousness, then it is God leads us home. Blessed indeed is the man whose whole being cries out for God. There is hope for us then. The Arabs of North Africa, when ranging far out in the desert, carry in the folds of their robes a little gazelle. When the party is desperate with thirst one of the riders will descend from his camel and place the trembling little animal upon the burning sand. Quietly it will lift its nose to the wind, then in a moment it will run away across the dunes. On and on, faster and faster it goes till the camels, goaded to action, are following at all speed. The mad race across the arid wilderness continues, perhaps for hours, until at last the little gazelle stoops down to drink the refreshing waters of an oasis. With the scent of water in her nostrils and a fearful thirst within, she runs instinctively to the waterhole. What moments of realisation in the relentless heat! Thus the Scripture records, "As the hart panteth after the waterbrooks so panteth my soul after Thee, O God." Jesus says, if this be your thirst, you shall be filled. Righteousness is not a mirage on the blurred horizon of the wilderness. It is found in the wells of salvation; in the Oasis of God. "Seek ye first," He says, "the Kingdom of God and *His righteousness*, and *all* . . . shall be added unto you."

> 'I hunger and I thirst,
> Jesus my manna be.
> O living waters burst
> Out of the rock for me.'

CHAPTER XV

THE NINTH NOTE

"Blessed is he, whosoever shall not be offended in Me."   Matthew 11
(Reading: Matthew 5, vv. 7-12)

WE are half-way through this first major lesson, or if you wish, half-way up the scale. We have four more notes to go, but we must not give these mighty notes, still sounding undiminished after nineteen hundred years, a merely human assessment. We cannot compare note with note and try to detect any variation of quality or imagine that one note is better than another. All are alike incomparable, but each is essential to the other in the full scale of Divine values. It is only the poor in spirit that are capable of spiritual mourning. It is only in the spirit of mourning, as chastened before God, that we arrive at meekness of spirit, and in that submissiveness seek with hunger and thirst for that righteousness that belongs to God alone. It is only as God rewards us, not according to our iniquities, but according to His loving kindness and tender mercies that the concept of the Divine mercy becomes a reality in our experience, affecting our treatment of others. Thus do the clouds clear, the conscience is cleansed, and the heart is purified till we have that indescribable bliss of nothing between us and God, and we begin to see Him, who once were totally blind to Him. Then having peace with God we enter on the ministry of reconciliation and begin to have the role of a peacemaker. It is in this public work that the final blessedness is reached, to suffer at the hands of men as He suffered, to be hated as He was hated, to be ostracised and resented as He was, in other words to be as He was, in this world. As we learn this lesson we have really begun to learn Christ, for "the disciple is not above his Master, nor the servant above his lord. It is enough for the disciple that he be as his master, and the servant as his Lord." It is at this juncture that Christ strikes the culminating note again. The ninth note makes the final blessedness our own. No longer is it "Blessed are they", but "Blessed are *ye*". "Blessed are *ye* when men shall revile you and shall say all manner of evil against you falsely, for My sake." This is the anthem of His joy in our hearts and on our lips, "rejoicing that we are counted worthy to suffer shame for His Name."

In our study, however, we are not yet come to this point, but with the goal before us let us press on to the next great word of the Master.

The fifth bell:

"Blessed are the merciful: for they shall obtain mercy." It sounds obvious but that is not what they always told us. "Tit for tat" is the way of the world, "and if you can give a bit more 'tit' than the 'tat' you were given then that's one up for you. After all, what's sauce for the goose is sauce for the gander. Why should I let him off with it?" We sometimes say. "It was he who started it. I'll just give him a bit of his own medicine and get my own back. That'll teach him and then we'll see if he will try it again!" This kind of talk reads like "gravel" on paper but much of humanity lives in very great measure behind such barbed-wire defences as these, and for that matter there is plenty of "tit" and a whole lot of "tat" in all of us.

At a high-level Communist committee meeting in one of the republics of Eastern Europe, one of the comrades spoke out of turn. At this the chairman shouted, "Comrade X, we shall never forget that!" An ominous silence ensued and Comrade X, retiring from the room, went out and committed suicide. "How extraordinary!" we might exclaim in the west. As one who endured three years of their brainwashing, I say, "No, not extraordinary but something that could well be expected. The explanation lies in this. Where there is no God, there is no mercy. In these regimes built on atheism the authorities never forgive you. If they release you, they always remember. Although allowed to leave Red China after three years' captivity, I was told that one day when the Communists rule Britain they will be able to deal with my question more fully. Mercy is a divine concept and it is only the mercy of the Lord that endureth for ever. We must understand that he who has little of mercy has little of God. The man who cannot forgive has almost certainly never been forgiven. Harboured vengeance is like fire in the bosom but mercy bestowed will be a benison at last, for mercy is that quality that refuses to give a person the harsh requital he deserves, believing that only God knows how to repay and is still willing to redeem. The world will insist on its pound of flesh and it will get what it deserves in its own terms at the judgement, for

with what measure we mete in that measure we reap. The last hope of a
man as he returns to his Maker is for mercy. If we fail to show it now, it
will be too late to expect it then. Have we learned this lesson? It is part
of the ABC of discipleship. John was a son of thunder before he became
the apostle of love. He could not bear to see the Samaritans shut their
doors in the face of his Master. "Let's call down fire on them," he cries,
but Jesus said, "Ye know not what manner of spirit ye are of." John had
forgotten the lessons of the Mount, thus did not know how to behave
himself in the valley. "I forgave thee all that debt," says the Master, and
shall we not forgive?

The sixth bell:

"Blessed are the pure in heart for they shall see God." The continual
cry of the unbelieving world is, "Where is thy God? You can't see Him,
neither can we!" How right they are, and why can we not see Him? The
cause is not in distance but in defilement. He is not far from any one of
us but sin has brought a cloud between. Filth in the spiritual blood stream
causes a film over our spiritual eyes. In fact all of us who have lived along
the shore know that our eyes have been affected. What kind of eyes are
the world's eyes? We are left in no doubt. "Eyes full of adultery that
cannot cease from sin." It is the flirty and the dirty thing that gluts our
vision. We must confess, we are a sniggering people. There is that within
each of us that lusts after the lewd and the crude, however sophisticated
we may appear to be. The advertisements and entertainments of our age
are sufficient evidence of the kind of bait we bite. Peter who had seen the
scavenging curs along the shore does not mince his words. "You are like
dogs," he says, and surely we are. We may get groomed up for the show
but like any other of our kind will turn to our own vomit again (1 Pet.
2:22). "How unsavoury!" we say. And have we only just discovered that,
for God has been accusing the filthiness of our flesh and spirit all along.
The Master is saying you will only be happy when your heart is pure and
only when you are pure will you see Him who is pure. No wonder we
cannot see Him. There is too much dust in our eyes and corruption in our
hearts. In fact no man hath seen God at any time. We must look to Jesus
and hear His word. He hath declared Him. He is sight to the blind. He
renews a right spirit within us, and then the scales fall from our eyes. Saul
of Tarsus, a blasphemer, a persecutor and injurious, says, "But I obtained
mercy", and thus made pure through the blood of Christ what does he

add, "and last of all He was seen of me". Such is the blessedness of the men whom God makes pure.

But what of intention? We aspire to a cross yet too often stoop to double-cross. God is still the only Person to keep His word. This also is purity and we shall not see Him without it. Prayer and preaching seem easier than purity, yet purity is placed before them both. If this is part of the first lesson, is not discipleship unattainable? Later in the New Testament we begin to understand that we are blessed with all spiritual blessings in Christ; that the law of the Spirit of Christ in us can do what the law of Sinai could never do. That the Christ before us is also the Christ within us, so that whilst He presents His standards in His teaching, He brings them into our hearts by His Spirit. Through faith His purity becomes our own, and in the very welter of life and sometimes at its lowest ebb, we can see Him and endure.

The seventh bell:

"Blessed are the peacemakers for they shall be called the children of God."

Somebody once asked, "And what does Jesus Christ stand for?" The answer he received was unexpected, "He doesn't stand for anything, He stands between." There is a difference between sitting on the fence and standing between. The former means I will have nothing to do with either party, the latter, I will lay my hand upon them both. That is what Christ did. As the apostle of our profession He came out on God's behalf to man. As the High Priest of our profession He goes in, on man's behalf, to God. His hand is upon us both. Because He made peace through the blood of His Cross, God and man now meet in Him. "God is propitiated: the sinner reconciled". How many persons and how many nations today need someone to stand between? Christ is the Son of God and every time we take a stand between persons at variance, for His sake, we proclaim His likeness and God calls us the sons of God. (Note the Greek here is "huios" the word for "son" rather than "child".) There is no task more liable to misunderstanding and abuse than that of the peacemaker. Once we begin this public work the final note of blessedness will soon be struck and persecution for Christ's sake begin. Whether we beseech men in Christ's stead to be reconciled to God or wheher we beseech them for Christ's sake to be reconciled to each other, hostility will be our lot. Moses in his day was the destined saviour of his people. On one occasion he stood between an Egyptian and an Israelite and defended his compatriot, but he was not appreciated. It says, "He supposed his brethren would have understood how that God by his hand would deliver them but they understood not." Another day he stood between two Israelites who were at loggerheads. "Sirs," he said, "ye are brethren, why do ye wrong one to another, but he that did his neighbour wrong thrust him away saying, Who made thee a ruler and a judge over us." This was their treatment of the man who esteemed the reproach of Christ greater riches than the treasures in Egypt. Such was their treatment also, only with more malignant intent, of the Christ Himself. "We will not have this man to reign over us." Such will be the treatment of the peacemakers who follow their Master today. They will be counted interferers, busybodies, tamperers, but rarely if ever mediators. To all this there is the amazing recompense of reward. He calls us the sons of God, and He who is the Son of God is not ashamed to call us brethren even though the sons of men may make us outcasts. Let us in all our life and witness be not ashamed to tread the middle road of the balance of truth even if we are splashed from both sides. We must never be partisan but seek to draw those who are divided together, remembering that the biassed outlook tends always to end in the gutters of life's road.

The eighth bell:

"Blessed are they which are persecuted for righteousness' sake; for theirs is the kingdom of heaven."

On the fringe of the Mau Mau country in Kenya, three young native women yielded their lives to the Lord Jesus Christ. They were publicly baptised and received into the fellowship of the local church. How sweet the moment when for the first time in their lives they remembered their Lord in the breaking of bread and the drinking of the cup with their fellow believers in that distant village. Shortly afterwards there was a Mau Mau raid and the three young women were taken off as hostages. Far away in the mountains the marauding band at last halted and examined their booty. The three young girls were set in the midst of the ribald circle of this bandit company. One was about fifteen, another perhaps fourteen and the third one only twelve years of age. What would these men do to them? After a little while a cup of blood was carried across to them and they were made to understand that the sipping of this cup was to serve as an initiation ceremony into the Mau Mau clan. In uncouth expectancy the men waited to see what these young Christians would do. Death was the only alternative. They would brook no defiance. The cup was proffered first to the girl of fifteen. Resolutely she refused it. With one magnificent utterance in the power of the Spirit she answered them, "Sirs," she said, "we have drunk of One Cup." There was a moment's hush as if these violent men were for an instant cowered by her witness. Then swiftly the blow fell, and the warm blood of a martyr soaked down through the stones and grasses. "O blessed are they which are persecuted for righteousness' sake for theirs is the Kingdom of heaven." She had struck the highest note in that last word of testimony. Hers was praise on the high sounding cymbals. She had sealed her witness with her blood.

This is where discipleship leads. Are we prepared to go through to such an abandonment? The ninth note is striking, but can we bear it?

"Blessed are YE when men shall revile you and persecute YOU . . . for great is *your* reward in heaven . . ."

> "O Cross that liftest up my head,
> I dare not ask to fly from Thee;
> I lay in dust life's glory dead,
> And from the ground there blossoms red
> Life that shall endless be."

CHAPTER XVI

HIDDEN CONQUEST

"As a man thinketh in his heart so is he."   Proverbs 23
"I verily thought . . . that I ought . . ."   Acts 26
"Let this mind be in you, which was also in Christ Jesus." Philippians 2

(Suggested reading—Matthew 5, v. 13 to 7, v. 29)

EVERY victory knows its secret; every conquest its untold story. There is no such thing as sudden triumph. Each man who overcomes before the world, has overcome himself long, long before. No one really wins in public who has not trodden down defeat in private. Failure to see this was the downfall of Israel's religious leaders. They sought a reputation yet were not essentially reputable. In the inexorable laws of God, the One Who made Himself of no reputation was the One Who ultimately ground them to powder. They stumbled at Him and were broken, and when the full weight of the Crucified fell upon them they were reduced to fragments never to integrate again.

Somewhere I caught sight of the following words, and as a Christian, I was immediately intrigued by their unconscious challenge. "As always before a big expedition, I tried hard to get myself back into good condition. I got up early in the morning, filled a knapsack with stones and took long walks up and down the nearby hills. And all the time I was thinking, planning, hoping about what would happen on this my seventh trip to Everest. This is the time you must do it, I told myself (for I was now thirty years old) you must do it or die." In this simple expression of dedication, Tensing unveils his own secret conquest of the mountain. He went to the summit of the highest peak not because of the strength of the day but because, when others were sleeping in their beds, he was tramping the local hills in the chill of the dawn, stones on his back. Before the public triumph he had to learn to be master of himself in secret. As the old proverb says, "Before honour is humility." It is only when I realise my need to master the ordinary thing that it becomes possible, one day, for me to attempt the *impossible* thing. If this is true in regard to a mountain how much truer when it comes to following the Man of the Mount. His stature is so sublime. He is the stone cut out without hands who in the day of His glory shall be as a mountain filling the whole earth. He is the Christ of the Mount; the personal embodiment of all that is involved when we say "God reigns". In Him is at once the impossible and the possible. The impossible standard and yet the enabling dynamic of His Spirit. He will teach us to climb but there will be stones for our back, and early risings. We must become men with only one mountain on our horizon, but if we will put our hand in His, if we who live by the Spirit will keep in step with the Spirit, then He will bring us to the heights of God in the morning.

The Law was severe but Grace is severer still. The Law demanded much but Grace demands all. The Law regulates the act. Grace purifies the motive. The Law left the people at the foot of Mount Sinai but grace brings us to the seat of Mount Zion. Jesus time and again utters these words, "Ye have heard that it was said by them of old time . . . but I say unto you . . ." Where the Law did not intrude, Grace is determined to control. The Law of Moses said, "Thou shalt not do this or that . . ."—a negative prohibition; Grace comes to us in Jesus Christ and says, "I will make you to become . . ." involving a positive recreation. Striving to obey the Law seeks to put God in our debt. Grace redeeming us, teaches us that we are now totally in debt to God. He does not look for any legal repayment but only loving response. We are not our own, we are bought with a price. Ours is now the discipline of glorifying Him in our body and in our spirit which are God's. It is no longer a question of seeking to keep the letter of the law but of having fulfilled in us the spirit of Jesus Christ. The Law was written on tables of stone but God has written now His own word upon our hearts. This is the difference between the Old and New Covenant. The "Old" started with our hands asking something from us—but the "New" begins in our hearts giving something to us. The Sermon on the Mount has to do in a very special way with the out-working of these standards by the inner man.

In the year 1662 when many godly servants of our Lord Jesus Christ were bitterly persecuted for their faithfulness to the Word of God,*

* The Great Ejection.

Joseph Allein was on his way to preach to the believers meeting at Luppitt, near Taunton, when he was summarily arrested and taken to Ilchester Jail. The indictment read as follows:

"That he upon the . . . day of . . . with . . . others, to the jurors unknown, did riotously, routously, and seditiously, assemble themselves together contrary to the peace of our Sovereign Lord, the King, and to the terror of his subjects and to the evil example of others."

From his prison cell he wrote, "Know, dear Christians, that the bonds of the Gospel are not tedious through grace unto us; that Christ is a Master worth suffering for . . . that Christ's prison is better than the world's paradise . . . that the influences of heaven, and shines of God's countenance, are sufficient to lighten the darkest dungeon."

His wife knew this was no mere pious language for she testified that, "All the time of his health, he did rise constantly at or before 4 o'clock, and on Sabbaths earlier, if he did awake. He would be much troubled if he heard any smiths, or shoemakers, or such tradesmen at work at their trades before he was in his duties with God; saying to me often, 'O, how this noise shames me! Doth not my Master desire more than theirs.' Neither did his fellow believers discount his witness for they knew him as a man of deep spiritual motive. When with them, he had this testimony. Writing of his heart's desirings he says, 'That in all I do, whether sacred or civil actions, still may I be doing but one work, and driving on one design, that God may be pleased by me and be glorified in me . . . I strictly impose upon myself from day to day—never to lie down but in the name of God, not merely for natural refreshment, but that a wearied servant of God may be recruited and fitted to serve Him better the next day. Never to rise up but with this resolution—Well, I will go forth this day in the name of God and will make religion my business and spend the day for eternity. Never to sit down to the table, but resolving I will not eat to please my appetite, but to strengthen myself for my Master's work. Never to make a visit but upon some holy design, resolving to leave something for God where I go and in every company leave some good saviour behind.' "

This devoted disciple of our Lord Jesus Christ died at the age of 35 just three years after his first arrest and largely on account of the privations he suffered in prison.

The record quoted here shows the discipline of a man living in the spirit of the Sermon on the Mount. It tells of high motive controlling the simplest actions of everyday. This discipline is the outcome of grace within, not a striving to attain a law without, for only the Grace of God can achieve what the Law of God demands.

.   .   .

In the Gospel of Matthew there are five main discourses of our Lord Jesus Christ. They are distinguished by the terminating words of the narrative in each case, namely, "It came to pass when Jesus had ended these sayings, parables, etc. . . ."* The first one is the Sermon on the Mount and is clearly *ethical* in its emphasis. The second is the instruction to the twelve before they were sent out, and might be termed as *evangelical* in the sense that Jesus tells His disciples how to make known the Gospel. The third deals with the seven parables of the Kingdom and is more *dispensational*, covering the whole period from the dawn of grace to the fall of judgement. The fourth is His introduction to the teaching of the local church and could be termed *ecclesiastical*. The fifth one is His warning for the Last Days and is *prophetical*. The order of emphasis is significant. How often we like to discuss prophecy, argue about church order, digress on the dispensations and exhort each other about preaching the Gospel. These are all important and our Lord neglects none of them, but first of all He puts forward the ethical principles of His Kingdom. If we are going to represent God the first requirement is that we should be *good*. If we are going to proclaim the Truth it is necessary first to speak the truth, indeed to have truth in our "inward parts".

In John's Gospel the emphasis is on entrance to the Kingdom. In Matthew the emphasis is on the character of those in the Kingdom. In John's Gospel Christ speaks of the birth of the subjects. In Matthew He speaks of the behaviour of the subjects. In John we become sons of the Father by partaking of the life of the Father. In Matthew we are known as sons of the Father by portraying the likeness of the Father. In John we find we cannot rise to sonship from a lower order. In Matthew we cannot be recognised as sons unless we exhibit the higher order. In John we are told we must be born from above. In Matthew we are told to set our hearts on things above. In John, Christ comes into us. In Matthew, Christ shines out of us. These

* 7, v. 28; 11, v. 1; 13, v. 53; 19, v. 1; 26, v. 1.

two Gospels must be taken together for they are but the two sides of one Gospel. In John we are brought into the sphere of His reign. In Matthew He brings the sphere of His reign into us. Whilst these truths do overlap in the two Gospels, it is helpful to trace some of the more characteristic features of Matthew's presentation in considering the basic content of the Master's teaching as He sat that day on the Mount.

The Sermon on the Mount is not to be relegated merely to the millennium. Its setting gives the key to its application. There are the few on the height and the many in the valley. In a short while they are going to be sent back into the crowd. They will be His Kingdom, God's bridge-head penetrating into a rebellious nation, indicative, in the wider sense, of a rebellious humanity. The disciples as subject to the God of Heaven are going to take the thought, life and behaviour of Heaven into the earth, to be both salt and light there. This is not a question of a far-away standard for a far-off era but of God's permanent standard applied to the present era. It is not sufficient to say there are Jewish overtones in the Sermon on the Mount and that Christ's teaching is just part of the process of presenting the Kingdom to Israel. When Jesus began to preach He said, "The Kingdom of Heaven is at hand." In this He was announcing something more than a dispensational turn of events. "The tense here is very important exegetically. It does not occur very frequently but when it does, it indicates an action complete in itself yet continuing in its effect, hence it could read, 'The Kingdom of Heaven hath drawn near completely, and abides so permanently'." This proclamation gives us the inherent significance of Messiah's advent and ministry. Thus John the Baptist employs it, for he was the final herald; and then as sent before Messiah's face the twelve declare it, and finally the seventy. We cannot take the sayings of the Mount and bandy them about. They are for us, and their relevance is enormous in today's world so dominated by the Communist's philosophy. Here is God's answer in the first lessons of discipleship, an answer that reaches into the very heart and motive of the individual and touches us on a level Marx never once perceived.

Our Lord Jesus Christ shows us that true practical righteousness rests on the fact of a relationship established between those who hear the Word of God's authority, and God Himself who wields that authority. This is a relationship not only of citizens to a King but of sons to a Father. This is the first major discourse recorded in the ministry of our Lord and in it

He introduces the Father. In the last recorded discourse in the upper room He introduces us to the Holy Spirit. This is a matter full of meaning. "Show us the Father," said Philip on that latter occasion, "that is all we need." In this he had put his finger on the touchstone of the whole mystery of spiritual hunger. Thus at Pentecost the Spirit was given to expound the Christ, that men seeing the Son might see the Father. In the Sermon on the Mount the Father, who had been mentioned but vaguely and by inference in the Old Testament Scriptures, is now brought into focus for the vision of faith. In these few recorded words on the Mount, Christ brings before us the Father's grace (5:45), the Father's perfection (5:48), the Father's reward (6:1), the Father's omniscience (6:4, 6:18), the Father's perception (6:42), the Father's abode (6:9), the Father's forgiveness (6:15), the Father's care (6:26), the Father's Kingdom (6:33 R.V.), the Father's gifts (7:11), the Father's will (7:21). Everything is built on that. To know the Father in the Son through the regenerating work of the Holy Spirit is eternal life. This is not so much longevity but a participation in the Divine life of the Godhead. It is a quality of life distinct from natural life and makes us *see* the Kingdom of God. Unbelievable possibilities are then opened up to us. Each form of life has its own level and is governed by certain instincts. Each is therefore ignorant of the life forms and life experience in the realm above it. To use a very simple illustration: on a farm a duck may eat a worm, and a fox may eat a duck, then the farmer may shoot the fox, but none of these understands the nature of the creature above it. The most it can know is a sense of fear from a greater and stronger entity than itself. So it is the Scriptures inform us that "that which is born of the flesh is flesh and that which is born of the Spirit is spirit"; also that "the flesh lusteth against the spirit and the spirit against the flesh". To understand the life of a worm we must be born in the worm's world; to understand the life of a duck we must be born into the duck's world, and so on. A man understands the things of a man, but to understand the things of God we have to be brought into a new realm, the Kingdom of God, and as in all other cases we can only enter this realm of life by being born into it. Thus to become a citizen of His Kingdom and a child in His family we must be born from above. Then we *see* and know this higher Kingdom into which as believers, we have been born. Jesus is telling us now what it really means to have God as our Father. It means that we are living constantly in a sphere of existence in which we are wholly transparent, in which God sees us through and through all the time. Living on the world's shore meant, to a large extent, putting a face on things and fighting for all we were worth not to lose it. In this way tremendous weight was put on externals—social and religious standing, reputation of all kinds, present advantage and impressions conveyed, but on the Mount where we are introduced to God's Kingdom, we have to look at everything from God's standpoint with the result that all is reversed. We are literally turned inside out and the inner life is seen to be fundamental, and the factor that must govern our external activity and relationships. If we reject this principle then all our outward achievement becomes a kind of "variety". It is no more than a fancy-dress and it must be remembered the party ends at midnight.

The key word in the Law, it has been noted, was "observe". It occurs, for instance, over twenty times in Deuteronomy. But the key word in relation to the Grace of God is "fulfil". Observing the Law has to do with the letter of the Law. Fulfilling the Law has to do with the spirit behind the Law. These weightier matters which Christ enumerated as "justice, mercy and faith", Christ came to fulfil. He came not so much to regulate man's conduct but to renew his heart. Thus to those who received Him and were made anew He gives the honoured designation. "Ye are the salt of the earth", "Ye are the light of the world". Here the "earth" is mankind in his unorganised mass and the "world" is mankind in his organised society. Salt is the Christian in his moral character permeating the mass through personal contact. Light is the Christian in his moral character illuminating society by its public impact. The former has to do with the Christian's invisible worth. The latter with the Christian's visible works. Salt has to do with penetration, light with manifestation. Salt brings out the true flavour of things, thus defining the nature of that with which it comes in contact. Light reveals the true colour of things, thus defining the characteristics of that upon which it makes an impact. Salt is a preservative from corruption; light a rebuker of corruption. The salt of Christian character smarts in the wound of sin. The light of Christian character searches out the secrets of sin. Christ speaks of having salt in ourselves (Mark 9:50) and He speaks of "the light that is in you" (Matt. 6:23). Christ reigning within a man; this is salt and this is light, and each emblem bespeaks the outworking of that rule. In whatever degree we fail to acknowledge that authority, in that degree we turn to grit and gloom. To be right with God within is the foundation of all right relationships without. Emphasis on *observance* leads to mechanical rituals. Emphasis on *fulfilment* brings us to the intuition of the Spirit which realises the very righteousness of God within us in a way the law itself could not do by reason of the weakness of our flesh.

During the last war, for one period, I worked with another Christian in the office of a quartermaster's store. As this was situated near the cookhouse the fellows there would make tea and put a bucket of the "precious liquid" into our room for our personnel. I used to take a cup with the rest of my colleagues but I eventually became aware that my friend John never partook of it. I was a little perplexed, so decided to ask him quite directly why he refused the tea. He replied simply and with evident conviction; and in a way, too, quite devoid of anything Pharisaical, that this tea was something the other fellows did not get. It was something taken out of the ration to which we were not really entitled and he therefore felt before God, that as a Christian he should not drink it. I was conscious that no matter how much sugar was put in the tea, it never tasted sweet again. John's salt had a savour that remained. If some feel this is negative Christianity, perhaps it should be said that once he was free from national service he prepared himself for a yet more vigorous encounter. He took the Gospel all the way to Tierra Del Fuego, that the light of God might shine through him in that far corner of the globe. If we are prepared to be salt in secret it will not be long before we are light in public. As our Lord unfolds His teaching He shows us the way in which the blessed men of the Beatitudes, namely, those who are the salt of the earth and the light of the world, fulfil the spirit of their Master and declare the likeness of their God. Where this is achieved there is a glorifying of the Father—and is not this the chief end of man?

Our Lord Jesus Christ now develops His instruction in four clear stages using the method of contrasting values. Then in His closing words He presents in three simple parables the challenge of His way of life to the listener. In summary we have therefore:

Chapter 5, vv. 17-48: Things outward and things inward; that is, matters concerning visible wrongdoing and the unseen evil intention.

Chapter 6, vv. 1-18: Things before and things behind; that is, matters concerning display in public and integrity in secret.

Chapter 6, vv. 19-34: Things below and things above, that is, matters concerning interests in earth and interests in heaven.

Chapter 7, vv. 1-12: Things of mine and things of thine, that is, matters concerning myself and others.

If we retain the musical parable we could say the Beatitudes are like an opening fugue and that what ensues is the development and exposition of this original Divine melody by the incomparable ability and excellence of the Divine mind. In detail this is demonstrated as follows:

Things outward and things inward: ch. 5, vv. 17-48; that is, matters concerning visible wrongdoing and evil intent. The questions raised in my conscience by the Lord's penetrating words are these:

—I know I should not kill yet is not my anger murderous?

—I know I should not commit adultery but does not my lustful eye constitute me an adulterer?

—I know I should not break an oath but should I not deal truthfully all the time?

—I feel justified in taking revenge, but the Master insists that I offer my other cheek, give my other garment, and go the other mile.

—I feel justified in hating my enemy but the Master insists that I love him; that I bless him and that I do him good.

He tells me that though in outward actions I may seem to acknowledge the Law yet in my motives I deny the very Spirit of the God who gave it. Now, I am not so much to look right, but to *be* right; to *be* perfect; to *be* as my Father; to *be* a son. It matters not only what I do, but why I do it. and what I really am.

Things before and things behind: ch. 6, vv. 1-18, that is, what we are in front of people and what we are behind their backs. The questions raised here are these:

—Do I try to look charitable before the crowd? Jesus demands that I be charitable in the secret of personal contact.

—Do I try to look religious before the crowd? Jesus demands that I be spiritual in the secret place of prayer.

—Do I try to look ascetic before the crowd? Jesus demands that I be a disciplined man in secret before God.

Man may take account of display in the open. The Father takes account of sincerity behind the scenes; and the question of recompense is altogether in His hand.

Things below and things above: ch. 6, vv. 19-34. By this we mean things on the earth contrasted with things in heaven. The questions raised are these:

—Is my heart set on an earthly treasure?
—Is my service to an earthly master, mammon?
—Is my care for my earthly life?
—Has the struggle to live become in itself for me the goal of life?

Earth's treasures must corrupt, earth's mammon must fail, earth's life must pass, but the treasure in Heaven remains, the Master in Heaven abides, the life of Heaven is eternal. Seek ye first the Kingdom of God, says the Master. Your Father will take care of the things below. Be free. Be still. Believe.

Things of mine and things of thine: ch. 7, vv. 1-12; that is, things concerning myself and others. The questions raised are these:

—Can I say I am always right and others are always wrong; that I must always be the judge and they the accused?
—Can I remove a speck of sawdust from another's eye with a plank still in my own?
—Dare I squander on others the gifts of God if they repudiate them?
—Should I not ask, then, the Great Other when I stand in need?— for I, though evil, give to others whom I love.
—Should I not do to others as I would they should do to me?

This, says Jesus, is the Law and the prophets. Indeed all this was fulfilled in Him, who was Himself the embodiment of all He taught.

A moment's thought will cause us to realise that in the development of this teaching our Lord Jesus Christ probes to the very foundations of our being. He completely overthrows us. He is showing that once His sovereignty is accepted He will go to the core of every problem in our lives and meet it with His own Answer. I can talk glibly of world problems. Actually I am my own problem. Therefore He begins with me. He starts with the individual and with the "hidden man of the heart".

We have here, then, two modes of life. The one is concerned merely with visible behaviour, purposeful display, material gain and selfish ends. The other is concerned with inward motive, personal integrity, things eternal and the care of others. One is manward, selfward, hellward. The other is Godward, otherward, heavenward. The last part of our Lord's discourse, which now follows, summarises the issues in an open challenge to the would-be learners at His feet. As the Master-Teacher, He deftly uses three simple parables and in a few immortal words crystallises for all time the choice that confronts every individual. He says that one way is the broadway leading to destruction. It is thronged with the many. The other way is the narrow way that leads up to life. It is trodden by the few. One mode of life is like a bad tree, corrupted within and yielding only blighted fruit. The other is a good tree, which out of the abundance and purity of its life, yields only excellent fruit. One way of living is like building on the sands, courting certain ruin. The other way of living is like building on a spur of rock where neither wind, nor flood can prevail. In John's Gospel our Lord is the Way, the Truth and the Life, Who brings us into the fellowship of the Father. Here He shows us the narrow *way*, the rocklike *truth* and the vibrant fruitbearing *life* that brings us into the likeness of the Father. To taste and see this goodness of the Lord is to find an Answer before which the atheism of the Communist fades into insignificance. The wild gourds of Marxism mean only death in the pot for humanity, but cast in one handful of the meal of God and His antidote is ours.

.   .   .

A little while and then His words are ended. No one speaks for the Master has spoken, and there is nothing else to say. Gradually they descend the Mount. They are the few. Soon they will mingle with the many on the broad way in the valley. There are multitudes there, but for them the way will be narrow always now. Beneath them is the rock of the mountain. Though they live amongst men, they can never build upon the sands again. They are the men of the Master, the sons of the Father and the representatives of the only Kingdom that will remain.

CHAPTER XVII

NO NEST, NO REST

"The foxes have holes, and the birds of the air have nests; but the Son
of man hath not where to lay his head."   Matthew 9

(Suggested reading: Matthew 8, vv. 1-27)

It was a hot, fine afternoon and the smell of fish drying in the sun came
surging up from the beach. The men and boys were out of the boats
and the nets lay repaired and ready for the night's fishing, stretched out
on the stones. In fact the shore was well-nigh deserted, for it was the
Sabbath and most of the fishermen were resting in their homes. The little
houses stood some distance back from the water's edge and in the silence
and the bright sunshine they seemed to add their own share to the calm
of the community. The house, however, which belonged to young Simon
and Andrew, was in a turmoil. The menfolk had been away much of the
time, and Simon's wife felt she could hardly face this new crisis alone.
Suddenly her mother had fallen ill and now as far as she could tell she
was dying with a raging fever. "If only Simon would come . . ." she
thought. "Surely the synagogue service is over by now . . . If they would
only call in they could see how she was . . . and then who knows, Jesus
might even be with them." She glanced anxiously at her mother lying
prostrate on the bed. How long she would last she did not know . . .

In our Primer of Discipleship the last word of the first lesson provides
the key to the first word of the second lesson. That word is "house".
The closing sentence of the Lord's teaching still rang in the disciple's ears.
He had said, "And the rain descended and the floods came, and the winds
blew and beat upon that house and it fell, and great was the fall of it."
Each disciple had a house to build. Would it be down there on the shore—
a life determined by the carnal standards of the Galilean fishermen—or
would it be on the rock of the mountain? On the Mount the Master spoke
of the conditions prevailing where *He* lived. Now He descends to see the

conditions prevailing where His disciples lived. Jesus had brought them so near to heaven on the summit but down there on the shore one could be so near to hell in the home. Christ's teaching is no escape route from responsibility. Doctrine cannot be loved for itself; it must be obeyed for love of Him. They must take heed to themselves now in relation to the doctrine of their Master. As learning, they are involved. He had talked about houses in His sermon; now they must return to their houses by the sea. With deliberate intent Jesus takes them back to the scene of their calling and into the very home of Simon Peter and Andrew. The sands are the same but these men are changed. They have been with Jesus and He begins to trust them now. On the way Christ acts. He cleanses a leper at a touch. He heals a man with palsy at a word and silences a raving demon in authoritative rebuke. He is not only mighty in word on the heights, but mighty in deed in the depths. Christ had spoken first to their heart; now He would act in their home. Sometimes, when Christ knocks at a door, folk will peer at Him through the windows to check if He is desirable, as if He came to plunder or maraud. Sometimes when He calls we feel His visit is inopportune. Our housees are in disarray and we wish He would come at some more convenient season, but when He arrived that day and stepped in out of the sunshine to the shadows of that fisherman's shack, He could hardly have been more welcome. The story of what followed is given in the Gospel not only of Matthew, but also of Mark and of Luke; and their combined narrative gives us a brief yet graphic picture of what took place. As disciples we must not mistake our Master's interests. He does not discuss the furniture or take up the local gossip. Not that He has no use for furniture or is uninterested in local affairs, but He has perspectives that flow from the heart of God. Now it is not His lips that move but His eyes. Matthew tells us, "He *saw* Peter's wife's mother laid and sick of a fever". Eyes that see are focussed by a heart that cares. Her need is His first interest. Mark adds they "tell Him of her" When His compassion and our intercession coincide, then things begin to happen in a home. Luke, accustomed as a physician to people's pathetic intreaty heightens the poignancy of their request and says, "They besought Him for her", supplementing with medical accuracy that the fever was "a great fever". The response of the Master is immediate. Matthew, writing the Gospel of the King, says, "He touched her and the fever left her." Here is His authority. Mark, writing the Gospel of the Servant, says,

"He took her by the hand and lifted her up." Here is His ability. Luke, writing the Gospel of the Son of Man, shows us the demeanour in which all this was performed. He says, "He stood over her." Here is His sympathy. This is how He deals with our fevers, and the disciples must learn this lesson for the day will come when they will deal with fevers too. They have listened to His precept, now they see Him in practice. No sooner has the fever left her than she arises. Matthew tells us that she ministered unto Him; Mark and Luke that she ministered unto them. There is no contradiction, for inasmuch as we act in love to one of the least of His children, we have done it unto Him. The main instruction inherent in the miracle, however, is this. She could not help until she was healed, and the disciple must understand he cannot serve God until he has been saved by God. We cannot go forth to teach until we have been taught. We cannot proclaim life until the power of death in us is broken. We cannot bring peace to others until the fever of sin has left us. In this incident Jesus makes little of the disciples' house but much of the disciples' home. Little of the dwelling but much of those who dwell in it. He made Peter's home that day a centre of healing power, and as the sun at last sank over the hills, out streamed a host of folk racked with pain and torn with demons, and there, gathered *at* the door they found that *from* that door rivers of blessing flowed. His presence in that home had made it immortal for God. It had become His house and a holy sanctuary. Surely men and their homes only become significant when God is in them, and there, that day, the very Scripture found fulfilment, for Matthew quotes, "Surely He hath borne our griefs and carried our sorrows."

All this is a very important prelude to what now takes place. It puts what our Lord Jesus Christ is going to say into its right perspective in our minds. In Matthew's account two would-be disciples now come forward. It is probably the following morning and they have been stirred by the previous day's events. The first is a scribe and says to Him, "Master I will follow thee whithersoever thou goest." Jesus does not deny his sincerity, but turning to him, He gently informs his naïveté. Men tend to be either "low down" or "high-flown", that is, either fox-like or bird-like. Some dig a place at the tree-roots and others feather their nest in the tree-tops, but the would-be disciple is informed that for the Son of man there is no nest; there is no rest. He has no place on earth He can call His home, for He is away from home. These would-be followers, like the two disciples in John's Gospel, have their motives brought under God's scrutiny. Jesus is asking these also, "What seek ye?" but they do not ask, "Master where dwellest Thou?" else He may have called them to come and see. We must learn that He has come to where we live, that we might go to live with Him where He lives. This is *His* heart's desire. "I go to prepare a place for you", He says, and in His prayer He asks, "Father I will that they also whom Thou hast given me be with me where I am." He can assure us of rest there but there is no rest here. If we have a house on earth then, there must be a tent pole through the roof and guy-ropes in the front garden. The disciple is a man who passes on with his Lord. This was brought home to me very forcibly in my own experience just a few years ago.

In early 1959, I was in Essex preaching. One evening I was on the telephone to my wife at our home in Scotland. She said, "We have a letter from Mr. and Mrs. Pucknell. They are feeling in need of furlough and wonder whether we would be prepared to go to Borneo. The work is at a critical stage and needs someone to stand in the breach if the believers are to be established." We rang off after just a few minutes and were left, each with our thoughts, four hundred miles apart . . . It was some six years since I had been in the Far East. Following my release from Communist imprisonment I had at first recuperated, and then later on, visited numerous centres in the British Isles. After our marriage in 1955 my wife and I had gone to Australia and New Zealand, returning eventually to Scotland via America nearly two years later. By July 1957, we at last managed to get a home together. Now in 1959 we had two small children aged two and three. The house was well furnished and the amenities the best we had known. We had also done some gardening and laid two lawns, so that with several arduous years behind us we felt perhaps for a while we could be at rest. But we served a Master who had on earth, no nest and no rest. Supposing we did go, I thought, would it not be hard on my wife? The house had only been in our hands so short a while and the home so hardly brought into being. Question after question began to rise but I had no cause to be surprised. Should not He who had vanquished our enemy lead us in triumph where He will? Had not I said, "I will follow Thee whithersoever Thou goest?" Dare I turn foxlike to the earth? I could only spread the matter before my Lord. Some days later I arrived home again, and it was somehow so very wonderful. We hardly needed to discuss Borneo, for when our eyes met we knew that here was something our Lord was wanting us to do together. A few weeks and the house was sold, our furniture was in store and we were ready to take off for the orient. I found that my wife had held to "things" far less than I had done. She never even mentioned the house again. Just once she told me how she thought of the little bulbs she had sown in the ground. Unbeknown to us two years later, in the heat of Malaya, she herself was to be all but sown in the earth . . . Moving from place to place had been very demanding, and weakened, it would seem, by our strenuous life in the tropics, she was suddenly attacked by a fearful virus. Almost immediately she became desperately ill and within about forty-eight hours she knew she was dying. Those were anxious days, but in the kindness of God, prayer was heard, and though it took many months, she did eventually recover. Afterwards, as she recalled the time when she was sinking, she said there kept running through her mind the words, "To me to live is Christ and to die is gain." It seemed almost impossible with the family about her, and with the prospect of returning to loved ones in Britain, to accept these words. As the struggle went on and her condition deteriorated, there came a moment, however, she said, of quiet surrender to His will, when she felt she could say in all sincerity, "Yes, Lord, 'to me to live is Christ and to die is gain'." The amazing thing is that from that moment she sensed that God was lifting her again . . . This was a time of learning for us both. It told us afresh that in the hour of crisis, there is no foxhole into which to run; no nest into which to fly; nowhere else to go; only Jesus. He is our only shelter, and our abiding place. When I call Him Master and Lord, it means I can hold to nothing else and no one else. All that I have, all whom I love, can only be held in Him. Do we know what we say when we volunteer the brave avowal, "I will follow Thee whithersoever Thou goest"? This is a course which always delivers us to death for Jesus' sake.

One of the things that concerned me when we first made our decision to pull up the guy ropes and venture ourselves and our babes in the Lord's hand to Borneo was the impression of foolhardiness this would present to our parents. Humanly speaking it seemed an appalling thing to do; but God is kind to us. At the very time of this inward conflict the text on the daily calendar read: "The sheep follow for they know His voice." Alongside it was a short comment by the saintly George Soltau:

"Do we know the voice? Can we be led by the voice? Have we the faith that can FOLLOW when the path seems so strangely crooked? There must be such a clear conception of the Lord, together with the cultivated habit of recognising His gentlest intimation, and obeying it without question. It is a splendid abandonment to the will of another, which has been called a 'holy recklessness' as to consequences. It may oppose human reason and circumstances, but if He calls—FOLLOW—' . . ."

Now the second would-be follower approaches and in his avowal he also boasts a true allegiance. He begins with, "Lord!"—but ironically enough the first step he wants to take is backwards. He must return home to attend a funeral. "Still, it *was* his father's funeral," someone will say. Yes it was his father's but note the way his request is couched. "Lord", that is to say, "Jesus, you are first, you are supreme, suffer *me* first . . ." It is rather like Peter who on the rooftop of Cornelius' house said, "Not so, Lord." It is a contradiction in terms. The disciple on this issue has to decide whether he is going to be a servant of dead men or a servant of the living Lord. This man had little appreciation of the power of Christ. There were only three occasions when our Lord was publicly confronted with death and He never let it pass Him. Jairus' daughter was just a child and still on her bed. He raised her there. The widow's son of Nain was a youth and his body already on the way to the cemetery but Jesus stopped the procession and raised him from the dead right there in the street. Lazarus was a step further still. He was actually in the tomb, had been dead four days and his body was already in corruption, but Jesus accepts the challenge and calls him forth. Yet here was a man who asked leave to bury his father when he could have asked Christ to raise him from the dead. No wonder our Lord replies, "Let the spiritually dead attend to the affairs of those who have died. Follow thou Me." The Lord is not callous of our griefs nor would He have us neglect our filial duties but when we call Him Lord, we acknowledge the prior claims of our living and heavenly Father, and the affairs of our dead earthly father become part of His concern. It is no good saying "Lord, I will follow but wait a minute I have something to attend to." Once He is Lord, He attends to everything and we as His disciples simply do what we are told. Lordship is absolute.

"We are going to put Jesus first," said the daughter of a friend of mine, "when we get married." "That is very good," her father said, "and who will be second?" "Well I suppose we will be." "Oh that would never do,"

he replied, whimsically, "Jesus must be second too." "Well, then we shall
be third." "But Jesus must be third too." The young girl, Christian though
she was, did not get the point. "But where do we come in?" she blurted
out. Her father looked at her kindly and being a man of long pilgrimage
he said slowly, "You don't come in . . ." It is so good if we can learn this
at the beginning.

From the fishermen's shacks on the shore He now brings them back to
the sea. They are learning to face the old environment with Jesus, learning
to meet the old circumstances with the new Master. So now He leads them
on to the sands and into one of their ships again. "And when He was
entered into a ship His disciples followed Him." He had given them a word
for life in the calm of the mountain. Now He was to give them a word
for death in the storm on the deep. As with the climbing of the Mount it
is only His disciples that follow Him to the ship. Difficulty and danger
alike sort out the crowds. The disciples were in their element now. If they
knew anything, they knew the sea. They could read the face of the lake
like the palm of their hand. They may not be very good mountaineers but
they were good fishermen. Jesus was a carpenter by trade. They would
look after Him for they were seamen. They had not yet realised that
their Master was "God of the hills" and "God of the valleys"; that "He
made the dry land and the sea also"; that He was Master in the heights
and in the depths. The words are very beautiful . . . "*There arose* a great
tempest . . . *He arose* . . . there was a great calm." Meanwhile they toil
and Jesus sleeps. It was all in keeping with His Word. "The Son of Man
hath nowhere to lay His head"; nowhere save the boards of a tossing
fishing smack. They were physically strong but spiritually weak. They
may be grown men on the shore but when it came to crisis they were only
babes in Christ. They thought they could make it alone but they had to
wake Him in the end. The truth is that once we have committed ourselves
to Him we can never do without Him again. The disciples would never
be able to say, "Master we got you across." They would have to say to
Him, "Master if it had not been for you we would have perished in the
deep." That is how it should be. All of God, all of grace. All of dependence. The disciple can never be greater than his Lord. If you dare to trust
your old skills again and show how clever you are, you will find that the
thing you thought you knew, you did not know at all. Professing ourselves to be wise we become fools. The natural man can never work for

the spiritual man and still have something to brag about. Jesus wakes and
administers two rebukes in order of importance. First He handles fear and
unbelief in the disciples' storm-tossed hearts. Then He handles the wind
and the sea on storm-tossed Galilee. Had He lifted them to the Mount
only to drown them in the sea? Had He brought them to the gates of
Heaven only to abandon them at the gates of Hades? "Lord save us; we
perish!" they cry. "Why are ye fearful, O ye of little faith?" He answers.
They had not yet understood what manner of man He was. They awakened Him. Now He awakens them. He shows them the true nature of their
dilemma. It was not the tempest without but the tempest within that
mattered; the dilemma of unbelief in a professing disciple of Jesus Christ.
It is interesting to note that the phrase "O ye of little faith" is a translation
of a single word in the Greek text and that it occurs four times in Matthew.*
Once on the Mount where Jesus tells them to take no thought for their
life, for their food, or for tomorrow, reminding them that "If God so
clothe the grass of the field . . . shall He not much more clothe you, O ye
of little faith." Then three times in connection with their journeys across
the lake of Galilee. First, here in Matthew eight, in the storm, then in
Matthew fourteen, where Peter begins to sink in the water, and finally
in Matthew sixteen, where the whole party appears to be stranded on the
farther shore without provisions. It is searching to realise that the rebuke
of the "little-faith-ers" is in each case linked with an impossible circumstance. How can we help being perturbed about tomorrow? How can we
help being afraid when the boat is going down? How can we help panick-
ing when we are sinking in deep waters? How can we help being put out
when we have nothing to eat? Anybody surely would show anxiety in
these circumstances. What the disciple has to understand is that when we
move with Jesus we move all the time in the realm of the impossible. We
operate as the Kingdom of God amongst the children of men. We are

* The words "little faith" stand in contrast in Matthew's Gospel to the "great
faith" of the Roman centurion (8, v. 10) and the "great faith" of the Canaanite
woman (15, v. 28). These Gentiles had little light but great faith. The Jewish disciples had great light but little faith. We do not need to know much to trust Him
greatly but if we do know much and fail to trust Him we are greatly to be blamed.
The Master's ideal of course is that we should have great light accompanied with
great faith. Paul is a good example here. On the Damascus road he first saw a great
light, then in the tempest of Euroclydon he showed great faith, crying, "I believe
God!"

in touch with the Source of Supreme Power. We can do nothing but He can do everything and this is really so. The disciple must never view events as out of control. Even the wind and the sea obey Him. His control is our calm. There is no nest on the deep but we are called to rest in Jesus there.

CHAPTER XVIII

NEW CLOTH, NEW WINE

"The disciple is not above his Master nor the servant above his Lord.
It is enough for the disciple that he be as his Master and the servant as
his Lord."   Matthew 10

(Suggested reading: Matthew 8, v. 28 to 10, v. 42)

THERE was not a ripple upon the water as the boat drew into the shore;
and the last dark clouds were already dispersing beyond the eastern hills.
One of the disciples, taking up the rope, jumped nimbly on to the wooden
jetty and gently drew the boat into the side. No one was to be seen, for
they had landed at a sequestered place some distance out of Gadara. As
the men stepped ashore they were subdued and said little to each other.
They had failed to weather the storm and knew it. The words of their
Master were still fresh in their ears. The rain had descended, the wind had
blown and they had proved no match for the tempest and its overwhelming flood. The crisis had revealed what manner of men they were; and it
had revealed also what manner of man was Jesus.

From the little landing stage, which protruded like an accusing finger
from the rocky coast into the placid water, there rose the bare slopes of
the mountain. Far up in the stillness they could see a large herd of pigs
foraging in the grass, and here and there a human figure perched on a
boulder or lying in the sun. Beyond the rough roadway that led away from
the jetty and over the cliffs to Gadara, stretched a scarred area of the hillside filled with stones and caverns, and dotted about with innumerable
footpaths. At some time or other it had been a cemetery but now appeared neglected and overgrown.

As the disciples walked with Jesus along the track, which wound up
through the scattered tombstones, they could not help but wonder where
He was leading. "Let us go to the other side . . ." That is all He had said.
Suddenly the calm which had followed the storm, and of which they were
now so conscious, was rudely shattered by blood-curdling shrieks. The
disciples froze in their steps and turned instinctively toward the sound. To

their horror two raving lunatics, stark naked, came bounding menacingly towards them like a pair of demons from the abode of the dead. They tried hard to stand their ground. They dare not panic a second time in a single afternoon. They glanced at Jesus. He remained unruffled and unsurprised. This after all was why He had come. This too was why He had been challenged on the lake. This was "the other side".

As the two demoniacs drew rapidly closer, the disciples could see broken rusty chains dangling from their wrists. On their bare flesh were streaks of fresh blood seeping from ugly gashes where they had cut themselves with stones. Their ferocity and the glint of evil marring their faces gave them that snarling, hunted look of a wild beast from the wilderness, half-crazed with hunger and jealous for its prey. No wonder the jetty and the road were unfrequented. No one was able to pass by. Just as the disciples were about to beat a hasty retreat to the boat, the unbelievable happened. In some uncanny way the devil-possessed men became conscious of Jesus, stopped in their tracks and grovelled in the dust before Him. As they did so they cried out in a piercing and agonising cry, "What have we to do with Thee, Jesus, Thou Son of God? Art Thou come hither to torment us before the time?" Jesus spoke but a word. The demons cringed. "Allow us to enter the swine," they whined.

As His followers looked in wonder at their Lord, in this further moment of mastery, they began to see that discipleship is not a question merely of seeking to be *good* in this world but of combating the "*god* of this world". Perhaps it was such an occasion as this that inspired John, one of the twelve, to write, "For this purpose the Son of God was manifested, that He might undo the works of the devil" . . .

"Go," said Jesus, and with that command He gave them their desiring. Almost immediately, startled shouts broke out from high up on the mountain. The eyes of the disciples strained to see what was afoot and then to their astonishment, a single convulsive movement gripped the entire herd of pigs and within moments the whole two thousand, like some great avalanche, came careering headlong down the slopes. In a welter of squealing and screeching they poured pell mell over the edge of the cliffs to disappear in a cauldron of foam in the sea below.

What Satan sought to perpetrate upon Christ and His disciples in the storm is thus portrayed in this frightening incident, as Satan's own inevitable fate. He is destined for the deep, for there is a lake, albeit of fire, prepared for the devil and his angels. No event could have spoken more eloquently to the disciples. It was a lesson they would never forget. They wrestled no longer with flesh and blood but against principalities and powers. But Gadara would not forget either, for in spite of the local hostility the Lord appointed these two new disciples to witness in their streets.

If the devil cannot possess, then he will paralyse, and in the next incident and its ensuing instruction the disciples are given an insight to that palsy of the spirit which gripped most of the religionists of their day. The hierarchy of Judaism and its attendant social set-up had taken the living God and presented Him to the people in sheer marble. He had become a lifeless image of their thinking, an idol cold and hard. The current concept of Pharisaical holiness was to be in touch with as few people as possible. This was on the public side. On the personal side, it seemed, that holiness was to be exhibited in being as unnatural as possible. Their two main emphases were thus self-segregation and self-abnegation. These were devil-induced and issued in spiritual paralysis. Yet the Creator has made us for company and given us all things richly to enjoy. Jesus came that we might have life and have it more abundantly and He expects His disciples to be fully alive and alert, in spirit, soul and body. Yet how often professing disciples are the world's most helpless creatures. They are morose, depressed, censorious, self-righteous and uncooperative. All that can be said of such people as they are carried hither and thither by their friends is that they are sick of the palsy. They are suffering from a devil-induced paralysis. If they are Christ's the devil cannot possess them but he does the next best thing, he oppresses them and makes them spiritual paralytics unable either to walk or work for God.

The key to freedom in this case is a true experience of the forgiveness of sin. When we have been forgiven much, then we love much and if we are lovers, we shall certainly be learners. As the four men lower their palsied friend to Jesus' feet it is precisely in this connection that the Saviour's healing work begins. The roof was broken but Jesus does not tell them to be careful of the tiles. He sees their faith and acts in grace according to the need. Israel was full of religious people who spiritually were flat on their backs—but they could hardly get to Christ for the sight-seers around Him and the roof of tradition shadowing Him. Mark adds to Matthew's record and says that they uncovered the roof *where He was*.

At the point where I am to get to Jesus that is where the tiles of tradition must be broken. Then let us come to His feet and our palsy of sin will be broken too.

The danger besetting the disciples was that they were liable to be drawn back into the old concepts of a harsh legal holiness and become slaves to the letter rather than sons in the Spirit; to become involved again in the outward form of things rather than go on drinking of the Spirit of life in Christ. It is interesting that just at this stage Matthew records his own encounter with the Lord Jesus Christ. At this juncture when the earlier disciples might tend to become stereotyped and try to fit in with the outlook of the Pharisees and other pseudo-pious elements, here comes this new follower of their Lord. Matthew, who is the author of this Gospel, first tells how the palsied man arose at Jesus' command and then he tells how he himself arose at Jesus' command. Matthew had a paralysis in his life rooted in sin also. He sat at the receipt of custom. This, for him, was a permanent position—but when Jesus came he changed his position and began for the first time in his life to move for God. We are immediately taken into Matthew's home and how refreshing it all is. He is a new disciple with a new Master. The restraints and handicaps of his previous position are all gone. He is completely uninhibited and this simplicity and godly sincerity is what Christ would have us retain to the end. How many so-called disciples, in the days of our Lord, went back and walked no more with Him? They turned again to their crutches and looked for a bed on which to lie, reverting to their old pattern of life. The paralytic carnalities amongst Christian disciples are enormous because we like a mould, a tradition, a pigeon-hole with which we feel integrated. Jesus Christ calls us to walk on the deep, to ride the heavens and cast mountains into the sea. In spite of His convention-shattering call, however, we still tend to prize formalities and reduce our contacts. We say in effect if only two or three will gather in our name, by which we mean share our convictions, then we shall feel secure. Thus we make a travesty of the new fellowship and the process of self-segregation from without, and self-abnegation from within begins all over again. We may feel we are holy and making spiritual progress but we live in a fool's paradise rather than God's. We are back to our bed once more.

Now as Jesus sits at meat in Matthew's home, two questions are raised which set these important matters in perspective. The first question is asked by the "segregationists", the Pharisees. The second question is asked by the "abnegationists", the disciples of John. The first party says, "I will have nothing to do with other people because they are sinners." The second party says, "I will have nothing to do with myself because I am a sinner." The first attitude results in isolation. The second attitude results in desolation. For the first outlook denies the possibility of a true corporate answer and the second of a true personal answer in the life we are called to live. In relation to discipleship both indicate the onset of a spiritual paralysis.

It seems that it was hard for the devil to fully possess a Pharisee or a disciple of John. There were, in a way, strong assertions Godward in many of them; thus the devil specialised in paralysis, making not a few of them life-long spiritual cripples who could not lift even a finger for God. No wonder some tile-smashing amongst the orthodox religious rooftops was necessary before a man could be lowered in simple faith to Jesus' feet. As these persons observed the spiritual liberty enjoyed by Christ and His disciples, they were filled with an annoyance and disdain which really arose from a spirit of envy. Their enquiries were thus specious in character and designed to influence the inexperienced disciples in such a way as to induce them to return to the "traditions of their fathers".

The first question was addressed to the disciples and concerned the Master. The second question was addressed to the Master and concerned the disciples. The Pharisees spoke first and asked, "Why eateth your Master with publicans and sinners?" By their very phraseology they repudiated any sympathy whatever with Jesus. To them, Jesus was unclean, for He had not conformed to their segregation—concept of holiness. They considered if Jesus were holy then He would eat with scribes and Pharisees and recognise who was who, in Israel. They had not understood that whilst they refrained from contact for fear of infection, Jesus insisted on it for He had come to heal. He answers them therefore very simply, telling them in plain terms—a doctor goes where he is needed. It somehow had not occurred to the Pharisees that the disease of sin is not so much transmitted by contact but inherited by birth—that every man, be he Pharisee or publican, carries his own defilement with him—that it is not what goes into us but what comes forth from us that defiles. It is out of the heart of a man that evil proceeds so that our malady is essentially "heart trouble" not "skin trouble". The Law did not profess to heal but

rather to diagnose and analyse the complaint. It ruthlessly exposed the
fatal consequence attending the disease of sin, although this was not
unmerciful. Rather it was to prepare the patient for the promised Physician and His remedy of grace. The Law in taking away *all* hope condi-
tioned the sinner to accept the *only* Hope. When the Law warned of
death it had life in view. The Pharisees had come to view segregation not
only as a precaution but as some kind of remedy. They were as people
shut up in their own house with doors and windows fastened, in the midst
of a plague-ridden city. Their own salvation through isolation had thus
become paramount and the mass of the people were abandoned to their
fate. Yet the Law was not devoid of mercy and its application even in the
Old Testament was not contrary to the needs of life. David when starving
was allowed to eat the shewbread which was not lawful and Hezekiah
was permitted to observe the passover out of season through practical
difficulties, and still be absolved from guilt. The sabbath could be broken
to feed an ass or for the performance of needful duties in the sanctuary.
So turning upon His questioners, Jesus says, "Go and learn what this
means. I will have mercy and not sacrifice; for I am not come to call the
righteous, but sinners to repentance." God never thinks more of principles
than persons—and the mercy which appears as a single thread running
through the Law—now under Grace is manifest as the grand design of
the whole canvas. The diagnosis is thus established and the Physician
has come. He is not concerned with instituting a quarantine but with
inaugurating a cure. To touch the leper no longer means defilement for
the "touch-er" but cleansing for the leper. What the Law could not do
the Spirit of Life in Christ does do. Virtue goes out of Him to the sinner,
not vice out of the sinner into Him. Evil is overcome of good. Holiness
in Christ is linked with life against which, the forces of death have no
power. We do not, therefore, shut ourselves away but can move through
the world's streets, the world's colleges and the world's factories in the
power and outflow of the life and goodness of Christ Himself. Whilst as
disciples of the Lord we must never go out on our own, yet the wonderful
thing is that in His company and by reason of His life, we can meet anyone
and go anywhere, and not only shall we be clean, but we shall conquer.
This is revolutionary and transforming and today, locked up as we are
in our age-long taboos of a counterfeit holiness, it is something we must
see afresh in the light of the Master.

The second question, asked by "the disciples of John", afforded the Lord an opportunity to give the next lesson to His followers. They asked, "Why do we and the Pharisees fast oft, but Thy disciples fast not?" The arresting thing in this incident is not so much in the subject of the question but in the identity of the questioners. John was the greatest man under the Lord, born of woman, and it is not surprising he had disciples. What was surprising was that they could stand in front of Jesus whom John described as "mightier than I" and question His leadership and, furthermore, do this in consort with the Pharisees. It only goes to show how that birds of a spiritual feather soon flock together. There is little or nothing to choose between the man who in his "holiness" keeps others out and the man who prides himself in a "holiness" which keeps himself under. Each reveals an attitude of independence of the grace of God and there is no holiness for sinful man without grace. But there is more in it than this.

As these men had listened to John's voice they were convinced it was the final voice but they had failed to realise that there must then come the final word, and that once the Word had come then the voice would die away and the Word remain. They saw in him a light but failed to realise he was pointing to *the* Light. They had appreciated his ministry as a prophet but had despised his ministry as "more than a prophet". They had received his message when he said, "There cometh one . . ." but had spurned it once he had proclaimed, "This is He." They had become enamoured of the herald but missed the King. They saw in John "a man sent from God" but were blind to the Son sent of the Father. The disciples of John had never reached out beyond him to Jesus. John was faithful but they were foolish. They had made more of the man than his message. They had failed to realise the introductory character of his ministry, and thus failed to repose their trust in Him who came after him. Thus in their minds John now belonged to them instead of they themselves belonging to Jesus. They had made a rallying point of a servant instead of finding their centre in the Lord. So it is that many who should be disciples of Jesus today are still only disciples of a John, and their loyalty to a reformer, a religious group or even an idea has displaced their loyalty to Jesus Christ.

As the Law was a tutor to bring men to Christ so John as the final voice of the dispensation was also a tutor to bring men to Christ. He so preached the Law in the power of God that men knelt in the sands of the wilderness and cried for mercy, then passing through the waters of Jordan publicly renounced their evil works. It was a flight from judgement and with the advent of Messiah they should have flown into the arms of Emmanuel, their Saviour God. The emphasis of John's ministry and the circumstances in which it was fulfilled, was thus one of austerity and humiliation in which prayer and fasting served as means to bring the soul low before God. These things were never ends in themselves or a criterion of holiness, but rather the reverse. Such measures had to do with the conditioning of a man's attitudes, that he might prepare a highway for the One who alone could bring salvation.

Now He had come as a Bridegroom for His Lover—but the disciples of John had become so preoccupied with the friend of the Bridegroom that they had failed to hear the Bridegroom's voice. They had lost the End in the idolising of the means. John's joy had been fulfilled. He had seen the descending and abiding Spirit upon the Lamb of God and had cried, "Behold!" Now he could decrease and Jesus fill the whole horizon. May be it was hard to understand behind prison bars but all was well—all the signs of Messiahship were demonstrated in the Anointed from the banks of Jordan, but the disciples of John—they would not have it so. They spoke of Jesus as "he who was with thee beyond Jordan" and expressed disappointment that all men should come to this stranger and not to their John. John tries to instruct them. "I am of the earth," he says, "and speak as a man upon the earth, but He that is from Heaven is above all." But the question of his wayward followers remained unsolved.

Why did they fast and that together with the Pharisees? The answer is, they shared a common delusion. They waited still for the Bridegroom when He was already before their eyes. They had been faithful to John but in clinging to a man they were left with only a corpse in the end. The commentary of Mark on this matter is poignant indeed. He writes, "John's disciples came and took up the corpse and laid it in a tomb", and then he adds, "and the apostles gathered themselves together unto Jesus". They were no more than dead men burying the dead. God's intention is that we should not be adherents of a departed prophet but followers of the living God.

Failure to understand Christ's answer to these two great questions has led many a disciple into the graveyard of self-segregation and self-abnegation. Those who are Christ's are people of a new fabric woven into

His own seamless robe. They are people of the new wine of the Spirit calling for new skins of witness. There is no comparison between the restrictions, fastings and observances under Law and the true spiritual discipline of Grace. Under the first, it is rebels in humiliation; under the second, sons in royal service. Shall then the children of the bride chamber mourn?

. . .

We have come to the end of the primer and are moving in an ever triumphant way. The devils recoil, the dead rise, the blind see and the dumb shout aloud for joy. The last reference to the word "disciples" in this illuminating progress of instruction and liberation brings us to the Master's heart. He sees the multitudes, as sheep without a shepherd and as whitened fields unreaped. He is opening up the horizons now. They have sat much at His feet, soon He will send them forth. How can they share His vision? How can they share His compassion? There is no doubt about the answer. He says to His disciples, "Pray ye therefore the Lord of the Harvest, that He will send forth labourers into His harvest." In prayer we come into God's counsel and learn to move with Him in His love. They are soon to preach but first they must pray. In praying for labourers they will be finally fitted as labourers. It is only when we have been in touch with God that He will trust us to be in touch with men. They will thus become the first answer to their prayers.

So He calls them to Him as disciples, and now sends them forth as apostles. He has taught them. Now they will teach others what He has taught. How can He trust them? These little men from the beach with their limited background and meagre education; all so untried and inexperienced. In a crisis they had panicked. When asked questions, they could not answer. They had no creed and no organisation. They were an unlikely group to announce the Messiah, the Mighty God, the Prince of Peace.

But God's thoughts are not our thoughts, nor are God's ways our ways. He has chosen the things which are not, to bring to nought the things that are.

What was the first word they had heard on the shore? It was, "the Kingdom of Heaven is at hand". What this meant they had now been told. It was enough. "Go preach," He says, and this same word they had received was all that they were told to say. "The Kingdom of Heaven is at hand" must be the message still. And yet what greater news than this! Messiah had come! The rule of God was present in His King!

Such was the beginning. They had not learned everything, but they had learned *the* thing. They had found the Answer for their personal lives in Jesus Christ, and with this knowledge their Lord and Master was prepared to let them go.

Part III

INTO THE MORNING

THE WIND IN THE TREES
THE BREAK-OUT
THE NAME AND THE NAMES
BACK TO THE SOURCE
WHERE FLOWS THE RIVER
THE MASTER BUILDER
STREAM OF HIS POWER
SINEWS OF FELLOWSHIP
RED SKY AT DAWN

CHAPTER XIX

THE WIND IN THE TREES

"There went forth a wind from the Lord . . ."   Numbers 11
"When thou hearest the sound of a going in the tops of the mulberry
trees . . . then thou shalt bestir thyself."   II Samuel 5

AWAY up through the gum forests towards the crest country of the Blue
Mountains runs a lone grey road. As it switchbacks through the sunlit
clearings and the shadowed glades, there are glimpses through the trees
of rugged cliffs and rocky heights. After some miles, well-trodden path-
ways lead in off the trail, each marked by a little mailbox perched on a
post. It is the beginning of the orange-groves and the homesteads of the
fruit growers, who cultivate the eastern slopes of the Great Dividing
Range.

Calling a halt at one of the houses, we knocked at the door and were
courteously received into a spacious old-style kitchen. We talked to the
family and then, in a little while, the elderly "orange boss" stumped in.
He was a rough diamond if ever there was one, a veteran Australian who,
like many of his generation, had fought his way to prosperity, through
cruel toil in the backblocks of the bush. He had known what it was to
drink in his day, and he still spoke with that half-broken drawl of a man,
who in younger years cared little for education. Yet in spite of his native
crudeness, there was a genuine tenderness in his demeanour and a kindli-
ness about him that quickly won the heart.

We listened with fascination, wondering what story lay behind that
rough exterior. In a few terse sentences he said enough to reveal that after
years of wild carousing, he had met the Master in the hills. Then with a
reverence that took the coarseness from his speech, he said with deepest
feeling, "And to think a man like me, by the grace of God, now has a
family that loves the Lord".

Rising with difficulty from his chair, he led me away outside into the
cool mountain air. Together we walked slowly over to a small clearing

just a stone's throw from the house. There, not long completed, stood a beautiful chapel. The old man and his family, assisted by other believing neighbours, had built it with their own hands. We slipped quietly inside and sat down together in one of the pews. It would have held, I suppose, a hundred people and everywhere one looked, the workmanship was magnificent. "It's a lovely hall," I exclaimed with unfeigned enthusiasm. The old man turned and I was suddenly conscious of his work-worn face. "Yes," he said with a brief glow of pleasure and yet with a sadness rising in his eyes, "they say its a lovely hall . . . but they *should* say, He's a lovely Saviour." I had not meant to sound superficial yet those few words silenced me and I was at once aware of a strange and rugged grandeur in this agéd saint; for beyond the building he saw his Beloved, and though handling these externals, the Great Eternal was the passion of his heart.

The Spirit of God was astir in the hills, fresh as the dawning, clear as the sun and strong as the floodwaters sweeping the plains. I had come from the city but He was nearer in the bush. Down there in the town, commerce and religion might hawk their plastic Christ, but here in the backwoods the old man's Christ was still the Living Stone. What price then our ritual by candlelight or our "revival" with "ragtime"? Of what consequence our denominational emphases or ecumenical deliberations today? To what purpose all our parochial routine? Some may choose to guard the grave clothes but one question still remains: "Where is He who has seen the Lord?"

As I look back through the centuries, I sometimes land at Neapolis and go up to the church at Philippi, or maybe walk the streets of Ephesus. I call on people like Philemon or drop in for a night with Mnason. And as I have fellowship in heart with my brothers and sisters of long ago, it seems that the gum trees of Australia are not far away and the old man of the hills a much loved friend of Paul.

Is it not the simple believer in the Lord Jesus Christ who is the key to the maintained testimony of the Church all down the years? Are not the twos and threes who have gathered in His Name through sword and flame the historical symbol of the abiding fellowship of the Body of Christ? Is not His continuing witness in the earth vested in those who are linked with Him in Heaven, while man's vain systems rise and fall, mushroom and decay? Is not the issue clear, that only that which is born of God endures?

One step of faith and we are caught up in the gale of His Spirit. Mounting the heavens we drink of the freshness of God. We find no cobwebs in His bright blue sky, and no wrinkles in His light-filled countenance. He is always at the zenith of His powers, rejoicing in His strength. His timeless span of everlastings, clouds not His perennial youth nor multiplies His age. He is a Bridegroom going forth of His chamber and as a strong man eager for the race. Ever moving, acting, planning, He is always at peace in the ease of His power. He is not fretted by a world of men though He holds them in His care. With Him is all the life surge of the Almighty, the tireless tempo of the God who reigns. He is independent of all things, though everything on Him depends. His Spirit is no natural force. He is not for harnessing. Rather 'tis He who holds the reins for "as many as are led by the Spirit of God, they are the sons of God." Our fellowship is with Divine Persons, with the Father, with the Son and with the Holy Ghost. We take our character personally and corporately from Him which is, which was and is to be. In trusting Him, His everlasting strength is ours.

And yet how grey we are, we so-called Christians with the jaded faces. How prematurely aged behind our stained-glass windows and medieval words. How low the fires of true initiative have burned in our poor hearth. What straws we clasp upon the ebbing tide. Stubble without sap, bones without marrow! Is this our category? In vain we clasp the relics, who should grasp reality.

And if we are not grey we are too gay, caught in the world's mad mill-race. With pride we sport ourselves as being "with it" when humbly we should seek to be "with Him". Thus do we stoop to a pop-song faith where film and feature supplant the Word of His power. We become all things to all men and then by all means win none. We have the Church at parties when the Church should be at prayer, and soon the club-centred community replaces the Christ-centred fellowship. This is the present pattern of descent, from the spiritual to the social and from the social to the carnal, until in the closing stages of collapse, whist drives and bingo are made the handmaids of the Church exchequer and giving to God is tied to the filthy rake-off of a human gamble. It is the way down into the depths of Satan and is trodden today by a myriad professors with Christ's own Name upon their lips.

But some will piously protest, "We are not grey nor are we falsely gay." Yet in the very protest, grows the seed of still another class of Christian—"We are *au fait*. We are not hidebound by ancient tradition or hoodwinked by modern trend. Ours is an expertise in things spiritual. We know the Word and we know the Lord. We preach the Gospel and observe the ordinances, and know what a church ought to be and how it should be governed. In fact we are the bulwark of the Truth in this day of declension. We have the greatest concern for the lost and set afoot all manner of activities to spread the message of Jesus Christ. We are the people who are zealous for divine interests. We constantly attend meetings. We have our quiet time, we give money to missions. We do not smoke or drink or go to houses of entertainment. We have been saved to serve and serve we will. Yet when all this has been said and done, the savour somehow is often foreign to Christ's spirit, for if the truth were known, we who cherish this assessment of our Christian life, are not infrequently self-centred, bigoted and bad tempered. We are slaves to tradition, secretly lustful, carnally indulgent and prone to jealousy. We are more concerned with discussing the Bible than obeying it; more occupied in criticising others than converting others; more engaged in making arrangements than seeking the will of God, more enamoured of our service than our Saviour, and in business life too often ready to betray the very standards we profess to hold. No wonder that so many "scriptural companies" are dead and dark, for where the wick of sainthood is left untrimmed, true fellowship must be extinguished at the last.

Yet still the Living God renews, our God of no decay. With unflagging strength He executes His destined purpose. In all our sky He is the Sun which knows of no decline; in all our wilderness, the Eternal spring, no drought on earth can dry. He that is born from above is therefore a child of no despair. In all our Christian life, both together and individually, we are called to move with God, and in the measure that we really do, then is true fellowship with God begun. This is not just an idea nor even an ideal. It is a divinely originated activity, rooted in a special relationship between man and his Maker, secured through the blood of Christ and the regeneration of the Holy Spirit. It is a walking in the light as He is in the light and as we do this together in His company, mutually submitting ourselves to Him who is our light, then do we become together, light in the Lord. This is a light that shall never be put out for it is the life of God in expression. This experience of fellowship flows from a common participation in the life of God and only in the recognition of that Source, and the drinking from it always, shall the saints personally and corporately be luminous for God. Those who believe unto the saving of the soul "are come" says the writer to the Hebrews, "to mount Zion and unto the city of the living God, the heavenly Jerusalem, and to an innumerable company of angels; to the general assembly and church of the firstborn which are written in heaven, and to God the Judge of all, and to the spirits of just men made perfect and to Jesus the Mediator of the New Covenant and to the blood of sprinkling which speaketh better things than that of Abel." Here is the full fellowship into which His grace has brought us. God alone conceived it. God it was who forged it. None but God can sustain it; and in His sight nothing that man can do will either add to it or detract from it. Our responsibility is to enter into the good of it by faith.

Yet we allow our fellowmen to tamper with our highest privilege. Though we have access, we pander to a bogus priesthood. Though saints are one, we cling to "shibboleths" perpetuating schism, and fondly yield to virtual witchcraft, expecting infants sprinkled in the Godhead's Name, to be inheritors of the Father's Kingdom. We limit prayer to chanted liturgies, and doleful repetitions, as if God's mind will change for beads and mumblers. We make the ministry professional and are glad to have it so that we might mind our own business. We let men institutionalise us, catechise us and proselytise us, control our conscience and consume our substance. We grant the interweave of alien causes with our church life, social, commercial, and even national, that have no links with Christ whatever, and all the time it is convocations, councils and committees, resolutions, recommendations and financial appeals, until little is heard of the Lord Jesus at all, and the fellowship of the Spirit is unknown. The denominational establishments permeated with liberalism, modernism and with-it-ism are now so broad-minded that evangelicals and modernists can exist and work side by side and we are left to ask in the Babel of it all, "Is there no word from the Lord?" Interdenominationally local church life tends to be treated as a sideline. We are asked to hold the ropes but too often when the blimp of the big effort is on its way we are left to collect the debris that remains. Once raise one's voice in censure and the accusation levelled is "You show no fellowship", when already the fellowship of the Church has been made a mockery and put to open shame.

Are these hard words? Perhaps not too hard, for it would seem that the King has very little function left to Him in His Kingdom as far as man is concerned. We make the plans and ask in prayer for Him to seal them. If they look like a success we glibly say His seal was given. In many places Church life is reduced to a roundabout catering for all tastes. It becomes a centre in itself and while its music plays you can jump on the horses and be taken for a ride. The whole land is strewn with steeples, but where is the living fellowship of God's people? The answer so often is, "Where there is no steeple at all."

Oh, why should we flounder like tired butterflies in this vast web of ecclesiastical confusion wondering why our heavenly wings still fail to lift us into God's pure air? There is no need, for there is one who has loved us and loosed us from our sins in His own blood and hath made us kings and priests unto God. Through Him we do have access by one Spirit unto the Father. We are sharers of a common grace and members of one another in the one Body. We are partakers of the one life, and servants of the one Lord and where this one Name of our Lord Jesus Christ is upheld and owned, there He has guaranteed His presence. Most true lovers of the Lord Jesus do at sometime or other escape the web, even if it be for an hour or two, and in some informal way taste the sweetness of His presence with others who believe. And if we are honest we must confess that these occasions, so often completely unplanned, remain with us as the most precious of all our spiritual memories.

What are the particular features of such times as these? My mind goes back to my old college with its turret tower and high gables in the Finchley area of London. In those days as I came up to school-leaving age, God touched my heart until my whole desire was to witness to Him. It was the dawning of a first love for Jesus Christ. Of course we knew but little, but Christ was real, and a few of us boys would gather to pray for a quarter of an hour before afternoon school in the library. I doubt very much whether you could call it "a meeting" but one of us would read a few words of Scripture, then we would all kneel together on the parquet floor. The prayers were spontaneous and extempore and we simply told the Lord about our life at school and the boys we longed to win. There was no embarrassment and nothing sentimental. It was simply fellowship together with the Living God. We did not feel inhibited. The Spirit of the Lord was there and gave us liberty. Nor could one say we were spoil-sports or puritanical; in actual fact one of the finest Christians of the group was the best batsman in the school.

Of all the things I loved most as a youngster, playing Podex stood high on the list. On a Friday evening I would go with our Bible Class into a park in Edgware and for some two hours, shout, gesticulate and hit that little leather ball for all I was worth. Afterwards it was orangeade and biscuits at the leader's house. I was just a teenager and it was one of the highlights of the week to sit round with those boys of my own age and talk about the Bible. Physically tired, we were ready to be serious and out would come our thoughts and questionings. Again in the quietness of that home and the freedom of that company there was that hallowed sense that God's presence brings. It was all so different, and to my young heart so much richer than a formal church service. We were glad to be there, nor was it the light refreshments that drew us. It was one of my early experiences of the fellowship and freshness of God, with no cassock to hide the preacher, or any prayerbook for me to fumble.

Once in a December not long after the war had started, I had a few days' holiday from the bank. It was a bleak time of the year to go cycling, but Des Honer and I decided to go on a trip into Hampshire. We went down through Bagshot and after a little while in Whitchurch, turned and came up through the country towards Reading. There were few people on the roads and the fields and hedgerows were bare and deserted. On coming to a wood we turned off the roadway and sat down on a log with the big trees arching above us. Through the leafless branches the wind sighed majestically yet sadly. Taking out our Bibles we turned to Isaiah where we read the words, "It was told the house of David, Syria is confederate with Ephraim. And his heart was moved, and the heart of his people as the trees of the wood are moved with the wind." With what dismay they heard that news but as we pondered the Scripture our minds went on through the years to the day of Pentecost when other hearts were moved with that mightier wind of the Spirit, and as we mused together, the Lord Himself drew near until the lonely copse became for us a 'Jehovah Shammah'.* Only a few days later Desmond entered the services. "I shall not return," he said to me solemnly, and turning to the date of his enlistment in Daily Light† I read the text to which he pointed. There at

* "Jehovah Shammah"—"the Lord is there" (Ezek. 48, v. 35).
† Daily Light—a symposium of Bible texts arranged for daily reading.

the head of the page were the words from Ecclesiastes, "The spirit shall return unto God who gave it." He took it as a word directly from his Lord. Later on, I heard of his witness in the Navy. He was one of the few who could tell a Bible story below decks, and command a hearing. Then one day the captain of his vessel, in utter devotion to duty, turned his ship into the path of a torpedo to save a merchantman. The result was that Desmond died as he expected and indeed as he would have wished, for the sake of others. I lost one of my dearest friends, but I can never forget that day when the wind sighed through the trees and the Lord Himself drew near.

In 1943 I was stationed in Nottingham. Our billet was a commandeered departmental store some four storeys high. Underneath the big building was a huge cavern extending deep down into the rock. Although it looked a veritable "black hole", yet for some of us it was a "secret place". At the far end of the cavern the hubbub of the men and the noise of traffic was hushed, and we could be still with the Lord. Perhaps it was in such a place the early Christians of Rome would gather and in the same simplicity, two or three who loved His Name and who desired to talk to Him together.

Then I recall a train journey from the north. There were three of us and we would soon arrive in London. We were all bound for different destinations and all had quite different backgrounds. Perhaps we would never meet on earth again. Yet in another way we were inseparable, for we all belonged to Christ. Ere the train steamed in and just as we sat, we bowed our heads, with our elbows resting on the collapsible table, and prayed to God. Others perhaps were quite unaware of what we were doing but once again there was that fellowship and freedom of the Spirit; only three, but sheltering together under Jesus' Name. I have been countless train journeys since but I always remember that hallowed moment with the Master there in that compartment.

It is now about seventeen years since that last incident and during this time I have travelled the world, lived and worked amongst strange peoples, mingled with all kinds of Christians and witnessed the work of God in many lands; yet wherever and whenever I have had the opportunity to quietly gather with my brothers and sisters in Christ, whoever they be, in this simple fashion, whether it be for prayer or Bible study, or for the remembrance of our Lord in the breaking of the bread, then I have found

that the Lord has always kept His promise and the sense of His Presence
has been sure.

If we are honest there is little doubt that most of us who truly know the
Lord Jesus Christ as our personal Saviour can think of many an occasion
of this nature, and whilst God may graciously come to us in more
organised services and formal meetings, yet are not our deepest corporate
experiences of God's presence when we meet simply as believers to wait
upon Him? Is it not then that we have that sense of a free and spontaneous
fellowship with Him and one another, and are enabled to give utterance
to our hearts' yearnings? Have we never considered that these experiences
are linked with those times when we move outside the trappings and en-
cumbrances of organised religion? This is a searching thing. For the tragic
irony is that though we know it to be so, too often we are prepared to
set along side of it and even above it a loyalty to some religious institution
which we call our denomination, or place of worship. In such institutions,
constituted so often not by the Word of God, but by various human ideas
and traditional practices, it may be we are prohibited from public participation in the services, informed what to pray, associated with actual
heresy in the rites performed and reduced to talking of "the church
within the church" as a justification for our presence there. Is this really
the portion of our Lord who purchased His Church with His own blood?

In the multi-coloured, milli-fragmented condition of Christendom there
is no answer provided when the Communists move in. Even were the
World Council of Churches to gather all the varied denominations into
one it would only be a bag of confetti ready to be scattered to the winds.
It would never be the bride. There is no such thing as the official Church
on earth; there is only the organic fellowship of His Body, and if you want
to see it in action, then have fellowship with one of these little known
companies who gather in simplicity about their Lord. They are more
numerous than people imagine. I have found them all over the world;
in Britain, in Denmark, in Norway and Sweden, in Germany, in India
and China, in Borneo and Hawaii, in Australia, in New Zealand and in
America. I understand there are about three thousand such groups in Soviet
Russia. They know very often nothing of each other, their form may vary
considerably, but to move in and out amongst such groups from land to
land is to witness in a very real measure the Body of Christ in action. It
is what Ter Tseegen has termed "the hidden priesthood". I recall his lines:

"The race of God's anointed priests shall never pass away;
Before His glorious Face they stand, and serve Him night and day.
Though reason raves and unbelief flows on a mighty flood
There are and shall be till the end, the hidden priests of God."

It is this unassessable quantity that challenges Communist governments today. There is not one Communist party that has been able to suppress the living fellowship of God's people. Organised "churches" in their denominations and federations, headed up in a headquarters and official leadership, are an easy prey to a totalitarian government. These ready-made organisations, being of human devising, only have to have the offices of the organisation filled with Communist sympathisers and the whole set-up becomes an organ of Communistic propaganda. The historical examples of this are now tragically numerous. Where denominations combine in a council of churches this only makes the task of the totalitarian state the easier. If this has not already taken place then the state will organise a union of churches for its own convenience such as that which the People's Government of China enforced under the "three-self movement." It seems at first that these little scarlet women ride with some security upon their respective beasts, but it is a delusion. After a short transitional period the beast turns round and tears her to pieces. In this we see in miniature the ultimate debacle of Christendom depicted in the Apocalypse. (See Revelation, Chapter 17.) Meanwhile the hidden priesthood still prevails and though individuals may be martyred, and local churches maligned and scattered, yet the living fellowship of God's children continues in homes and cellars, in woods and in caves. All history bears witness to this fact whether we look at the catacombs of Rome, the tundra wastes of Soviet Siberia, or to the scattered islands of the seas.

One lovely afternoon aboard a fishing smack, I stood and watched the mighty cliffs of Kalsoy rising in breathless splendour from the sullen bosom of the sea. Some fifty yards from the boat I spotted a small shelf of rock just above the level of the tide, and behind it, a flight of hewn steps winding up through a precipitous defile, to the hamlet of Trollanes above. As the engine slowed, we began to wallow in the big Atlantic swell and so immediately made ready to go ashore. With care we managed to cast off in the small rowing boat and pull away to the dark shadowy waters lapping the seaweed at the foot of the giant crags. All seemed so still and sinister, save for the rise and fall of the sea and an occasional friendly

shout from the landing place. Once we were close in, we jumped up to
the narrow ledge one by one, on the crest of each succeeding roller. One
tense moment poised over the heaving depths, then strong hands hauled
us aloft. As we clambered up the steps and the sea fell away beneath us,
countless guillemot wheeled in flight above the seething cauldron of the
adjacent cove, and their distant cries echoed eerily around the buttresses
and caverns of the rock. All out of breath from the steep climb we walked
at last through the turf-roofed cottages of the tiny village. Away beyond,
the wide green amphitheatre of the hills swept up to a rim of broken
ridges and jagged pinnacles. On lower slopes there was some evidence
of cultivation but the soil is meagre and as elsewhere in the Faroe Islands,
the richest harvest is always reaped from the sea. In the glorious sunshine
we tramped up through the grass to the lofty promontory from which the
lighthouse scanned the far horizons of the northern seas. From that point
of vantage the cliffs dropped sheer, a thousand feet, to the sea below and
we peered down at the myriad birds nesting in the hollows and along
the numerous ledges, white with the droppings of the years. We were
told by the islanders, how in season, they dangle from their ropes to catch
the birds and then sell them in Thorshaven, the capital. Far away the
northern capes of Esturoy, Kunoy and even Vidoy could be glimpsed
reaching out into the Atlantic. Trollanes I thought must be the last
community this side of the Pole. To me the isolation seemed complete.

And yet at evening time, as we gathered with the villagers in a cottage
home, there was no sense of loneliness or frustration. They were content
in Jesus Christ their Lord. Of the fifteen permanent residents, almost all
were true believers, worshipping and working together in fellowship.
On Lord's Days, as brothers and sisters together, they would break the
bread in His remembrance. Often they would read God's Word and pray
together. They lived in Trollanes as a true local expression of the great
Body of Christ to which they belonged. Nor were they a solitary example,
for up and down the fjords of the Faroes there are no less than twenty-
seven such companies. Apart from the Lutheran State Church—there are
virtually no denominations in the Faroes—almost all the evangelical
believers meet together, simply as Christians, in their different villages.
The gatherings are marked by a spontaneity and simplicity and in those
distant islands one breathes again the fresh air of the Spirit that fills the
pages of the New Testament.

In an old book given to me in Thorshavn, I found these words. In the particular setting I felt it was more than mere coincidence that they should come to my attention:

"A band of faithful men
Met for God's worship in some humble room
Or, screened from foes by midnight's starlit gloom
    On hillside or lone glen,
To hear the counsels of His holy Word,
Pledged to each other and their common Lord.
    These, few as they may be,
Compose a church, such as in pristine age
Defied the tyrant's steel, the bigot's rage;
    For when but two or three
Whate'er the place, in faith's communion meet,
There, with Christ present, is a church complete."

Anon.

CHAPTER XX

THE BREAK-OUT

"Prove Me now herewith, saith the Lord of hosts, if I will not open you the windows of heaven, and pour you out a blessing that there shall not be room enough to receive it." Malachi 3
"Launch out into the deep, and let down your nets for a draught. And when they had done they inclosed a great multitude of fishes: and their net brake." Luke 5
"No man putteth new wine into old bottles: else the new wine doth burst the bottles." Mark 2

THERE was a nest in the tree and we two boys were full of excitement. With the first spring sunshine the fresh leaves everywhere were unfolding their tiny hands and now, roaming along the hedgerows, we had suddenly spotted it. What were we to do? "See if there were any eggs in it of course!" That was our immediate reaction. "And what would we do with the eggs?" It remained to be seen. With some effort I clambered up through the closely matted branches and there for the first time in my young life, I saw the loveliest sight of three or four little blue eggs lying close together in the downy heart of the nest. I felt like a thief, but we took two, and on the way home stopped to hide them in a secluded outdoor place for we were not sure how our parents would view our first attempt at bird-nesting. After some days we returned to our hideout and there were the eggs. They were safe but already cold and uninteresting. We never looked at them again. We had kept them for their shell but unwittingly had killed the little life maturing within. We did not realise that the shell was never made for keeping, but only as the transient guardian of a life that was yet to be. We were just children. Perhaps that was why we wanted the shell. If we had gone back to the nest we would have found some lively chicks cheeping for their food and learned, may be, that life abandons even the shell it produces once its function is fulfilled. Could there be greater folly than to pick up the pieces from the leafy floor and catching one of the chicks try to enclose it and put it back from whence it had broken out? Keep it long in that position and it would die. A child with a cruel streak might even attempt it. The amazing fact is that there have always been those in the history of the Church who have felt it their duty to do this very thing. In pursuing this thought we recall that it was under Constantine that the so-called Christian Church first rose like some great spiritual Humpty Dumpty to sit upon the Imperial wall. How great the fall was ultimately to be only time would tell. In spite of all the efforts of the centuries, and they are being renewed with even greater vigour today, all the king's horses and all the king's men still fail to put this Humpty Dumpty together again. It is, of course, an impossible task; but not only so, it is a meaningless one, because were they for one moment able to arrange the scattered fragments into an organised whole it would still be nothing but a shell; the life has long since fled.

At the turn of the century Warsaw buzzed with religious controversy. Some of the priests of the Roman Catholic Church had disgusted their fellows and the local populace with their drunkenness and immorality. So serious was the situation that Zebrowski, popularly known as Father Stephen, took the long journey to Italy to implore the Pope to denounce these defaulters personally, and save the reputation of the Roman Catholic priesthood in the Polish capital. To Zebrowski's utter astonishment the Pope dismissed his report and this resulted in a deep sense of moral cleavage between the two men. When the moment came for Zebrowski to kiss the Pope's foot he resolutely refused. Returning to Poland with fourteen other priests, he founded another Romanist communion called the "Mariawita". This venture set its face against immorality, thus trying to do by example what authority had spurned to enjoin. In the course of time, Zebrowski was designated as the Mariawita Bishop of Warsaw. As the day of his enthronement drew near he had occasion to make a journey through the countryside. Before he could reach his destination he was caught in a tremendous storm and obliged to seek shelter in the cottage of some local peasants. The warm-hearted couple received him and, seeing he was a Bishop of the Roman Catholic Church, besought God that night that He would open the Bishop's eyes to see that it is Christ alone that redeems, and that unless He is received as Saviour there is no church on earth that can give a person peace with God. The Bishop rose the following morning and passed on his way, but something was already happening in his heart. Deep within himself he knew that the outwardly

beautiful, though inwardly empty ritual of his church could never save
his soul. Into his heart came the words of Holy Scripture, which he had
studied over the years. He knew that Christ had died for him and borne
the full punishment of his sin. What then was he as a priest trying to do?
Add something to what Christ had done? What blasphemy! Had He not
died for sin once and for all? Ere the day of his enthronement came he had
placed his trust firmly in Christ as his only, and all-sufficient Saviour.
Finally the great day dawned. He was up early and soon all was prepared
for the unique occasion. Six thousand people had gathered in one of the
big squares in Warsaw. The solemn moment came and in the course of the
ceremony the host was handed reverently to him. Quietly the crowd
waited for his blessing. As he looked upon the wafer, Zebrowski suddenly
declared in a loud voice, "Christ is not in this host, but He cometh soon
to judge the living and the dead." There was a stunned silence, as in fear
and horror the meaning of the words went home. Then pandemonium
broke out. Some rushed forward and would have killed him had they
not been restrained. After a while the riot subsided and order was restored,
and it proved possible for him on an improvised platform to answer
for his faith before the vast concourse of people that had now gathered.
As he spoke, a great stillness settled over the immense crowds. In simplicity and sincerity he told them of what God had done for Him in showing
him the way of peace and forgiveness through simple faith in the Christ
who had died for him. His uprightness as a man was widely known, and
being so universally respected, many in the crowds were deeply affected
by what they heard, and cried out like the conscience-stricken Jews on the
day of Pentecost, "What shall we do?" Whilst sure as to his faith, there
were things about which he was still perplexed; but God gave him insight
and he soon perceived from the Scriptures that those that believed were
to be baptised by immersion, and that baptism was not a means of
regeneration but an act of witness and obedience by those who have
already come to the Lord. With this obedience in view, he asked the
Baptists to baptise him, but he was disappointed for they insisted that he
join their church. It is interesting to note his answer. "I managed with
difficulty," he said, "to escape from two churches and do not as yet see
my way clear to join a third. All I see just now is that I should be baptised
on confession of my faith." At that juncture, when rather like Saul after
his conversion he still had scales upon his eyes, God once again had His

"Ananias" ready. Mr. E. H. Broadbent, that renowned missionary and traveller of Eastern Europe, in the overruling providence of God, arrived in Warsaw just at that time. Hearing of Zebrowski's dilemma he went to see him. Together they made their way down to the River Vistula and there Zebrowski was baptised. The news spread and soon one hundred and seventy others followed him into the waters, confessing Jesus Christ as their Saviour and Lord. As with Martin Luther, Life had broken through an obsolete and putrid shell and, having done so, had dared to cast it away. "What is this new sect?" asked the Tsarist police. Zebrowski opened his Bible at Acts, chapter two, and pointed to the words, "And the disciples continued steadfastly in the apostles's doctrine, and fellowship, and in breaking of bread and prayers." The police were baffled, but finally wrote down in their records, *Zwolennici Nauki Peirwotnych Chrzescijan*", which means "Steadfast Followers of the Doctrine of the Primitive Christians". From place to place the liberating power of the Spirit moved. Groups of believers meeting in simple fellowship began to spring up. It became yet another historic example of the reassertion of life discarding a crippling and unscriptural form. This in most cases is called heresy or derided as a new cult but this true story, together with countless others, declares the inevitability of the breakout of life from a crust of decaying tradition and ritualism. It must break through or perish. Life on the move must produce its own form. We cannot dismiss such movements by calling them divisive or condemning them as disruptive. It is an organic development. Dare to superimpose on a living organism an encasement of regulations, procedures and taboos unassociated with the development of life itself, and crisis will ensue. Either life will wither and slip away or else the regulations, procedures and taboos, however "pious", however "religious", however "scriptural", will be blasted to the four winds with iconoclastic force. Then it is that the guillotine of orthodoxy emerges and the hue and cry of heresy begins. The defences of life, however, are dynamic, for who can defeat the Lord's anointed or halt our God when He is on His way?

Whilst in Borneo a few years ago, we were living in Tanjong Aru near the capital of Sabah (then British North Borneo). One day Ian Morrison, the representative of the Bible Society, knocked on our door. He had just flown in on the Borneo Evangelical Mission piper plane from the distant jungle. As we talked, he told us of a great movement of the Spirit of

God amongst the native people in the interior. God had taken up one of the tribesmen with no more than the Gospel of Matthew in his own language and had thrown him like a flaming torch into the dry tinder of heathendom. Many had been converted and believers were now building their own meeting huts in the clearings. So great was the development of this work of God, that a priest of a strong ritualistic church group in the area was sent in to investigate, and bring the many newborn souls into the fold of its communion. Away in the forests he eventually encountered this Spirit-filled tribesman. Sensing somehow that the yielding to these intruding hands would mean an embrace of death, the native leader looked for direction from his Lord. He was not disappointed, for in a moment the answer came. "We would rather die before the face of God," he said, "than abandon life."

The Swiss historian, Walter Nigg, in his book entitled *The Heretics* makes an interesting comment. He says, "The history of heresy has shown that Christianity is richer in content than its ecclesiastical embodiment; the Gospel holds potentialities which have not yet come to the surface." This is undoubtedly a true observation. The organisational fabric of a church group whilst able to trace a historical sequence which looks back to days of spiritual power is rarely, if ever, in the good of that power today. What is more, any attempt by one of its rank and file to return to the days of power by paths according to the Word of God, yet independent of the present hierarchy, is viewed as dangerous, destructive and even cultist. An Anglican rector, speaking some two or three years ago of the new life surging through the veins of the Church of England, said with obvious disappointment that in spite of such hopeful signs "safe men are being appointed as bishops and fire-extinguishers as deans. Today," he said, "when a man is appointed bishop he goes not into the vanguard of the Church's life but as it were into the guard's van where the brakes are." Both in the secular and the religious sphere, very rarely is official government combined with progressive leadership. Established rule is nearly always reactionary. Their task too often is to control; their concern too rarely the will to grow. That much-criticised yet stimulating thinker Austin-Sparks puts it very succinctly, "Upon a living movement of the Spirit, born with fire in the heart of some prophet—successors, sponsors or adherents build an earthly organisation, and imprison the vision in a tradition. So a Message becomes a creed, a 'Heavenly Vision' becomes an earthly institution, a movement of the Spirit becomes a work, which must be kept going by the steam of human energy and maintained by man's resourcefulness. Sooner or later any real, or seeming departure or division from the recognised and traditional order of creed or practice will be heresy, to be violently suspect, repressed, and outcast. Too often what, at its beginning, was a spiritual energy, producing a living organism expressing something that God really wanted and to which He gave birth has become something which the next generation has to sustain and work hard to keep going. The thing has developed a self-interest and it will go hard with anyone, or anything interfering with it or seeming so to do. The Spirit has become the prisoner of the institution or system and the people become limited spiritually as a result." He is surely right when he says, "The history of Christianity from the latter days of the apostles is the history of prisons. Not literal, material prisons, though there have been not a few of these, but prisons which are the result of man's inveterate habit of taking hold and bringing into bondage. How many times has the Spirit broken loose and moved in a new and free way only to have that way brought under the control of man and crystallised into another Form, Creed, Organisation, Denomination, Sect, Order, Community etc. The invariable result has been that the free movement and life of the Spirit has been cramped or even killed, by the prison of the framework into which it has been drawn or forced; . . . and the grapes of Eschol turn to raisins in our hands."

The mighty movement of the Spirit of God in England in the eighteenth century, and the subsequent events, provide a solemn illustration. In the May of 1738 the Wesley brothers came to know Christ as their own Saviour and began to preach the Gospel as it was preached in the days of the Acts. Thousands came into the joy of forgiveness and into the deliverance from the power of sin, and the brothers record, "One and another came to us asking what shall we do, being distressed on every side as everyone strove to weaken and none to strengthen their hands." The counsel they received was that they should associate themselves together to pray together, to receive the word of exhortation, and to watch over one another in love that they might help each other to work out their own salvation. Wesley describes these gatherings thus: "Many now happily experienced that Christian fellowship of which they had not so much as an idea before. They began to bear one another's burdens and naturally to care for each other. And speaking the truth in love, they grew up into Him in all things who is the Head, even Christ, from whom the whole body fitly joined together and compacted by that which every joint supplied, according to the effectual working in the measure of every part, increased unto the edifying of itself in love." Prayer was greatly encouraged, the sole authority for both belief and behaviour being the Word of God. John Wesley wrote these great words. "What I nightly wish is that you all may keep close to the Bible. Be not wise above that which is written. Enjoin nothing that the Bible does not clearly enjoin. Forbid nothing that it does not clearly forbid." Here indeed were local churches in the making. The Life of God enjoyed by believers in different localities caused them to grow and bring forth fruit unto God. Planting there was, and watering too, but God was everything, for He was the One who made the seed, and He the One who made it grow. What men subsequently did in organising this promising vineyard out of existence is well known today. John Wesley's nightly wish has not been realised. The Spirit broke forth but the synthetic skins of men could not contain the precious wine and much was spilled. This is not written invidiously nor designed as a special criticism of Methodism. In fact, it is not written for the purpose of criticism at all but rather as an illustration of the tragic truth that virtually all the great denominations of our day are nothing more than sepulchres of movements that once were Spirit-born. Can we point to a single one that has not *"Ichabod"* for an epitaph?

In a world drugged by the opium of capitalism and scourged by the lash of Communism, what then is the Christian's task? Are we to perpetuate the factors of decay existent in our ecclesiastical systems, haggard and distraught with the adulterous spirit of the age; or are we to rise in the Holy Spirit who gave us birth, and moving with the Spirit who leads the sons of God, break up the very ground in which we grew till fruit is found for God? The Pharisees could discuss Jesus, they could question Jesus, they could criticise Jesus, but they never brought a soul to Jesus' feet. It took some earnest simple folk with faith in their hearts to break the roof apart and bring the sick of the palsy there. Some might wonder who would pay for the tiles, but meanwhile sins are forgiven and a man set free in the liberty of God. For many today, faithfulness to the present fabric is more important than faith in the great Physician. The Pharisees held the tiles together as long as they could but when the stone cut out without hands finally fell upon them, they were ground to powder, tiles and all. It happened to their religious system then. It has happened many times since and at the last the whole of Christendom will know that doom. Once again, we must assert, only that which is born of God can possibly remain. To say this in the present climate of opinion concerning church matters will hardly be regarded as palatable, but let us not forget the words of Tyndale as he faced the hostility of the Satanic forces of his day entrenched in formal Christianity. As the precious sheets of his freshly translated New Testament went forth from the Continent to England he said, "The scribes and Pharisees have thrust up the Sword of the Word of God in a scabbard or sheath of glosses, and therein have knit it fast, so that it could neither pierce nor cut . . . Now O God, draw this sharp Sword from the scabbard. Strike, wound, cut asunder the soul and the flesh, so that man being divided into two and set at variance with himself, may be in peace with Thee to all eternity." There is only one thing more ruthless than death and that is life. Thank God that whilst the flames that burnt the martyrs die, the candle that the martyrs lit shines on. Shall we forget the price they paid and turn again to Rome? O God forbid that we should abandon life!

We must not imagine, however, that the break-out and the break-through of the Spirit of Life is always immediately manifest in a public way or in a prominent movement of power. Rather does the Spirit of God begin in the personal and the more intimate sphere of the lives of the two's and three's. The routing of the Philistines often begins with a Jonathan and his armour-bearer. The breakthrough comes first in our own individual lives, when in the crisis of life, we are not prepared any longer to bow the knee to the traditions of an effete religious officialdom, but dare to believe God for ourselves; dare to act upon the Word of God ourselves, and allow the Spirit of God to speak directly to our conscience withour reference to self-appointed ecclesiastical adjudicators.

A personal friend of mine told me of a most harrowing and heart-searching experience he endured in South-East Asia during the last war. As the Japanese pursued their conquest in that theatre of conflict he, with many other British troops, fell into their hands. Herded together in the hot and steamy atmosphere of the camp; made to work on a low diet, and live in unhygienic conditions, it was not long before cholera broke out amongst them. This presented a very critical problem to the Japanese officer in charge and he decided to set up a separate compound for those men who contracted the disease. This became little more than a death camp. As the crisis grew, the Japanese commandant asked for volunteers from the British prisoners to go into the death camp and tend their dying comrades. Nine men volunteered. Of these nine, two were professing Christians, my friend, and another man whom ironically, proved to be a member of an opposing communion. Normally speaking, in Britain, there would be no comings or goings between these two Christians or the groups they represented. One by one, the nine volunteers began to succumb to cholera and die with those whom they had gone to nurse, yet still the two Christians survived; then one day one of the cholera victims vomited violently into the face of my friend. The two Christians looked at each other. This must be the end. On the fringe of the camp, however, there was a quiet spot amongst the bushes. In the stillness they knelt together in the fellowship of their common Lord. It was a great moment. All barriers were gone now and their Father heard. Slowly the cholera outbreak subsided. Only three of the nine volunteers emerged to tell their story. Two of the three were these Christian men. In the crisis, traditional differences were forgotten. They had entered together into that essential fellowship which is the undoubted birthright of every child of God.

Here I would quote from C. F. Hogg's leaflet on *Fellowship*. His words are an endorsement of our theme.

"This fellowship of Christians is spiritual, not formal; it is not the result of human planning, much less of human scheming; it is an organism, not an organisation; vital not mechanical. And since it is the result of a living, directing power it cannot be confined within artificial bounds. There are no straight lines in living nature . . . Straight lines appear in crystallisation, where life is not. Crystals can be very beautiful in orderly design, but this is the result of pressure exerted from without, not of inworking life."

So it is, that once the artificial bounds are broken and men are free to move in faith together, then in the stress of life the Spirit of the Lord leads them out into a fresh experience of God. Yet we would ask, "Must there always be a 'death camp' before we realise this living fellowship which is ours in Christ?"

CHAPTER XXI

THE NAME AND THE NAMES

"And Jacob . . . said, Tell me, I pray Thee, Thy name. And he said,
Wherefore is it thou dost ask after my name?"   Genesis 32
"And Manoah said . . . What is thy name? . . . and the angel of the Lord
said, . . . Why askest thou thus after my name seeing it is secret?"
                                                          Judges 13

BUT these are rather like conclusions. What of the origins? The mists of
time and the acrid theological smog of our day have so beclouded our
spiritual concepts that Christian fellowship for us tends to bear little
resemblance to that fellowship described in the Word of God. In one
sense this may not be altogether our fault for in this twentieth century we
are historically a long way downstream from Pentecost, and the mudflats
of contemporary religion are extensive to say the least of it. Notwithstanding, it is incumbent on each believer, in this closing period of the dispensation, to return to the Source. In the lonely days of my imprisonment in
China when the sense of isolation from fellow Christians was very great,
I was much comforted by the words of the hymn—

> "A monument of grace
> A sinner saved by blood
> The streams of love I trace
> *Up to their fountain, God.*
> And in His sovereign counsels see,
> Eternal thoughts of love to me."

This is what John was saying when he wrote to the first-century
believers about fellowship. He took them back to the Source and pointed
to "that which was from the beginning, which we have heard, which we
have seen with our eyes, which we have looked upon, and our hands have
handled, of the Word of life, for the Life was manifested . . ." And then
he says, "That which we have seen and heard declare we unto you, that

ye also may have fellowship with us; and truly our fellowship is with the
Father, and with His Son, Jesus Christ." Here is the Source of all fellowship in the Spirit. This is the Fountain Head.

Fellowship is not something nebulous, but intensely practical and real.
If we use another metaphor we can say it is a wheel with a hub. Through
the life of the Spirit and the work of Christ we, as spokes, are first rooted
centrally in God. Then as we hold hands with each other we present a
firm circumference to the world in which we move. The rim may become
defiled at times and sorely abrased but if we stand firm in our Centre, then
is our movement sure. Human fellowships centre about a human personality. Divine fellowship centres in Divine Personality. If our fellowship on
earth is associated with a human name, it will not exceed the concept of
a human coterie. If we are bound together by a human enterprise then we
shall not surpass the scope of man's endeavour. The true fellowship of the
child of God centres in God alone and those who are so bound to God find
that the activities of such a fellowship issue out from God, take their
direction from God, are upheld of God, and lead home to God. This
fellowship with the Father and His Son; this fellowship of the Holy
Spirit, is thus of unfathomable depth and of limitless vision. In it regenerate
men take their place in relation to their Centre and only thus do they have
relation to each other. If they make one of their number a centre, then
they have denied the fellowship of God. If our fellowship is with Him,
then it is with no one else outside of Him, and our fellowship with one
another is because we are in Him, and He has hold of us, and His life is in
us. My Christian fellowship is not concerned so much with what *I* hold
but with *Who* holds me. Not so much with a creed but with the Christ.
It rests not so much in an agreement on the doctrine of redemption but in
a common interlock with the Redeemer. Not in an equality of light but
in our sharing the eternal life of God. If I can say to my fellow believer,
"The life you have is by the grace of God the life I have", and if in the
power of that God-given life we walk according to the light we have,
then we have fellowship one with another and the blood of Jesus Christ,
God's Son, cleanses us from all sin.

We hear about the Personality Cult today. In the East the massive
pictures of Communist leaders are paraded through the streets, or at the
other extreme, an idol of "illustrious" name is carried hysterically through
the crowds. There is a name on everybody's lips, whether it be that of Mao

Tse Tung or that of a heathen deity. The significance of a name is that it gives to that centre through which men have fellowship together, an essential identity and recognition in their minds. Their idol, living or dead, is made theirs in a personal way through its name. Once named, they can call on him, or they can wish him well. They feel they know him now; that they can really worship him now. It is hard to worship a god or a demon without a name. It is hard to know anyone or make him known, if he bears no name.

What a man is, is expressed in his name. In his lifetime he either disgraces it, or glorifies it, but without it his very existence is called in question. In the disclosure of a name a man reveals himself. He becomes known who before was unknown. It is not to everyone a man will tell his name. Sometimes the disclosure of a name is not only an unveiling but a committal. We quickly identify names with character. In our minds certain names are unsavoury for they conjure up in our minds the memory of unsavoury persons. Others are revered and precious to our ears for they are linked with a quality of life in someone we shall never forget. Some names are devised on earth whilst others are conceived in Heaven. Every babe is born nameless but when a man dies he has specific identity and he hopes the name he bore on earth will be written in the record of the Lamb on high. God is concerned with names, for the person he creates must be identified, but first of all He is concerned for His own Name, for He is the Invisible God. He is Spirit. It is by His Name that He must be identified to His creatures. Angels veil their faces, cherubim hide beneath their wings, for what creature can see God and live? Yet if no man has seen God at any time how then is God known? From all eternity He has been known by His Name. That Name is an everlasting Name. By it His pre-eminence is asserted for it is "a more excellent name". By it His glory is proclaimed, for says the Scripture, "His Name is glorious". Divine Names are ever expressive of Divine character, and down the milleniums it is through His Name that men have been drawn to Him and by His Name that He has drawn near to us.

Angels have names. There is Michael, portrayed as one of God's great contenders. His name means, "Who is like God?" He challenges Satan concerning Divine interests. There is Gabriel. He is seen as one of God's great informers. His name means "God is mighty" and he proclaims to human beings Divine intentions. There are names in the heavenlies which are known on earth but then there are also names on earth which are known in the heavenlies. "Though Moses and Samuel stood before me yet my mind could not be toward this people," says God. These men were distinguished by their prayers before His Throne. Demons are interested in names. They have their mediums and antagonists. Judas Iscariot, no doubt, was a name of peculiar interest to Satan, though Sceva and his exorcists were only nondescripts. What does the evil spirit cry? "Jesus I know, and Paul I know; but who are ye?" "Surely a good name is better than precious ointment, and rather to be chosen than great riches!" God sets a priceless worth upon the Name He bears, and great importance on the names He gives. One aspect of His great reward is the bestowal of His own new Name. Unchanging in Himself, He wears a changeless Name, but our poor names he loves to change, for His new men are given new identity. We who were once in Adam are now in Christ. We who were once in darkness are now in light. The earthly has been called to bear the image of the heavenly, thus God has brand-new names for all the men he makes again. Abram becomes an Abraham, Jacob an Israel, Simon a Cephas, and Saul a Paul.

God has so much to say in a name. It may express not only a man's nature but his destiny. It may point to current conditions or carry a prediction of judgement. It may express an experience, or epitomise a ministry. It may be the instrument of intercession, authority or fear. Sometimes we ask, "What's in a name?" As far as God and His Word are concerned all is set forth in a name. There are almost three thousand proper names in the Bible and each has its own significance, yet above them all there towers one matchless Name, a name divinely given, a name for ever unexcelled, the Name of Jesus.

The Bible then is a book of *the Name*, and *the names*; the Name of God and the names of men. In relating this to the question of fellowship we find that there are two basic scriptural concepts of fellowship in the New Testament; a sharing in a common wealth, and a partnership in a common cause. The former is the Greek word *"koinonia"* and the latter *"metoche"*. The former seems to have a richer content than the latter but it is interesting to note that *"metoche"* is used in the Septuagint version of the Old Testament, in Psalm 122 and verse 3, where we read that "Jerusalem", which was of course the place of the Name, "is built as a city whose fellowship is complete". Fellowship in the Bible is almost always associated with a name. Men and women are either people of *the* Name or people of *another* name. They are either centred in the Living God, or in a man, dead or dying. We need to ask ourselves then, "In what kind of circle do I move?" Having discerned this, we must then ask ourselves, "Who or what is the centre of it?" Are our secular and religious associations divinely originated or humanly contrived? "The Lord is our Sun and Shield. The Lord will give grace and glory," says the Word of God. Are we in His appointed orbit, stabilised in all our life and movement by His gravitational pull and His centripetal force or are we out of His orbit altogether? To be out of His orbit is to become a "wandering star". It is to come into the orbit of another; it is to be drawn into the great deep and "the blackness of darkness for ever". It is only night there, whereas in the sphere where He is altogether central the Word says, "There is no night there", for He is its Sun and "the Lamb is the light thereof". It is the desire of God that our fellowship on earth should anticipate in character our future fellowship in Heaven. That the One in whom His eternal delight is centred, might be the focus of our faith and joy in Time. That together with the Father, in the Holy Ghost, we might centre our whole heart in the Son who ever brings us to God and God to us. But men love other names and other centres. They would have other persons. They would have Jesus, but with Him, Moses and Elias too and tabernacles for them all. They would have Paul, and Cephas, and Apollos. They would have Jesus plus many a splendid preacher and many a "lawful" doctrine till finally Christ is but an adjunct to their official centre, and a co-opted authoriser of their official rallying point. Thus servants of the Lord become greater than the Lord Himself, and the words they speak, more than He who spoke the Word. This is a modern way of Cain. It is the way out from God. If we return to Genesis we shall see how it all began.

CHAPTER XXII

BACK TO THE SOURCE

"Thou, Lord, in the beginning hast laid the foundation . . ." Hebrews 1
"The devil sinneth from the beginning."   I John 3
"Have ye not known? Hath it not been told you from the beginning?"
                                                              Isaiah 40
"Moses suffered you to put away . . . but from the beginning it was not so."
                                                              Matthew 19

MAN had humble but great beginnings. Though made of dust, he yet was
made for God, and his first abode, the Garden of Eden, was essentially a
place of fellowship. Man had all things in common with His Creator.
God planned that He and man should reign together, work together, that
they should walk and talk together; that in all things they should move
in harmony; that man might know no separate way. In this partnership,
God planned to subdue all things to Himself in the sphere of the earth,
where for the moment chaos reigned, owing to His righteous intervention
against Satanic ambition. In the midst of the garden we see how the Lord
supplies a two-fold ministry. There is the tree of life and there is the river
of life. The first grows up within the garden. The second flows out
beyond the garden. They are natural symbols testifying of spiritual
realities. They are the evidence of eternal things transcending, yet coming
to us through temporal things. In a world plunged into chaos they represent that which survives both satanic intrigue and Divine judgement. A
world "created not void" had been reduced to emptiness that God might
fill it and become its all in all. Whatever natural life there may have been
in that erstwhile creation it did not come through, but that which spoke
of the life of God did. Through every crisis God survives. Soon his man
would face his own crisis. In the appointed time, though immediately
after the fall, restrained, man would taste both of the tree and the river. The
tree speaks to us now of Christ as an object of faith. Man must taste and
see that the Lord is good, whereas the river speaks of Christ coming to
us in sovereign grace. "Everything shall live whither the river cometh."

It is something with which we ourselves have nothing to do. These ministries are supplied all down the years of this present age, until in the eternal state the tree and the river of life are identified as at the beginning, with the authority of God. The river flows from the Throne and the tree still grows upon its banks for the healing of the nations. Now all this is very important for the understanding of fellowship. God is the centre of His garden as He is of His Heaven, and the ministry of life finds its source and administration in Him alone, who is both Lord and God.

Satan then, in the dawn of time, comes and by subtle means, seeks to introduce an alien centre on earth just as he sought to introduce an alien centre in Heaven. He comes anonymously and in disguise. Successfully he draws man away from God and to himself. This is the nature of all activity which is satanically inspired. In immediate and positive action God provides, in the blood-sacrifice of innocent creatures, an adequate covering for Adam and Eve; and by this means, together with His certain promise that the woman's seed should bruise the serpent's head, He makes Himself responsible for man's recovery and guarantees to him both the way of his return and the defeat of his tempter. Yet notwithstanding such abundant grace, a line of unbelieving men arises, determined to maintain its interests in the earth independently of God. With what penetration did God's first questions strike the human conscience! To Adam he said, "Where art Thou?" To Cain He said, "What hast thou done?" Once defined, a man's *location* and his *action* are enough to show the evil of his heart. Although Adam returned in faith, accepting the Divine provision, yet of Cain the record says, "He went out from the presence of the Lord." Now what did he do? His first reaction at severance from God was unrelieved despair. Judging God after his own thoughts he said, "My sin is too great to be forgiven. I shall be a fugitive and a vagabond in the earth." In other words he felt he had on earth neither "face" nor "place". He was a man of no God, no focus, no conscious destination. Having refused God as the rightful controller and centre of his life he now resolves to create a new centre. He builds a city the centre of which is Cain and the name of which is Enoch. He thus seeks to perpetuate his cult by naming the city after his offspring. Enoch means "teacher". This would be a centre where what Cain thought and what Cain taught would prevail; where Cain's view of man would be the basis of the new culture. Under Cain's wilful leadership, the masterful line of his posterity quickly tamed the curséd earth, establishing man's three main occupations, agriculture, the arts and industry. Each of these spheres had its big name, being inaugurated and developed respectively by Cain's renowned descendants, Jabal, Jubal and Tubal-cain. But this society for all its apparent progress could not escape the doom inherent in its origins. Born in the act of murder and inspired by him who is a murderer from the beginning, violence and bloodshed became its hallmark. In the fifth generation, the seed of its founder, bringing forth after its kind, blights the life of Lamech with its bitter fruit. "I have slain a man," he cries, "to my wounding and a young man to my hurt." As these developments were taking place, a grandchild was born to Adam. At this time Adam was two hundred and thirty-five years old and Seth, the father of the child, a hundred and five. It may be the alien centre of the Cainite culture was already well established. Whether or not this was the case, Adam, Eve and Seth, with the revelation that God had given them, had had ample opportunity to consider the consequences of their sin and their true position before God. For Adam there had now been over two centuries of silence, yet he, with the remnants of his broken family, clung on still to the promise of God, though ever aware of the certainty of death. This is now reflected in the deep spiritual exericise of Seth at the birth of his son. This was a gift of life but Seth called him Enos which means "mortal". This is all the more significant as we have no evidence that any person, as yet, had actually died of natural causes. Yet it is precisely at this juncture that the Bible says that "men began to call upon the Name of the Lord". Up to this time men had been named, women had been named, children had been named, rivers and cities had been named, but God in the experience of the fallen race had not been re-identified to his creatures by a name. Here then is an act of grace. To man, increasingly conscious of his mortality, the Lord discloses himself in such a way as to enable them to call upon His Name. This is the reassertion of the True Centre in human experience. It is God's next step in the recovery of man; and for the few who believed, God had once again become the home and goal of humanity.

Approximately one half of the known history of man is covered in the period dealt with in the first eleven chapters of Genesis. In those chapters two lines of people emerge, each with their own focal points, each with their own faith, each with their own god. They represent two opposing fellowships. The one is the fellowship of light, centred in God as Lord and

Redeemer of the race, and the other is the fellowship of darkness centred in the devil, the usurper and deceiver of the race. The first is held together in the Name of the Lord. The other is marshalled under any name that might serve the purposes of Satan at any particular juncture of history.

Following the cataclysmic judgement of the flood, the Cainite concepts of God and human society were perpetuated in the sons of Ham; whereas the Sethite faith, centred in God, was perpetuated in the line of Shem, so that God was known first of all in the post-deluvian era as "the God of Shem". Of the sons of Ham there arose a man called Nimrod, who is termed "a mighty rebel before the Lord". The beginning of his kingdom was Babel and in the Cainite tradition he founded a city which was to be a world centre. He culminated his ambition in a vast "space project", namely the building of a tower that would reach to heaven. The significance of this is clear when we read their godless manifesto. "Let us build a city and a tower whose top may reach unto heaven; and let us make us a *name*, lest we be scattered abroad upon the face of the whole earth." In contrast to this we see the Everlasting God choosing a solitary man, and in grace, leading him out of idolatry and corruption, to a simple dependence on Himself. This was a descendant of Shem, called Abram, living in Ur of the Chaldees, a man whom God later describes as "Abraham, my friend". To him God says, "Get thee out of thy country, and from thy kindred and from thy father's house, unto a land that I will shew thee and I will make of thee a great nation, and will bless thee, and make thy name great and thou shalt be a blessing." In other words he took a man and asked him to have no other centre but Himself. He was to find no focus for his life in country, home or relations. It was as if He said, "You are to have no one in all the world but Me. In this you will find your destined greatness as a man on the earth. Others may make much of men, much of themselves, much of their own. Others may have alien interests, foreign centres and worldy fellowship. Others may serve the satanic ends, but I have called you and it means that only in Me is real destiny, true greatness and lasting blessing to be known; and what is more, in you and in your seed shall all the nations of the earth be blessed." Then it is we read that Abram builded an altar unto the Lord and called upon the *Name* of the Lord. From that day, we can say, the fellowship of believing men and women took a great step forward, and when Paul takes up the whole question in the Spirit about two thousand years later, he writes concerning

Christians, "Ye are all the children of God by faith in Christ Jesus and if ye be Christ's, then are ye Abraham's seed and heirs according to the promise."

As the inspired narrative of the Holy Scriptures unfolds we find that what first came to light in Seth at the birth of Enos; what was confirmed in the personal witness of Shem, and what was ultimately demonstrated in Abraham and his household is now developed at a national level. Whereas at first it was individuals who called on the Name of the Lord and then later godly households, now a whole race is joined to the Lord and is constituted by Him and for Him a holy nation and a royal priesthood. Whilst quickly falling from their destined status we nevertheless see in Israel in the wilderness, an entire nation under the direct government of God. Furthermore we see that the honour of His Name is their special charge and by the time we come to the end of the Pentateuch, the Lord their God is entrusting them with His plans concerning His Name on the earth. As they move on towards the land of His promise He says, "Then there shall be a place which the Lord your God shall choose to cause His Name to dwell there." Israel was to be God's bridgehead in a rebel world. Now the basis of the fellowship of this "church in the wilderness", as Stephen termed it, was redemption; and it was realised in their experience, by the God of Israel being present in the midst of His redeemed people, gathering them, teaching them, guiding them, disciplining them, until He brought them into their inheritance. Thus was He sanctified in them before the eyes of the heathen. His desire was that they should know no other Centre but Himself, no other authority but His own, no other Shepherd than Jehovah. It was to be a theocratic rule. So through the years we follow them till we come to Jerusalem. There with the temple built and inaugurated, the staves are drawn out of the ark. The way of their pilgrimage is completed now. There the God of Glory fills the sanctuary and all Israel bow in worship at His feet. This is a great prefiguring of the climax of the ages when He who is greater than Solomon shall sit upon the throne of His glory and, with his train filling the temple, shall rule from sea to sea and shore to shore. Solomon in his prayer is deeply sensitive to God's mind in all this. Before the people on that day of dedication he cries: "Have respect unto the prayer of thy servant, O Lord my God . . . That Thine eyes may be open toward this house night and day, even toward the place of which thou hast said, My Name shall be there."

Such then was the fellowship of Israel, centred in the Lord Himself who would meet them and hear them at the place of His Name.

In the history of the nation, however, we find those elements who were never prepared to rejoice in the Name of the Lord, but wanted to set persons, idols, ordinances and relics above the Lord who brought them. They introduced alien emphases and false rallying points, and raised divisive standards for the allegiance of the dissident, thus breaking the ranks of the nation and bringing down the wrath of their jealous God, who would not give His glory to another.

Some of the instances are full of instruction. One of the earliest false centres was the golden calf. The subtlety of this deception lay in presenting "Jehovah" in Egyptian religious terms. "These be thy gods that brought thee up out of the land of Egypt", says Aaron, and then adds, "Tomorrow is a feast to the Lord." In other words the gods of the heathen are but tangible expressions of the basic idea of God. There is only a difference of form, but not of fact. Could there be any greater blasphemy! So in the intellectual world of our day, God is being reduced to creature-dimensions. He is described in philosophical clichés, which, whilst professing to be down to earth, are like wisps of cloud that toss and turn in every current of opinion. The general trend is to equate primal natural forces with Deity, a confusion which ends in making energy a substitute for Divine personality, evolution an expression of the will of God, and the Communist Utopia, the realisation of the Kingdom of Heaven. Such are the pretensions of men, some of whom profess godliness though they deny the power thereof. Theirs are great and swelling words, but when analysed, prove to be no more than age-old fantasies fashioned anew in borrowed Egyptian gold. The tragedy for the Church is intensified, because along the wilderness way there is many a traitor-priest, who, like Aaron, raises an altar to the vain concoctions of the creature. "Out came a golden calf," he vapidly explains. And such is contemporary culture, marked from head to toe by the same nonchalant irresponsibility. We mix the ingredients of our decadent society in the witch's cauldron of unbelief, and as our values slur and slump together, out comes a grotesque expression of our life. Hence in philosophy, art, music, literature and even religion there is distortion, excess, rowdyism, deception, incoherence and unbridled licentiousness. To the golden works of our sin-soiled minds and hands, we bring our treasure store of admiration, interest, verve and vigour, time and talent. We even bring our faith testifying that here at last are the gods which give release. That is exactly what they said about the golden calf. "These be thy gods, which brought thee out of the land of Egypt", and as in that distant yesterday, "the people sat down to eat and drink, and rose up to play", so it is today. But God is not mocked. A little while and the bones of an entire generation lay beneath the shifting sands of Sinai. On the ritualist level of the religious godshelf, the apostasy of the golden calf devotee is something more obvious, though none the less evil. In twentieth-century Britain, thousands still centre their thoughts in images, amulets and crucifixes. I cannot forget my revulsion on one occasion at seeing a Protestant clergyman in Scotland genuflect before a grotesque hulk of wood suggestive in a crude kind of way of Christ upon the Cross. Though we may scorn the calf of Egypt, yet modern art still draws its worshippers to such idol "messiahs". "Beauty and strength are in His sanctuary" but these are attributes intrinsic in His Person. We shall not add to them, not yet to Him, by shamelessly deifying the tawdry carvings of our hands. Our Saviour needs no monument. He made atonement, in His blood.

On another occasion when threatened by Philistine invasion the Israelites rallied to another centre. This was quite different from the golden calf. Here was something made to Divine specifications. They said, "Let us fetch the ark of the covenant of the Lord out of Shiloh unto us, then when it cometh among us, *it* may save us." Here they made that which spake of His Presence the saving factor, instead of the Saviour Himself. This has been done time and again in the worship of the Church. The sacraments (especially the Lord's supper), for example, which speak so profoundly of our Lord, have been taken up as saving elements in themselves and in many a church group have become a rallying point for fellowship or a plea for division, as if acceptance with God, be it in the temporal circumstance or in the eternal state, could ever depend on bread and wine. The history of First Samuel shows conclusively that the Israelites were impotent so long as they centred their confidence in a mere thing, however sacred, instead of in the Living God.

In the days of Gideon there was a mighty movement of the Lord, and clothed with God's Spirit he won great battles for God. In later days when the movement and its effects seemed more established there was a lot of popular sentiment and good-will shown towards Gideon and although basically a man of faith yet he committed an unbelievable folly. The ear-rings of his enemies, the Midianites, were at his behest made into a memorial which was finally erected in his city square. Everyone seemed to think it was a "nice idea" and an acceptable way of commemorating what Gideon (that is to say, the Lord) had done. It was hardly on its pedestal before people were making excursions to see it and even paying reverence to it. It quickly became a rendez-vous of religious pilgrimage and before it was realised, a man, his deeds and his memorial, became a centre. Though Gideon's deeds were wrought in gold yet he himself was still of Adam's clay. Before long there arose from his very loins Abimelech, "the bram-ble king", who murdered in cold blood all but one of his sons, killing seventy persons on one stone. Suffice it to say that in a work of God, if the emphasis once shifts from God to man, then tragedy ensues and un-imagined shame is soon incurred. We cannot tamper with His Name and guiltless be.

During Hezekiah's reign we see another unexpected alien centre turning men from a true focus of faith and worship in the Lord. Amongst the relics in Jerusalem was the closely guarded treasure of the brazen serpent. Had not men looked at it and then been healed of the serpent's bite? The narrative gives us the amazing information that "unto those days the children of Israel did burn incense to it . . ." Thank God in Hezekiah we find a man whose whole horizon was filled with Jehovah. He made one derisive pronouncement upon it. "Nehushtan!" he cried, "a piece of brass!" "But surely it *was* the brazen serpent", someone might say, "and even Christ referred to it when speaking of salvation". What we must always remember is, that it is not that which speaks of Christ that saves, but Christ Himself. Not even the Bible can save, for though it is the Word of God, quick and powerful as the Spirit's Sword, it is not a talisman or a magic wand. Nor can a catechism save, though it may well contain the Truth of God; nor even sound doctrine, though it point to the Cross, but the Christ of the Cross Himself.

The Lord wanted to be all in all to His people but they would not let Him be so. Thus the time came when judgement fell, the glory departed, and the place of the Name was desecrated and burned with fire. Eventu-ally, in spite of a return from captivity and a period of revival, decline again prevailed, the prophets were silent and a generation of time-servers and political opportunists filled the temple courts. Such was the scene at the time of Christ's advent. It brings us to the deeply significant words of our Saviour, spoken to the Samaritan women at the well. "Women, believe me, the hour cometh and now is, when ye shall neither in this mountain, nor yet at Jerusalem, worship the Father ... the hour cometh and now is when the true worshippers shall worship the Father in spirit and in truth; for the Father seeketh such to worship Him."

Israel after the flesh, and as a nation on the earth, was to be set aside for the present. She had despised the law and done despite to the covenant. Her people had slain the prophets and were soon to crucify their Messiah. He had come unto His own to be a Prince and a Saviour in their midst. He longed to be the object of their faith and worship, to shepherd them, to rule over them; and through them, to pour out blessing on the nations. But they received Him not. They had not known the time of their visitation. Their house was desolate. Yet the purposes of God would not be thwarted. Rather would they be matured. Now He would seek a spiritual Israel, a holy nation and a royal priesthood from those who, in former times, were not His people, nor could be, but who now, by grace, would become the people of God.

But how could they come to know Him? This miracle would be wrought through that which men despised—by the preaching of His Name! How would He save them? They would enter His salvation by calling on His Name! No other Name but His would spell forgiveness to the lost. In that Name would men rejoice and be baptised. In that Name would they witness, suffer, triumph and endure. How would He meet with them? His promise was for the Gentile now, as well as for the Jew. "Where two or three are gathered together in my Name there am I in the midst of them." Thus would He become the centre and the focus for all His believing people. Thus would He gather them about Himself, no longer in Jerusalem, much less in Samaria but still in the place of the Name. One day a trump will rend the skies and we shall gather unto Him to scatter from His side no more. Then shall the Bride in constant union with her great Beloved worship for ever, owning no Name but His.

CHAPTER XXIII

WHERE FLOWS THE RIVER

"He opened the rock and the waters gushed out, they ran in the dry
places like a river."   Psalm 105
"There is a river, the streams whereof shall make glad the city of
God . . ."   Psalm 46

IT was a Lord's Day morning in the far west of China. Having received
word from a Chinese believer that a group of Christians met to worship
the Lord in the heart of the idolatrous city, I set out to find them and to
enquire of their witness. After walking some distance through the dirty
streets, and past many a sad sight of destitution and misery, I came at last
to a small alleyway leading in behind some houses. It was a dark muddy
tunnel beneath the buildings and I was glad to get through it and out
again into the open air. I found myself in a desolate square surrounded by
drab dwellings of one kind and another. On my right I noticed a room
which, devoid of any doorway or formal entrance, looked straight out
on to the courtyard. It was a place formerly used for idol worship. In one
corner of the room was stacked a pile of disused religious furnishings,
but of this I was barely aware, on account of the other furniture in the
room. There was something very moving in its stark simplicity. In the
centre of the small chamber, but set a little towards the light which slanted
in from the courtyard, stood an occasional table, about two feet square. It
was laid for a simple meal, although the neighbours, even in their poverty,
must have thought it rather frugal. There was just one plate, and on it
a thin wafer of bread. Beside it was a cup, or to be more accurate, a jug
of wine. Around the small table, at a distance of several feet, were spaced
about ten stools. I had come to the place where the Christians met. One
by one the seats were filled. The believers were surprised to see me but
welcomed me sincerely as one of themselves, in trusting the Lord Jesus
Christ as my Saviour. The meeting though obviously convened for a certain
hour of the day was not, however, conducted by any particular person.

I learned afterwards that they believed quite literally that this was the *Lord's* Supper. It had been instituted by Him. He it was who had invited us. He it was of whom the emblems spoke. We were but His guests. He would lead us in remembrance and worship by His Spirit. We had not come so much to see each other but to meet our Lord. We had not come to listen to each other but to seek His face, and to hear His voice speak to our hearts. These earnest believers counted wholly on His promise that if they would gather in His Name, He would be there. In silence then we waited on the Lord. After a while one and another suggested hymns for praise, and different believers prayed audibly. Then with our hearts poured out in adoration before the Lord, the wafer of bread was passed round. Each one of us in turn broke a small piece from it and ate it, remembering Him who gave His body for our sakes. Then the little jug was passed round too, and we thought together upon Him whose blood was shed that we might be forgiven. After this the meeting went on for a long time and we continued to worship and meditate upon His Word. The gathering was quite unhurried and everyone seemed content to be there as long as the Lord in our midst continued to draw out our hearts to Himself.

Over the following weeks I was frequently in the home of one of the more mature believers of this little church. The hearts of the saints were warming, for we spoke often now of the Lord and thought much upon Him together. One evening as four or five of us were conversing in this Chinese home, we began to look into the first chapter of Matthew. We were so helped in this that we decided to come together the next evening to look at chapter two. Drawn by the Spirit of the Lord into His Word, we now gathered evening by evening, until different ones joined us and the blessing began to reach out to other Christians. We continued with growing interest night by night through the book of Matthew until the little church was enlivened and enriched in a very real way. Hidden sin and personal difficulties in the lives of the believers began to find solution. We gathered now in a more public way and still more gathered with us in a bigger room. Some of the believers who came to the meetings were lepers. This would horrify a congregation in the West and quickly disperse it, but somehow it seemed of no moment in China. Soon a number of Christians asked to be baptised. It was a matter of great interest to me to see how such a request would be handled. Whilst I was witnessing with these Christians, all decisions of the little church were in their hands. They would seek God's wisdom. I was simply their brother in Christ. I had not come to have dominion over their faith, but to be a helper of their joy.

One cold winter's morning not long afterwards, I joined the little band of believers and together we wended our way outside the city wall to the riverside. On the stony, dried up part of the river-bed they pitched a small booth for changing. It was rather an unusual occasion, for those to be baptised were mostly, if not all, lepers. Some had ugly nodules protruding from their faces. Nearly all were mutilated in some way. It was something that no words can describe, to see those men go down into the river in obedience to their Lord. Out in the cold waters flowing straight down from the Central Asian Plateau, stood a more mature Christian leper waiting to receive them. There, in public confession, they passed beneath the surface of the river, being baptised in the Name of the Father, and of the Son, and of the Holy Ghost. As they came up out of the water on to the dry part of the river bed, their knarled faces were radiant with joy. Once they had changed their wet clothes, we climbed up on to the bank and broke bread together in a little room near at hand, which had been acquired for the occasion. So we met again around our Lord as we did each Lord's Day, only this time there were over twenty of us.

It was not long after this that I took my journey westward in the appointment of the Lord, up into the high country of the Tibetan Borderlands. It was hard to say good-bye. We did not know whether we would meet on earth again, but God had knit us all together with eternal bonds, in those unforgettable days of fellowship around His own dear Son.

About eighteen months later, however, I did have occasion to return from the plateau, this time with my fellow-worker, George Patterson. There were matters to attend to in Szechwan ere we travelled deeper into Central Asia, and whilst only in the province a week or two, it gave us opportunity to contact this little church again and other believers also in West China. It was very reassuring to find this tiny church even more established and launching out now into aggressive evangelistic work. From the very poor quarters of the first courtyard I had visited, they had now transferred to a fine airy room rented in a big bank building. One day when I was in the town, I went along to this new meeting place to see what they were doing. There was a fine crowd of Chinese folk brought in off the streets, listening to the Gospel being preached from a pictorial chart by the leper brother who had bapised his fellow-lepers in the river those months before.

Through this church we were able to contact another church with a similar witness in a city some days' journey away by road. We called quite unexpectedly on these believers who met in a large downstairs room of a private house. I suppose there must have been up to fifty Chinese present. As the meeting was in progress, our entry proved rather an interruption, but they received us courteously and made us feel very much at home. We had met none of them before but there was no sense of awkwardness by reason of our intrusion. The meeting appeared to be open for individual believers to take part in prayer, praise, testimony and ministry, and after a while we were asked whether we had any testimony to bear to the Lord Jesus Christ. We both spoke and eventually the meeting closed. Afterwards one of the brothers approached us and, speaking on behalf of the whole assembly, told us that they would receive us to their fellowship as true believers in our Lord Jesus Christ. Little did we realise that as we spoke, our sincerity and soundness of faith were undergoing the scrutiny of the company. On enquiry we were told that they had recently baptised nine believers in the nearby river and were now about forty strong. They said, "You are the first foreign missionaries ever to visit our church." They were anxious also to know whether Christians were meeting in this way in Great Britain and how any such companies came into being. They had a great heart for the Lord and His work and when at last we bade them farewell, in one of our bags we found a gift of money to assist us in our task of taking the Gospel to the Tibetans.

How many of these groups were in China at the time of the Communist take-over it is impossible to estimate. They accepted no designation and acknowledged no affiliation. As Europeans we could hardly find them apart from personal contacts who knew of them, or who had been blessed through their witness. To what degree a Communist government could ultimately suppress such gatherings is very open to question. There was the breath of New Testament days in their fellowship and activity. Theirs was a genuine desire to centre their all in Christ, and to own His Name alone.

In the course of my travels in many countries over the past twenty years it has been my custom to search out and meet with many such companies as these. At different times in history and amongst different races, God raises up time and again individual Christians and local churches who maintain a distinctive testimony to the Lord Jesus. They have, maybe, no contact with similar groups and may be completely oblivious of each other's existence. Their gatherings may differ in form to some degree and local custom may tend to colour their procedures, but in spite of such diversity, when one sees a company desirous of confessing Christ as their Lord and Head, when they genuinely acknowledge the leading of the Holy Spirit in their midst to gift and guide, when the saints are free to exercise their God-given priestly office in intercession and worship and are not ruled artificially by ordained ministers or official leaders, then one senses the difference.

In our day when ecumenical councils and papal compromises hit the headlines, and business mergers are matched by church amalgamations; when Church and State unite to bless Imperial arms; when church dignitaries ask us to be honest to God and say what we like about Him; when the blood of Jesus is trodden under foot and put to an open shame by so-called spiritual leaders, then I would sooner stake my all with God and His despised minority. In a state of ruin and decay, of boasted knowledge yet spurious devotion, of what does God take note? Malachi gives us the answer: "Then they that feared the Lord spake often one to another: and the Lord hearkened and heard it, and a book of remembrance was written before Him for them that feared the Lord, and that thought upon His Name." This is the fellowship He owns.

It is surely not without significance that this is the last Word to Israel before Christ comes and the building of His Church begins.

CHAPTER XXIV

THE MASTER BUILDER

"What house will ye build me? saith the Lord." Acts 7
"I will build . . . I will build . . . and I will set it up that the residue of
man might seek after the Lord, and all the Gentiles, upon whom my
Name is called, saith the Lord, who doeth all these things." Acts 15

WITH these illustrations before us let us now turn to the record of the New
Testament and trace the development of this great theme as it has been
realised in the early Church. Fellowship is not a static idea. It is action.
We have fellowship by doing. Fellowship is something shown; something
extended. It has been well said that "Life" is the medium by which
Christian fellowship is known. "Light" is the means by which it is maintained; and "Love" is the mode by which it is made manifest. Fellowship
in the Bible is always expressed in service, whether it be toward God,
towards fellow believers, or towards mankind at large. Our fellowship
lies first with the Source of all our life; then as the life of God flows into
us, so we are borne out together in that stream of life, bringing life and
light to men in our love of the Lord. All Christian activity, if real, is an
expression of our basic fellowship with the Father and His Son, in the
communion of His Holy Spirit. There is therefore nothing independent
about the believer who is in the good of this Fellowship of God. He is
organically linked with the Source, and through Him, to every other
believer whoever he may be. Paul puts it thus: "Holding the Head, from
which *all* the body by joints and bands having nourishment ministered,
and knit together, increases with the increase of God" (Col. 2, v. 19).
"Christ is the Head from whom the *whole* body fitly joined together and
compacted by that which every joint supplieth, according to the effectual
working in the measure of *every* part, maketh increase of the body unto
the edifying of itself in love" (Eph. 4, v. 16).

These words are rooted in first principles and leads us to consider the
foundational teaching of our Lord set out in the Gospels, for He speaks of

both the Building and the Body there. "The Acts of the Apostles" is the historical account of how the early believers realised these great truths in experience. The Epistles are the interpretation of that experience revealed to the apostles by that same Spirit who was the Originator of their initial and living contact with the Lord and his Word. The Biblical metaphors therefore employed to define the fellowship of the Church are not just helpful illustrations from human life, but an actual unfolding of the Divine life which is in Christ Jesus our Lord and which flows to, and unites together, all those who are partakers of His Divine nature. In view of this it is good to let their weight fall freshly upon us so that our human demurrings might be silenced, and all our carnal groupings be dispersed. What does the New Testament teach?

There are many sheep but there is only one flock under one Shepherd.

There are many brethren but they are all disciples learning from one Master.

There are many stones but they are all integrated into one building and knit into One Chief Corner Stone.

There are many servants but they are all under the one Lord of the Harvest.

There are many branches but they are all growing from the One Vine tended by the one Great Husbandman.

There are many lovers but only one bride being prepared for the one Bridegroom.

There are many priests but only one High Priest our great "Melchisedec" over the house of God.

There are many members but only one body functioning under one Head.

Men have devised many other heads, links, grounds and reasons for fellowship. Some of us may call ourselves Lutherans, Wesleyans, or even Darbyists, establishing our fellowship around Jesus plus a reformer, or some other name of spiritual renown. Some choose to create their fellowship around a common experience, such as the Pentecostalists, and the burning question of almost every meeting is—"Have you received the baptism of the Holy Ghost?" The fulness of the Spirit's blessing is a wonderful thing, but dare we make a clique of people who have had "it" as distinct from those who have not had "it", or who perhaps do not seek

"it" in those terms at all? The Bible teaches that the baptism of the Holy
Ghost is the way I am brought into Christ and become a member of His
Body. The gift of the Holy Ghost has to do with how Christ is brought
into me. The former is always corporate in emphasis, the latter personal.
Yet both aspects are but complementary facets of the same coin of testimony. If we share the experience of the apostles in the Acts, then we are
obliged to share their interpretation of those experiences. This interpretation is found in their epistles. Our understanding of apostolic practice
must be based on the apostolic teaching. If we wish to live in the atmosphere and experience of the early Church it is not sufficient to simulate it;
we must be subject to the whole scope of instruction they received. Whilst
varying circumstances and manifestations accompanied the early experiences of the Spirit's work in the Acts, what emerges is that there was no
stereotyped pattern of experience. On the other hand, there is one
principle regarding the receiving of the Spirit running through each incident, namely that God always sealed a bona fide faith with the gift of the
Holy Ghost. He did not come to men merely on the profession of faith—
but real faith was always vindicated, as Peter says, "God which *knoweth
the hearts*, bare them witness giving them the Holy Ghost . . ." With this
the Epistles unanimously concur.* Were this not so, then some believers
must be in the Body of Christ and others not. This is schism and leaves
loose hands and legs strewn in confusion through Christendom's blood-
drenched fields. Is not the emphasis rather on fulness? In his letter to the
Ephesians, Paul says at the beginning, that they were sealed by the Holy
Spirit on belief in the Lord Jesus Christ.† At the end of the Epistle he

---

* This is especially evident in I Corinthians. The Epistle is addressed to all that
call upon the Name of Jesus Christ our Lord (ch. 1, v. 2). To such Paul writes in
ch. 6, v. 19, "What? know ye not that your body *is* the temple of the Holy Ghost which
is in you, which ye *have* of God, and ye are not your own?" Ch. 10, v. 2; 12, vv. 7,
11, 13, 18, read together, show that Paul taught that *all* believers were baptised by
the Spirit into the one Body and that *every* believer was a member responsible to
function in it. In Galatians ch. 3, vv. 2, 3, 14 show that it is through the hearing of
faith that the Spirit is received. To the Romans, Paul writes, "Ye *have* received the
Spirit of adoption . . . the Spirit himself bears witness with our Spirit"; and to the
Thessalonians he speaks of God who *hath* also given unto us His Holy Spirit. The
Epistles teach that all true believers therefore are indwelt by the Spirit. The events of
Acts, ch. 10 led to this exposition which became foundational in all subsequent
teaching concerning the Spirit of God and the child of God.

† Eph. 1, v. 13, R.V.

exhorts them to "be—being filled with the Spirit.*'" That is the tense. The former is an experience common to all who trust Christ and occurs only once. The latter a continual inflow and over-flow, varying according to the spiritual condition of each believer. Why then a denomination and, more than that, a multitude of sects within the general "Pentecostal" category?

The concept of true fellowship being the esoteric privilege of the "spiritually élite" is not however confined to Pentecostalism, but permeates most of the "Holiness" groups and also the Salvation Army circles. It is also found in those companies where "overcomers" are viewed as a separate and privileged section of the Church. Whilst there are degrees of reward at the judgement seat of Christ, we are clearly told to judge nothing before the time. It is hard for the simple believer to accept that those who propound these kinds of doctrines are in actual fact the superior ones, much less, that the true fellowship of the Church is to be defined in such restricted terms. Birds of a religious feather will inevitably flock together, but flocking together by natural instinct, and on account of kinship in ideas must never be confused with true spiritual fellowship brought into being by God's calling and constituted by the incorporating power of God's Spirit. It is not our degree of light or our depth of experience which is the basis of Christian fellowship. It may affect its intensity but it is never its basis; and to make it the basis is to do despite, be it all unconsciously, to the atonement of our Lord Jesus Christ. The fellowship of saints is the inalienable right of the whole flock of God, for Christ has purchased it, in its entirety, with His own blood. It includes not only the maturer sheep, but every lamb as soon as it is born into the care of the Great Shepherd of the sheep. It is not a question of our faithfulness but of God's faithfulness, for "God is faithful by whom ye were called unto the fellowship of His Son . . ." Our fellowship is in Christ alone. There is one Lord. This is our common confession and there is no other.

On the other hand, some Christians will allow themselves to be bound together on what is little more than a concept of Church government. Presbyterians, Congregationalists and not a few of the so-called "Christian Brethren" are coloured by this approach in their relations with other professing Christians. The only Scriptural reason we receive each other is that we have been received, and if we re-examine the ground of our own

* Eph. 5, v. 18.

reception by the Lord, we shall be left in no doubt as to the ground on which we are to receive each other. We hear people talking sometimes about being a good Presbyterian, or may be a good Congregationalist, or even a good "Brother". With this mode of expression is the implication that being good in this way means to hold the tenets of the sect faithfully and be one of the thorough-going and reliable members of the "special fellowship". The Bible does not call this good. It calls it carnal. The reason is that God is good, and nothing that divides His family is born of Him or can really serve Him.

Some hold the vain belief that they are *the* Church by historical descent and apostolic succession; they cling together on this imagined golden thread of history, but forget that a spiritual heritage is never bequeathed via the dead bones of an institution. The life and power of God, much less His authority, are not an heirloom handed down by church officials through the dusty ecclesiastical centuries. God gives His Spirit freely all down this age of grace and bestows the most authority in each generation on him who is most subject to His Lord. God is, after all, no respecter of persons. When spiritual men arise outside the pale of the established churches it brings disturbance and perhaps dismay; and though extraordinary phrases have been invented to rationalise the situation, the idea of "separated brethren", "protestants", "non-conformists" and other less salubrious titles does not make the situation really more acceptable. It is not adequate to say such persons are of the Soul of the Church but not of its Body. Unofficial saintliness is always hard for orthodoxy to endure. Like all other myths these concepts are silenced by the mouth of the Master. The chief mark of His sheep is that they hear *His* voice.

Some believers seem to adhere to one another, that is at least for a while, by separating from everybody else they deem unclean. We see the last terror of this negative approach to fellowship, amongst the extremer elements of the Exclusive Brethren. The original principle is that "separation from evil is God's principle of unity". Had this been accompanied by the positive and Scriptural teaching that identification with Christ is God's principle of unity then every turning from sin would be a turning to the Saviour, and would result in sitting together in fellowship at Jesus' feet. As it is, the negative principle carried to extreme results in a collective monastic emphasis and a segregational position. There is a fleeing from the world and an increasing fleeing from one another until the life of the "fellowship" is in a state of continual convulsion with the expulsion of, and withdrawal from, every believer who is judged as defiled by "evil associations" or "erroneous doctrine". This is a mockery and a travesty of fellowship. It is no longer a sharing of life in which individuals love each other, care for each other, serve each other and attract new members into the common life, but a harsh steely mechanism to exert control, tyrannise the weak and crush any divergence from the ruling party line. It is in essence no longer spiritual, but political. It is the oppression of one class by another in the realm of religion. This fanaticism has been seen also in what are essentially similar systems, namely Roman Catholicism and Communism, systems in which mutual spying and reporting are an essential part, and in which "the heretic" is ruthlessly purged in the name of God, and if not in the name of God, then in the name of social good. In these three systems, the confessional in one form or another is the weapon by which the leadership exerts and maintains control. Confession may be to the leading brethren, it may be to the priests or to the party, but in each case, control over the minds of the rank and file is by means of a perverted concept of "criticism and self-criticism". It is important to note that whilst early believers were exhorted to confess their faults one to another and proper apology and reparation upheld under both Law and Grace, yet we have no evidence that mutual and public confession was at any time the normal content of the gatherings of the Church. In I Corinthians, chapter fourteen, where we see all the church in that city together in one place, the brethren are exhorted to come each with a psalm, a doctrine, a tongue, a revelation or an interpretation, but they are not asked to come each with a confession or a criticism. The proper disciplining of genuine evil is of course provided for, but fellowship is never interpreted as the convening of a public confessional, whereby a clique of inquisitorial leaders maintains a mastery over those of weaker conscience and less forceful temperament. This is not a holding of the Head but the holding of a whip. In church life this invariably means that the flock is not fed but flayed and fleeced, and finally completely scattered. The sheep then run either to the shelter of the fold nearest at hand, which may or may not be helpful, or else they are found after years of wandering, as castaways along the desolate shores of disillusionment.

Some of us make the mistake of insisting upon baptism as being essential to the basis of church fellowship. The heretical teaching of baptismal regeneration, of course, abuses and distorts baptism in this way, but we do not refer to this alone. The normal sequence of Christian experience in New Testament days was faith, baptism and then active participation in the work and witness of the local church, but even though this was so, baptism *itself* was not viewed as the door into the Church. Both the ordinances, whether baptism or the Lord's Supper, are a proclamation of death. They are never a means of obtaining life, and precisely because of this, they can never be the passport to that fellowship of persons who have eternal life as a gift from God. It is only when we are already personally identified with Christ in His death and resurrection, that either baptism of the Lord's Supper have any meaning. In baptism, I declare in a personal way, that I died with Christ; and in the Lord's Supper we declare in a corporate way (it is "the bread which *we* break") that Christ died for us. Only when we are in fellowship with Him, in newness of life and as waiting till He come, do these ordinances have any significance. Thus if they only have meaning when I am in fellowship with the Lord and His own, they can never be the entrance fee to the fellowship, nor can they be the focal point of it. The Baptists observe the ordinance of baptism in a Scriptural way, but err in making it a rallying point for their denomination. Although sometimes a broad-mindedness and a big-heartedness is shown towards other believers, it still remains that Jesus plus an ordinance is not the ground of our fellowship and we have no right to create an artificial fellowship on earth which contravenes the nature of the fellowship above, where Christ alone is central and Jesus is "all in all".

Of course, there are many others and when we come to the more heretical cults then men will cling even to "a day", or a misinterpreted prophecy, like the Seventh Day Adventists or the so-called "Jehovah's Witnesses". Some will unite around sheer legend like the Mormons and Christian Scientists. But whoever we are, in whatever degree we insist on an additional rallying point; in that degree do we deny the True Centre, and refuse to acknowledge the true fellowship of all believers in the bonds of Christ.

If a person with a denominational viewpoint shows a good spirit of fellowship beyond his own communion then this is the work of the grace of God and the enlightenment of the Spirit. It is in spite of, not because of his denomination. Have you ever been in a crowd of Christians conversing together? Gradually one and another will meet a Christian of his own demonination. "Are you C. of E.?" one will say, "O, so am I." "No, I'm from the Methodists." Someone overhears this and then says, "O, I am a Methodist too," and soon there is an increased animation in the conversation because people are reverting to type and finding that common ground of fellowship to which they are more accustomed. But unquestionably it is lower ground. Why can we not be content simply to be lovers of the same Lord together? Why does it give us a fillip in our personal contact and conversation to find someone of *our* denomination? Is it not because our so-called Christian fellowship has a content other than Christ? Our salvation rests on Christ alone. We acknowledge that without difficulty, and condemn any suggestion of grace plus works, whatever kind they be. Should we not be stricter with ourselves and search out the error of our attitudes on this question of fellowship? If salvation rests on Christ alone then so must our fellowship. We should repudiate any other content. Anything extraneous makes it sub-Christian and ineffective for God. What dilemmas we create! We talk about our Baptist brother, or our Anglican brother or may be our Presbyterian brother. These are surely ambiguous terms, each suggestive of a lesser and a greater communion. Some will even say they belong to "the Brethren" when Christ has said of His own "all ye are brethren". Are we then to refer to such as "Brethren brothers" or "Brethren sisters"? To what designations we come once we cease to hold the Head! It is this rent garment which makes us a laughing stock before the Communist world. The "live and let live" denominational and inter-denominational outlook of our day is a totally inadequate answer. It is not a question of getting together and organising something to show our unity. As evangelicals we sometimes try this, and even put up a banner over our summer convention tent, bearing the words, "All one in Christ Jesus". Apart from the quotation being used out of context, it really means very little, if for one week we relax our denominational barriers but then go home to maintain them for the rest of the year. The liberals, too, have their way. Assembly after assembly of the World Council of Churches is convened, but of what consequence are the speeches of the leaders if the members of the churches they represent, and perhaps even they themselves, are not born again and united spiritually in Christ. Neither is it a question of any of us saying, "I am of Christ", as if no one is a real Christian but we ourselves, or our own kind. What is needed is a spiritual descerning of the children of God; a determined disregard of the man-made loyalties of organised religion, and a forthright extending at all times of the right hand of fellowship to every one who believes on the Lord Jesus Christ as his personal Saviour. This is not as difficult as it sounds, for those who are His have the witness within themselves. "His Spirit bears witness with our Spirit that we are the sons of God". We can say with John, "We know that we have passed from death unto life because we love the brethren." To live out that God-given fellowship is victory. It is "the victory that overcometh the world even *our* faith." Note, not "my faith" but "*our* faith". This is that fellowship which, though it be but a grain of mustard seed, tumbles the devil's mountains into the sea.

If we take a fresh look at the only two mentions of the Church in the Gospels we shall see that our Lord Jesus Christ is the author of both.* In Matthew, chapter sixteen, He gives us the first view of this mighty building, which, under His own Master-hand, is to rise in grandeur and prove impregnable before the very gates of hell. Everything that man achieves is subject to death and decay. But Christ through death has annulled him who had the power of death and taken the keys of death and of Hades into His own control. The Church, built on Christ confessed as the Son of God, will rise on this Foundation according to the Divine plan; and death, the last enemy, will never lay it low. Christ being the foundation determines that the nature of the superstructure shall be consistent with His own nature. Christ as the builder determines what materials are to be used and the mode of their integration. He says, "I will build . . ." and the prerogative of direction and management are His from first to last. He will not relinquish the control of building operations to another. As the chief cornerstone, He is Head also of the corner, and crowns the whole. So from first to last, all is His; all is of Him, and all is for Him and thus it should be, for He purchased every stone. Divinely conceived and divinely consummated, it is secured for all eternity as a vehicle of Divine glory. This initial view of the Church embraces the whole history of its formation, beginning with the descent of the Spirit at Pentecost and concluding with the day of the Rapture, when the Lord Himself shall descend with a shout and we shall all be changed and caught up to meet Him in the air. This view of the Church is the *total* view. It brings the Church before us in its entirety as introduced by its Founder.

* Matt. 16, vv. 13-20. Matt. 18, vv. 15-20.

The second mention of the Church is in Matthew, chapter eighteen. Here the details are quite different. This reference portrays to us a specific and visible company of persons, vested with authority, acting in unity; a company in which each member is responsible to listen to the voice of the whole. It is local in character, the key words being "where" and "there". "*Where* two or three are gathered in My Name *there* am I in the midst of them."

Our Lord Jesus makes no other direct reference to the Church He was to build, though He does mention the temple of His Body, which in its wider application may look beyond the resurrection to the Church also. These two fundamental statements concerning the Church give us on the one hand the *total* view, and on the other the *local* view. If we proceed through the New Testament, we shall see that all the practice and teaching of the apostles in relation to the Church, flows from these two basic concepts laid down by our Lord Jesus Christ. It is true to say that in the New Testament there are simply no other concepts of the Church to be found. This is demonstrated particularly in the two major Epistles on the Church, namely, First Corinthians and Ephesians. Ephesians gives the total view, speaking of the Church which is His Body. First Corinthians is concerned with the local view. In it various local problems are dealt with and when Paul takes up the metaphor of the body, he is careful to omit the article before the noun, when he writes to them, "Ye are the body of Christ." That is to say, a local church is to be in miniature a picture of the whole, although, of course, it can never be itself the whole, in this present day. The consistency with which the Holy Spirit maintains this distinction is very marked and much of our distress over disunity stems from our unwillingness to view the Church of God from God's own standpoint. The confusion in the churches today can be identified quite directly with the disregard of these basic principles. Men either go astray on the concept of the "total Church", or on the concept of the "local church". The Roman Catholic communion is the chief example of this first error. For long centuries it has tried to maintain that its communion is co-extensive with the True Church as a whole. That means it believes that true Christians must of necessity be communicants of its particular church. All others are viewed as being in varying degrees of error and unbelief. This delusion is gradually being exposed today as vital evangelical ministry and healthful spiritual life is evidenced amongst those found beyond the frontiers of these pretensions. On the concept of the local church the error rises chiefly in viewing a particular denominational church, as a branch of a central organisation, possessing a headquarters staff, and a ministering clerical hierarchy. This makes the "local church" responsible, primarily, to a head on earth instead of the Head in Heaven. As a federation of churches allied to a "Jesus-plus" rallying point such a denomination unifies its communion through adherence to a creed, or acceptance of certain practices and principles. It is thus patently not Christo-centric and is obviously neither "total" nor "local". It falls somewhere in between and thus loses Scriptural warrant for existence. Others go to the opposite extreme on the question of the local church and say they are *the* local church. Actually all the believers in one locality are in principle members of the local church. We have for instance references to "the church of God in Corinth", which clearly embraced all believers in the city. They may not actively engage in their appointed function as part of the local expression of the Body of Christ. They may not publicly identify themselves and gather with the Lord's people in His Name. They may even join themselves to other religious causes and become partisan, but they pertain to the local church nevertheless and should come under the shepherd care of those spiritual elders in the locality. Though they seek pasture in other folds and other fields, they are still the Lord's sheep and no one else's. As the saints gather in the Lord's Name locally, however, it is presumptuous to infer that their active communion is co-extensive with the full content of the local church, for often there are many hidden, and many wayward ones. They may be an expression of it, but in practical fact are generally no more than part of it, sometimes only a fragment. It is, therefore, exceedingly dangerous and almost always incorrect to say as we so gather that we are *the* local church. What we do know is that where Jesus' Name is owned alone and there is a genuine spiritual desire to gather in keeping with His character, He has promised to be there. In the larger communities of the Roman Empire, churches often gathered in homes and the household church not infrequently become the nucleus of a more thorough-going local testimony to Jesus' Name. So today it would be tyrannical, and often against God's interest, for church elders to insist that people travel miles to a central gathering because they want to view the gathering as "*the* local church". On the contrary, under the leading of the Spirit in fellowship with existing testimony, household churches could be commenced in suburban localities, and become the commencement of a wider local witness.

As we read the Acts and the Epistles, it is quite clear that State churches, national churches and regional churches are all contrary to Scripture, for such churches are neither local nor total. The Bible teaches plainly there is only the concept of the total church embracing all believers in this dispensation of Grace; and the local view embracing all believers in the locality where we live at the present time. As the total Church is linked to her Head in Heaven and is dependent upon Him and built up of Him, so the local church, a picture of the whole is directly dependent upon and responsible to Him too. Each local church is a candlestick individually lit, continually supplied and in case of default, personally removed by the Son of Man. He is in the midst of every church standing in relation to each believer; and He is in the midst of the churches standing in relation to each church. It is He alone who holds the stars of the churches in His hand. There are no other ecclesiastical links. Just as individual believers enjoy their fellowship together in Christ, so must the churches. There is nothing else on earth to bind us. Now the solemn thing is that if we are not willing in simple faith to walk in the light of the Lord's own teaching on the Church, then we shall find ourselves ensnared in man's view of the Church. In some countries there are national religious councils on which representatives of the different denominations sit. Such councils are usually recognised by the governments of the countries concerned, and in the less democratic countries legislation and policy concerning religion are passed on to the churches at large through such an organ, infecting the whole with contemporary political interests. A "World Council of Churches" is clearly the organ through which a World Government organisation will seek to control the church life of the masses. The shadow of things to come has been clearly portended in the course of recent events in China. I quote the very excellent summary on this question published by the Evangelical Missionary Alliance. There is now a great deal of material collated but little is really published on this stupendous matter. As one who has been in the midst of the struggle I commend this brief outline as a clear statement of the relevant facts. It is headed, 'The Chinese Government and the Christian Church'. *

* Quoted from *Seeing the Invisible: Can the Chinese Church Survive?* by kind permission of the Evangelical Missionary Alliance.

"The Religious Affairs Bureau, a Government department, has worked through the Three Self Patriotic Movement* in carrying out its policies in relation to the Protestant Church. These have been very subtle and very effective. They first found willing, though misguided agents, in Mr. Y. T. Wu and his former Y.M.C.A. colleagues. Mr. Wu has recently stated: 'Without the Communist Party there would not have been the Three Self Movement of the Christian Church, nor the new life of the church, and we Christians would not have received education in socialism, and the opportunity to surrender our hearts to the Communist Party . . . I love the Communist Party . . . The Church greatly needed cleansing (of the "destructive poisons of imperialism and anti-Party, and anti-socialism thinking") and so for several years now the Three Self Movement has carried on this work of cleansing the Church, but this was a work which could not have been carried on without the support and direction of the Party!' Those are plain words! And they make it very clear who has dictated the stages in policy by which the Party has gradually secured a stranglehold on the Christian Church. All that has happened between 1950 and 1958 has been the development of a carefully co-ordinated plan. This plan has been in four clearly defined stages of action.

(i) The Manifesto Stage

There was first of all the Manifesto stage; the wording of the Manifesto published in 1950 was drawn up by Government officials and a group of Church leaders led by Mr. Y. T. Wu. The document clearly committed the Christian Church to purging itself of 'imperialism' (meaning the foreign missionary movement), to rendering its first and highest loyalty to the State ('Love country, Love Church'—in that order!) and to unquestioning obedience to the Party. The immediate effect of the publication of the Manifesto was official pressure on the churches to oust the missionaries and to achieve immediate self-support and self-government. By the end of 1951 these aims vere virtually accomplished!

(ii) The Accusation Stage

The second stage may be called the accusation stage. With a view to ferreting

* The Three Self Patriotic Movement means "self-government, self-support and self-propagation" for the churches under the leadership of Mao Tse Tung, chairman of the Chinese Communist Party. It was conceived and launched by the Communist-led government of People's China as a means to register and control all church groups and organisations. By ruthless manipulation of church leaders and church affairs, the Three Self Movement became the spearhead of Satan's attack against true believers in the Lord Jesus Christ and all evangelical missionary activity. Whenever a church or denomination failed to register with the Three Self Movement, then it was denounced as reactionary and an enemy of the people. Maligned and misrepresented, some puppet or quizling leadership would be seized upon and used to represent the members, spiritual elements being then forced underground or publicly disgraced.

out opponents and intimidating all anti-Communists in the churches, every congregation throughout China was forced to hold 'accusation meetings' at which pastors and leaders were pilloried, accused of pro-imperialist sympathies, denounced and handed over to the Government for punishment. This might be ex-communication, prison or a period of years in a labour camp. From 1951 to 1956 there was a series of campaigns affecting the whole nation, designed to purge out all opposition to the regime. During this time some sections of the Church made a last ditch stand against the Three Self propoganda directed at the missionary movement which was being vilified in every possible way. Mr. Wang Ming-tao of Peking had been an old foe of the Three Self leaders on the grounds of their liberalism in theology. Now he found himself opposed to them again on similar grounds and set about proving that what they were denouncing as 'imperialist poison' was nothing more nor less than the evangelical doctrines of the Christian faith. Without question the chief target of the Three Self leaders has been the evangelical element in the Church. It is evangelicals above all others who are suffering today for their loyalty and obedience to the Word of God. Mr. Wang Ming-tao and his wife are in prison again after a brief period of release—and hundreds more as well. People sometimes sit up all night compiling lists of 100 or 200 self-criticisms in obedience to orders and to save themselves!

(iii) The Rectification Stage

The third stage came in 1958—the rectification stage. By 1957 Chairman Mao Tze-tung felt confident that he had the nation well under control and he therefore loosened the reins a little to free criticism of the Government—meaning constructive criticism. The outburst of abuse that arose from all over the country, including men in high position, was a shock to China's rulers. There were even riots in several cities. Christians too joined in out-spoken criticism and Marcus Cheng even dared to criticize the Government in the very presence of the Government leaders in the People's Political Consultative Council—the Chinese 'House of Commons'! Immediately the campaign to rectify wrong thinking was set in motion. The campaign affected the whole country but the Church came in for a very close scrutiny through the Three Self organization. Hundreds of Christian leaders were accused and denounced as 'rightists', had their licences to preach withdrawn, were sent to labour camps in remote parts of China and even executed. Some were driven to suicide. There are certainly thousands of faithful Christians in prison or in labour camps to-day, including forty graduates of Dr. Chia Yu-mings Spiritual Life Seminary in Shanghai. One of the former staff members of this seminary and a companion were sent to Tsinghai on the Tibetan border where they were made to live in a straw hut in bitter cold, and without adequate clothing or food. These two young women had to collect and cut up firewood on the mountain side until their health broke down. Why? Because they were 'rightists' and refused to respond to indoctrination, so true and steadfast was their Christian faith. Large numbers of Christians have been sent up to Tsinghai, apparently a kind of Chinese 'Siberia'. One third year medical student who proved uncompromising in her faith and who refused to accuse a certain pastor has been relegated to the role of a college servant. She declares that she is very happy in her witness for Christ and that 'if my sufferings could hasten the coming of the Lord, I would gladly die!' Christian students often say to one another when parting, 'We may meet inside (prison) next time!' Friends are sometimes able to visit Christians serving prison terms, and report that they are very cheerful and rejoicing in the Lord. There have been several conversions in prison through the witness of Christians.

(iv) The Unification Stage

The fourth stage began in the autumn of 1958. Worshipping congregations in most towns and cities were reduced to one or two. In Shanghai the number of churches was reduced from about 200 to about 20; in Peking from about 50 to 4. The supernumerary ministers were sent to work in the communes which by that time were in full swing throughout the rural areas of China. In those areas the conscription of the entire population for forced labour in the communes has so disorganised normal social life that it is hard to see how any church life is any longer possible. Sunday as a rest day has been abolished. In the course of the amalgamation of city churches, churches of very different liturgical and theological traditions have been forced to unite, and it would seem that an attempt is being made to do away with denominational distinctions. These are, it is said, the last vestiges of 'imperialist' influence in the churches. Mr. Chou En-lai insisted on this in the 1950 conference with church leaders. There is to be a single hymn book, a single liturgy and a single organisation. All books of reference are being scrutinized and only those favouring church reunion and socialism are being passed for use. All property is being turned over to the Three Self authorities. The largest church building in Shanghai has been turned into a factory! To-day the world witnesses the spectacle of the Protestant Church firmly in the iron grip of the Government. Christians have all been urged to 'surrender their hearts' to the Communist Party. Their highest devotion, as was intended in the original Manifesto, has been yielded, not to God, but to the Party. Thank God therefore for those who, facing hard labour, long terms of imprisonment and even death, still dare to say with their Lord, 'Get thee hence, Satan: for it is written, Thou shalt worship the Lord thy God, and Him only shalt thou serve.' "

The choice then before us today as believers in the Lord Jesus Christ is —"Are we going to live out our Christian lives and express our Christian fellowship along the lines laid down for our guidance in Holy Scriptures or —are we going to be inveigled step by step under the deception of Satan in preparing an instrument of organisational unity which will serve the purpose of a totalitarian power?" The church on earth today may resemble the dry lifeless bones scattered up and down the valley described in Ezekiel's prophecy. We feel there must be a remedy, thus we are tempted to manufacture what are really only plastic sinews and produce an artificial church union on an ecumenical and social appeal. This is not God's answer. His word through the prophet is, "*I* will lay sinews upon you . . . *I* will cause breath to enter into you and ye shall live." Only thus did Israel become again a mighty army. Some will say, "But what of the Lord's prayer for unity amongst His own?" Let us pause and re-examine the words: "Neither pray I for these alone, but for them also which shall believe on me through their word; that they all may be one; as thou, Father, art in me, and I in thee, that they also may be one in us; that the world may believe that thou has sent me. And the glory which thou gavest me I have given them; that they may be one, even as we are one. I in them, and thou in me, that they may be made perfect in one . . ." (John 17, vv. 20-23).

First let it be noted that He was praying for those who would believe on Him through the Word. It was for their unity and union with God he prayed—not for the amalgamation of millions of nominal communicants who have no use for the church except it be for the convenience of christening, marriage and burial.

Then it is important to see that His request was to His Father. He is not asking for men to manufacture a unity, but for His Father to create a unity. This unity is something quite specific as to its nature. It is spiritual. It is to be of the same kind as He enjoyed with His Father. A unity and a union arising out of their very nature and realised in the Holy Ghost. This is what He longed for us to know and prayed that we might experience. "That they all may be one; *as* Thou, Father art in Me, and I in Thee that they *also* may be one *in us*."

In addition to this He was looking right down history. The whole dispensation of grace stretched before Him. He longed that all believers down all the years might be one. No church organisation, federation or even Council of Churches could achieve this. Once a person dies his name is struck off any church register. He is no longer viewed as being in fellowship. Thus nothing which mortal man can do in the realm of his religion can perpetuate a unity of believers. Death puts an end to that. Yet the Church which Christ builds—He says the gates of hell shall not prevail against it. What then is the answer to the conundrum?

Thank God the answer has been given. On the day of Pentecost, the Spirit which proceeded from the Father descended. The Father heard and acted on the prayer of His Son. Through this One Spirit we are all baptised into one body and this is effected in everyone who believes on the Lord Jesus Christ all down the years. Thus by one mighty Act of God we are all one in Him, partaking of that unity in the Spirit which the Father and Son ever enjoyed. Thus we say *our* fellowship *is* with the Father and with His Son. Our communion *is* in the Holy Ghost.

We are called now by faith to enter into the good of this wondrous answer from the Father—not to make the unity but to keep the unity of the Spirit in the bond of peace, to observe that which is already ours in Christ. It is not a matter for discussion by ecclesiastical dignitaries but a matter for daily action on the part of each member of the Body as he meets and works with his fellow members.

We live in a day of a red sky, and little scarlet women are already riding their various beasts. Here and there a united religious force is struggling hard to keep in the saddle of the political monster beneath her. China is only one example. There the beast is already making her desolate and naked. This is the beginning of her retribution. Swiftly it falls, for the blood of the martyrs is on her hands. The religious flesh of the Three Self church federation is doomed to be devoured. The red authorities will burn her in their fires. Such are the signs of the times. It is a red dawn and foul weather is not far away. The quickening drift of the big established denominations into the blood-stained skirts of Roman Catholicism, defiled as she is with the spiritual fornication of centuries, becomes more and more apparent. The Pope appeals not only to Christendom at large, but also to the great non-Christian religions, showing the scope of Rome's ambition and those with whom she will stoop to ally herself. Here are the precursory pointers to that final scarlet woman of a world religion seated on the seven hills of Rome. In Hitlerism and Communism we see those elements which portend the emergence of the final beast of world dominion, which this great whore will attempt to ride. Today we do not see the ultimate things but only those things which speak of them. As the development becomes more evident the challenge to the true believer will become more clamant. A clear-cut choice will have to be made. Religious Babylon will need to be left behind; the fellowship of darkness openly repudiated. From reports received, the active cleavage is already under way. To whom shall we go? Thank God our Lord Jesus Christ is waiting to receive us. "They shall hear My voice," He says, "and there shall be one flock and one Shepherd".

If we will kneel down in His presence and seek His grace and wisdom, we can begin this very day, with a new attitude towards other believers and towards His great work in the world. Through the power of His Spirit we will refuse to be embroiled in vain connections or serve sectarian ends. We will refuse to bow before the golden image of present-day ecumenism but with a clear-cut faith that lays hold on the Head alone we will encourage one another to acknowledge Jesus only, as our Lord and Saviour, and seek to love and serve all men for His dear sake. This is the pathway of discipleship. This is the challenge of His fellowship.

CHAPTER XXV

STREAM OF HIS POWER

"He overturneth the mountains by the roots.
He cutteth out rivers among the rocks and
His eye seeth every precious thing." John 28

(Suggested reading: Acts, Chapters 1-11)

BUT a little while and those piercéd feet would no more tread the hot and
dusty streets. Just forty days and then the cloud would bring Him to the
Majesty on high. His work on earth was done. His work in Heaven would
soon begin. Here, He was the sacrifice. There, He would become the
Great High Priest. Here, He had died once. There, He would ever live to
make intercession for His own. Meanwhile what would He do to perpetuate his memory? He gave no further thought to this. A loaf of bread,
a cup of wine—enough for all the years. What steps would He adopt that all
His mighty words and deeds might still remain? Once having penned His
word in hearts of men, He leaves no diary of His days. The works of God
are all secure, for all He does He does for ever. But what of the Kingdom?
"Lord wilt Thou at this time restore it to Israel?" 'Tis not the blood of foes
He seeks, but through His own blood shed, must now the great credentials
of His royal authority emerge? But how shall the "movement" be preserved? There is no movement. He is not come in His own Name. There
is no impetus to foster on the earth. He is bringing men to God and sons
to glory. He has called the many and chosen the few, but not as a man
does He seek a following. He came not to suggest a better way or to
aspire to deity in the pantheon of world religion. His teaching was not
an alternative, or a rival cause. He does not compete for human loyalty.
He is not a revolutionary nor even a progressive speaking beyond his
years. He organises, therefore, no party and publicises no programme as men
count programmes. Must all then be lost? Yes, it would seem so. *Anything
that man would make of Jesus Christ is all usuitable to God.* The world at
large never saw Him beyond the tomb. Christ after the flesh has passed

from view. The "movement" died at the crucifixion. All forsook him and fled. The cry of "Hosanna" is drowned in the curse of the cross. Now God is free to act solely on the ground of grace and through His Spirit. Ere Jesus passes to the skies only one task is His. It is to fill the hearts of His own; to be their Lord and God; to be their centre; and gathering them again and again about Himself, to become established as their all in all. So He talks with them, and walks with them. He floods their hearts, that they might lift their eyes to heaven and see Him always there at God's right hand. It is with this activity that the closing days are filled. He desires to leave on the earth a company whose every hope is in Himself, the God of their salvation. The disciples were assembled, the doors were shut. Without were fightings, within were fears. "Then Jesus came and stood in the midst and saith unto them 'Peace be unto you'. And when He had so said, He showed unto them His hands and His side. Then were the disciples glad when they saw the Lord." This was the essential character of His dealings with them. It was so then and it is so now. "After eight days *again* his disciples were within . . . then came Jesus, the doors being shut and stood in the midst and said, 'Peace be unto you.' " The peace of any Christian company is in this alone; the Presence and centrality of Jesus Christ, their Lord. Out of this experience, our confession is declared; doubts vanish from our minds and we begin to cry, "My Lord, my God." A few more days and then He meets them in the dawning. The darkness is past and the true light now shineth. The Shepherd has been smitten and the sheep have been scattered but gradually He has gathered them. He found some at the tomb; some in the upper room; some on the Emmaus road. Now He contacts His little band upon the shore. That is where He found them at the first. They have run again to their own level, that lowest of all levels, the level of the sea. But He is the great Shepherd of the sheep brought again from the dead; and He finds them now. Twilight recedes before the sunshine of His face. There is a longing gaze across the water; a disciple's whisper in the boat; and someone says, "It is the Lord." And so He draws them to Himself, till in the warmth of the fire, lit by His own scarred hands, His fisherfolk revive. Here again is anticipated the character of the Church, so soon to be. Jesus, the crucified and risen Lord, in the midst, showing His love, drawing out hearts and lighting up their souls with the flame of His Spirit; such is His ministry along earth's shores and down the sands of time. Now once more to the heights, for the Scripture reads, "The eleven disciples went away into Galilee into a mountain where Jesus had appointed them." I wonder what mountain that might be? Was it that mountain where first they heard His Word and sat silent at His feet? Though aspostles, they were still very much disciples; but now as taught again, they are being sent again to teach. It is the great commission; but see the circumstance in which this new command is given. There is Jesus, and about Him, this little group of men. Their fears are mingling with their faith, but they are kneeling now in worship. Christ again is central. Central to these who were to form His Church. Central to heaven, and central to the earth; for all authority in every sphere is His. And from this central point on the unnamed hill the Master directs their eyes to the vast circumference of the earth. "Go ye therefore and make disciples of all nations," he says, "baptising *them* in the Name of the Father, and of the Son and of the Holy Ghost." Here is the hope of the Living Fellowship of the Spirit. From all nations He would draw men to Himself that they might know the true God as their Father, the Living Christ as their Saviour and the Holy Spirit as their Comforter; that all His disciples from every race might be baptised in the common recognition of that Name. That they might know no other God, no other Lord, no other Spirit; that they might be one in the Name. "Teaching them," he says, "to observe all things whatsoever *I* have commanded you." Christ as God manifest, the Living Word made flesh, is likewise to be the only authority, the only point of reference in all the nations through all the years unto the end of the age. These words of the final Mount we dare not dilute or dispensationally dismiss. They are absolute for the age of grace. The emphasis is sure. All authority. All nations. All things. Always. The hallmark of our entire experience—"I am with you." Christ all in all.

In the period therefore between the resurrection and Pentecost our Lord indicates something of the kind of life the Church would enjoy. By His frequent appearances He shows that its dominant feature is "Christ in the midst" and in His teaching He reveals, during those forty days, that this is the Kingdom of God in the Holy Ghost. Whilst He was on the earth the rule of God was present in Himself and the Divine sway reached out claiming all those with whom He came in vital contact. Now He was going away to take His seat at the right hand of God, possessed of all authority. On earth, those who owned His sway would be baptised by one Spirit into one Body, to become the vehicle through which the sway of God would still be knowable in human experience. In acknowledgement of the Name, the Church would fulfil the unique function of communicating to men on earth those things decreed in Heaven. There is no other sphere on earth where the rule of God is directly operative. Outside of this, all is in the devil's hands. As John says, "We know that we are of God and the whole world lieth in wickedness." It is therefore a matter of prime importance that the authority of our Divine Head be ever recognised in the Church, for the Church's distinctive testimony is, that Jesus Christ is come in the flesh; that Jesus Christ is Lord. This is the burden of Peter's message on the day of Pentecost. It was the very first thing the Church had to say. "God hath made that same Jesus whom ye crucified both Lord and Christ." If the Church once loses that witness, it is useless to God. In the opening days of its ministry therefore this emphasis is meticulously maintained. The results of the first day's preaching give further evidence of this fact. Christ as the great Baptiser on the day of Pentecost, through the Spirit, retains the entire initiative in this work of God. Three thousand souls repent and believe but the apostles do not view this as good campaigning or successful evangelism. They simply spoke as the Spirit gave them utterance and "*the Lord* added to the Church such as should be saved". As the story of the Acts unfolds, all is in the hand of the Lord. The Spirit He has shed abroad cuts through the parched desert of Jewish orthodoxy bringing life to thousands. The fear and fellowship of the Name take hold of the people. By His Name the apostles heal. In His Name they preach, saying, "Neither is there salvation in any other for there is none other Name given among men whereby we must be saved." In that Name they pray till they are filled afresh with the Spirit and the very place in which they gather is shaken. Time and again we read "they continued in one accord" for truly theirs was an obedience to one Lord and a drinking of one Spirit. This fellowship and unity in Christ spread terror amongst the enemies of the Gospel. None durst join themselves to them. If imprisoned and let go, they returned to their own company. The reality of the fellowship left no blurred frontiers. It was clearly defined from within and without. Even their persecutors held the Name in awe, for when they forbade them to preach, it was always a prohibition to preach in the Name of Jesus. Thus "with great power gave the apostles witness to the resurrection and great grace was upon them all". The early chapters of the Acts bring us into the wondrous freshness of God. There is no fatigue. It was not the disciples but their enemies who were exhausted. Satan could not keep pace with the mighty tide of the Spirit. The Lord was sweeping all before Him and His blood bought people were willing in the day of His power. All is marked by spontaneity. They gladly shared together such things as they had. They came together with a God-inspired enthusiasm and an overflow of sheer joy, and they knew no other activity save the teaching of the apostles' doctrine, fellowship, the breaking of bread and prayers. The Spirit was as the bursting forth of an Eternal Spring and out from Christ, in the midst of His own, flowed living waters testifying to the fact that the Holy Ghost was now given and Jesus glorified as Lord. The ministry of the early Church brought men to Him, and to no one else, for He was their only centre and source of blessing. The cause was not theirs, but His. They had no proselytes to make, no establishment to uphold. The Pharisees might fight to keep their place and nation, and compass sea and land to claim a convert, but the disciples moving in God's stream of power were irresistible, and in the ease of that majestic strength, led countless men and women to the Saviour's feet. It is only as our hearts overflow that the spiritual drought about us is broken. In the days following Pentecost, Jerusalem, for the first time in its history, knew floods on dry ground. And as the river, which maketh glad the city of God, burst all its banks, blessing flowed out to the Gentiles. Then the word of the Lord Jesus began to know fulfilment. "Neither in this mountain nor at Jerusalem shall men worship the Father, but they that worship Him shall worship Him in spirit and in truth."

Such intense activity on the part of the Holy Spirit very quickly aroused Satan's hostility. This was expressed in two ways. He attacked from within and then from without. From within he used the perversion of Ananias and Sapphira, following it with the dissension of the Hellenists, as to their widows. From without he stirred up persecution from the orthodox Jewish establishment which culminated in the fanatical purges under the direction of Saul of Tarsus. It is interesting to see how the Holy Spirit deals with these obstacles in His path. In the case of Ananias and Sapphira, we see judgement beginning at the house of God. This was a sin unto death and the apostles did not pray for it. These persons fell immediately into the hands of the living God. They were beyond the reach of prayer. The Lord exercised His own prerogative and removed them sovereignly from the scene of testimony. As Jeremiah says, "He was

unto me as a bear lying in wait, and as a lion in secret places." In the case
of the dissension, where subtle racial, and even family issues lay below the
surface of the problem, prayer was the answer. The Church has its
problems and God has His plans. Prayer is the means whereby we are
brought out of our problems into His plans, and here through prayer a
suitable answer is effectively realised. Whilst we never see in the New
Testament the spiritual ministries of the evangelist, pastor and teacher
set forward in an organised system, it is instructive to note that when it
comes to the material requirements associated with the testimony, that
there is in the prayerful choice of personnel by the main body of the
Church, and the official appointment by the leadership of the men so
chosen, to their specific service. Whilst overseers are appointed of the
Holy Ghost and emerge to recognition from amongst the flock by reason
of their ministry, those responsible for the material things of the Church
are looked out by a common concensus of opinion and appointed by the
spiritual shepherds. Whilst this is anticipating the development of the
Church, yet it is here that these principles are first discernible. In the mercy
of God the apostles did not apply this mode of selection to the spiritual
ministry. As in the temple, there was wood for things of wood, and gold
for things of gold.

Satan's use of deceivers and murmurers, being now successfully coun-
tered, the evidences of divine power wax greater and greater. "The
number of the disciples", we read, "was multiplied" and "the Word of
God increased" until "the number of disciples in Jerusalem multiplied
greatly". It is understandable therefore at this juncture that Satan attacks
from without. He takes as his tool Saul of Tarsus imagining that he was
a vessel of wrath. In this, his limited knowledge of Divine sovereignty is
clear, for Saul of Tarsus was one, of whom God later said, "He is a chosen
vessel unto Me." Until now there was a sense in which the local church
had been identified with the total Church. Jerusalem still appeared something of a centre, but the Builder of the Church had determined that this
was not to be so. Whilst beginning at Jerusalem, the goal was to bring
the Gospel to the uttermost parts of the earth. Of the temple, He said, "Not
one stone would be left upon another." Now He was to build a habitation
of God through the Spirit, composed of living stones from all nations and
gathered down all the centuries of the dispensation of the grace of God.
Under the persecution of Saul of Tarsus the Church of God at Jerusalem

becomes a scattered Church. Satan's intention was to disperse in defeat, but the outcome was only the increase of the Church, for in the inscrutable wisdom of God there is that scattereth and yet increaseth. As the scattered disciples went everywhere preaching the word, conditions were created which, under the sovereign hand of God, were to see the church-local emerge as a separate entity in different places. In Acts, chapter nine, we read how Satan suffered a devastating defeat in the conversion of Saul. The evidence of the far-reaching effects of this victory is seen at once. "The Church," in its scattered condition, "had rest throughout all *Judea* and *Galilee* and *Samaria* and was edified; and walking in the fear of the Lord and in the comfort of the Holy Ghost were multiplied." This verse speaks volumes to us if we have ears to hear. It marks the breaking down of immense barriers by the creation of the living fellowship of Christ's Body. The three provinces of Judea, Galilee and Samaria were all poles apart from each other, nationally, religiously, socially and commercially. Judea had no dealings with the Samaritans. Galilee was called Galilee of the Gentiles, and despised. There was the contention between the capital and the provinces, the pure-blooded religious Jew of Jerusalem and the half-bred Samaritan who clung to Samaria. Remarks like that of Nathaniel, "Can any good thing come out of Nazareth"? show how entrenched was local prejudice. Yet now in so short a time amongst these very people there had come into being an unbelievable unity. People, who before were at loggerheads, were now at rest together, in the Lord, and being continually built up in their spiritual lives. The secret is seen in their description. The first thing was that they were walking in the *fear of the Lord*. That is, they were united in a common reverence for, and submission to their Lord and Head in Heaven. They had a common centre in Him at the right hand of God. In studying a book we sometimes emphasise the historical background. The most important thing in the study of a book of the Bible is its spiritual background. The spiritual background of The Acts is the Man Christ Jesus at the right hand of God. There is the hidden, yet glorious centre of this new creation. There is the key to the amazing transformation in their mutual relationships. The second thing was they were walking in *the comfort of the Holy Ghost*. As holding their Head in Heaven they knew on earth the fulness and blessing of the ministry of the Holy Ghost in their experience. They had nothing else to bind them together and nothing else was needed. The New Testament teaches us that the Head in Heaven and the Spirit on earth are God's all sufficient provision for the worship, fellowship and witness of the Church. Thus being edified in a Divine way, they were miraculously multiplied yet again.

The immediate outcome of this was that some of those scattered abroad eventually travelled as far as Antioch, and although up till now the Gospel was preached to the Jews only, they suddenly, under the constraint of the Spirit, began to preach to the Gentiles. We might ask, "What did these primitive believers preach?" They preached a person rather than a doctrine. They told out to the dark Gentiles of Antioch the wonders of the One who filled their hearts. It says they preached the Lord Jesus. The result was remarkable, yet altogether in keeping with the amazing development of the earlier period. Having preached Jesus as Lord, the hand of the Lord was upon them; and then it says, a great number believed and turned unto the Lord. All was thus of the Lord. He was the Initiator of it all and He was the theme of it all. As He said at the beginning, "*I* will build my Church." This was not an outcome of a special mission from Jerusalem, nor was Antioch viewed as a daughter church of the one at the capital. The local church that came into being at Antioch was not a branch of the "home church" or a mission station of the Apostolic Headquarters on Mount Zion. All these concepts are completely foreign to the account in The Acts. This was not the work of man but the work of God. This was living seed wafted abroad on the wind of persecution taking rest in alien fields and bringing forth fruit after its kind. God's work is never mechanical. The increase of man-made articles is by artificial duplication, but the increase of that which is divinely created is by organic reproduction. As news of the happenings at Antioch came to the ears of the church at Jerusalem, it brought, undoubtedly, its own amazement. The Spirit was already moving away and beyond the apostolic leadership. They were not swift enough, or flexible enough, to flow out with Him but clung to the old centre which was ready now to vanish away. The church at Jerusalem was no longer the Church total, it had become a church local. With Antioch it was but one amongst a growing number. Yet being essentially a spiritual company, they sent one of the saintliest of their number to investigate what they had heard. It is said of Barnabas here, that "he was a good man and full of the Holy Ghost and of faith". It is salutary to see how a spiritual man reacts to a mighty work of God, with which he and the group of his association have nothing to do. Immediately deep answers to deep. It is at once evident to him that here is something that is not the work of man. It is not merely a fruitful evangelical venture or even the outcome of a well run series of meetings. As he walks through the gates of Antioch, and meets in that far northern city men and women radiant with Christ, he sees what the narrative calls the "grace of God". This is something originating wholly in God and being a man whose whole heart rejoiced in God, it says, very simply, "He was glad." This is fellowship in the Spirit; to be glad to have seen God at work wherever that may be, though it be beyond our ideas of things, and outside the scope of our own witness. O, to be always glad when we see the grace of God at work! Now what did he do? Did he say, "Well this is excellent. Now you will have to get linked up with Jerusalem. You realise the apostles are there and that is really the church headquarters. We would like a list of your church members and a bi-annual report and in due course we may be able to appoint a minister to take care of you and you will be constituted a diocese under the Apostolic See"? Nothing is more foreign to the account we have. God's thought for the care of His sheep is diametrically opposed to man's. What does he do? He does not even mention Jerusalem. No, he exhorted them all that with purpose of heart they would cleave unto *the Lord*. The Lord had died for them. The Lord had purchased them with His own blood. He was the only Shepherd and the true Bishop of their souls. The Lord had brought them to Himself. They were not to be centred in men, however spiritual, especially men they had never seen. They were to be centred in their new found Lord and in Him alone. He who was sufficient to save them was sufficient to keep them. The result of this further preaching was not only the strengthening of the believers but the adding of even more to the Lord. Barnabas was moving with the Spirit and the Spirit worked on ungrieved. Now, far from going back to Jerusalem for help, he goes to Tarsus for Saul. The apostles' guidance had been that Barnabas should go as far as Antioch, but this was said in fellowship, and according to the light they had. It was not dictatorial. Barnabas was a servant of God, not of men; and now, exercised directly by the Spirit, and not deployed by any remote control from Jerusalem, he reaches out for a fellow-labourer prepared of God. When they return together to Antioch, how do they conduct themselves? Do they lord it over God's heritage? Is Saul appointed by Barnabas to the charge of

Antioch? Again nothing could be more alien to the text. It says on the contrary, "It came to pass that a whole year they assembled themselves *with* the church and taught much people. "Thus on coming in to the locality from without they in no way intruded, nor did they take over the group but as "with them" they fed them. There were two things resulting from this God-inspired ministry. One was that the believers became so identified with the likeness and Name of Jesus Christ that they were called Christians. Note they did not call themselves Christians. Nowhere in Scripture does a believer call himself a Christian. It is always a name which the unbelievers gave to the believers. Perhaps it would be well if we left it like that today. It is not, what I say I am, that counts but what I evidently am. Some of us may say we are Christians and call that testimony. In many cases it would be better if we kept our mouth shut. The Antiochan believers were different. They did not so much say what they were, but they were so obviously Christ's that they called them "Christ's ones". The other outcome of the ministry was that the Church was taught to listen to the voice of the Spirit speaking in the assembly. They were not sermon-tasters or address-criticisers. They were taught to listen to the voice of God and to discern a word from the Lord. Inasmuch as they were gathered unto Him, then naturally they looked for Him to speak. Thus when Agabus stands up at the close of the year's ministry, his Spirit-inspired utterance is immediately recognised, and far from Antioch coming under the sway of Jerusalem, the position, if anything, is just the opposite. The saints at Antioch in the bonds of mutual fellowship, send relief to their brothers and sisters at the capital. Such are God's ways in the expansion of the Church. All is seen in these early stages as spontaneous, alive and fresh from the hand of God.

But have we no appetite to move again with the Spirit? Is there not a man amongst us who will confess that Jesus Christ is Lord? Is there not a company who will own Him as Head? We answer, "Of course there is!" But too often, like Peter, when the vision comes we start to say, "Not so, Lord." Our church life and our personal thought lie wrapped in the tiny napkin of our traditions. Yet look! A mighty sheet knit at the four corners is coming down from heaven to earth. What does it say? It tells us the purposes of God are always bigger than we know.

CHAPTER XXVI

SINEWS OF FELLOWSHIP

"Our bones are scattered at the grave's mouth, as when one cutteth
and cleaveth wood upon the earth."   Psalm 141
"I will lay sinews upon you and will bring up flesh upon you and cover
you with skin, and put breath in you, and ye shall live; and ye shall
know that I am the Lord . . . And . . . lo . . . the sinews came."
                                                      Ezekiel 37
"All the body by joints and bands . . . knit together . . ." Colossians 2

(Suggested reading: Acts, 13-15; I Corinthians 12; II Corinthians 8)

THE long lumbering caravan of mules and yak, some two hundred of
them, straggled higgledy-piggledy back down the hillside into the grassy
ravine. Up near the top of the pass, the first animals, lurching wearily
under their heavy loads, were picking their way doggedly through the
broken rock towards the sky-line. Suddenly the silhouette of the first
beast broke into the blue and we knew that we were over. A few more
minutes and we peered into a big broad valley, down the centre of which,
meandered the silver thread of a mountain stream. The valley was almost
deserted and a sense of great loneliness came surging back from the
distant hills. Slowly we descended to the valley floor, which although
almost fourteen thousand feet above sea level was carpeted with the soft
green of the summer grasses. As we traversed the dusty trail, worn into
ruts by the pack animals of forgotten years, we could see it stretching
on before us like a ragged scar cut diagonally across the bare shoulder of the
treeless heights. In the great between, and scattered all along our way, were
innumerable bones, picked clean by the vultures and bleached snow-white
in the sun. In the keen atmosphere of so high an altitude they could have
lain a century. Whose bones might they be? Hapless sheep caught by the
lone night wolf or perhaps some mule or yak unable for the next stage,
left to die. Could these be bones of men; the silent witness of an old
nomadic feud, fought to the death under the frosty star-filled sky? For

us these questions must remain unanswered. They keep their mystery, locked up for ever in the timeless wastes beyond the Er Lan Shan* . . .

As young Ezekiel trod the sandy trails of Mesopotamia into exile, there is little doubt that the straggling line of prisoners would frequently file through such a bone-strewn valley. With haunting memories of Central Asia still fresh in my mind, and far away feelings and emotions still rising as I think of such great places in the earth, my heart goes out to the sons of Israel as they stumbled in despair, on towards Babylon. Some would sense that they could never reach to journey's end. They would glance uneasily at the vultures circling high; and the silence and loneliness of the burning horizon would be nearer to them than the sound of their shuffling feet. A few more dust-filled days and then, maybe, their bones would strew the trail, and who would gather them? Can it be that as the long sad years of exile slipped away, and memories of Jerusalem begot in the heart of the prophet, a burning passion for the re-birth of his nation, that the Spirit took up the indelible impression of the wilderness way and showed to him how God could make even dead bones live, to declare His praise. There is something very real and very moving about Ezekiel's words when he writes: "The hand of the Lord was upon me, and carried me out in the Spirit of the Lord, and set me down in the midst of the valley which was full of bones and caused me to pass by them . . ." As he speaks of that open valley he says of the bones, "they were very dry . . ." This is not imagination. There is pathos here. It harks back to reality.

Then God makes an amazing announcement. He identifies the bones with Ezekiel's kith and kin and says of Israel, "I will lay sinews upon you . . . I will put breath in you . . . ye shall live." So bone came to bone and knit together, flesh and form appeared and life was given, until they stood upon their feet an exceeding great army. There are two historical fulfilments of this prophecy. One at the close of the seventy years captivity and the other at the close of the coming "Great Tribulation" when Israel re-born and reconstituted as a nation will enter, at the return of Christ in glory, into the millennial Kingdom. Between these two great historical fulfilments there is also what might be called a spiritual fulfilment pertaining to the Spiritual Israel of this age—the Church of God. After the embalming of our Lord's body and its confining to the tomb, Israel, and the remnant who trusted Him, were indeed as bones scattered at the

* The watershed between the plains of West China and the Tibetan plateau.

grave's mouth. The devil as the roaring lion had devoured, the flock had been cruelly dispersed and the casualties were as dead men's bones. But then, rising from the dead, Jesus Christ our Lord began to lay sinews upon them, as we have seen. He taught them of the Kingdom and of their mutual relationships as bowed to a single Authority. He taught them to engage in prayer together, to share with one another, to care for one another and thus are they found at the day of Pentecost. Then the life of the Spirit is breathed into them and their form appears. They are incorporated and stand up together an exceeding great army. First the twelve stand together, then three thousand, then a further five thousand and they rise impregnable before the adversary and all his hosts.

This spiritual fulfilment is attested also in the Epistles, especially in Ephesians. In Chapter two, verse one, we are as dead bones, dead in trespasses and sins. Then we are quickened with Christ. In Chapter four and verse four we are seen as a body, constituted a living organism through the one Spirit. In chapter four, verse sixteen, we see the co-ordination of the whole, so that we can say in verse thirty of chapter five, "we are members of His Body, of His flesh, and of His bones". Then in chapter six, we stand in this unity as an exceeding great army challenging the might of principalities and powers in all their dark array.

How can it be then, that Christendom presents a picture of isolation and dislocation and leads us back to the grave's mouth, a scattered and a life-less people? When Saul of Tarsus was converted, there and then he received his first lesson concerning the constitution of the Church. The question that His Lord asked was, "Why persecutest thou Me?" In touch-ing the members, he had touched the Head. When later he was given his special revelation about the Church his heart was open to the great truth of the Body, for it was already woven into his experience. Can it be that we have failed to exercise the sinews of our fellowship? Do we not creak as we meet and dismally submit to arthritical conditions and spiritual atrophy.

The sinews of fellowship in the unfolding story of the Acts of the Apostles are strikingly in evidence. A glance at some of them may spur to action and set our languid limbs walking and working once again in Jesus' Name; for what we need today is not a better blue-print of Church anatomy, nor a post-mortem on the dead corpse of Christendom, but a Scriptural key that will unlock to us the secret of spiritual vitality inherent in the Spirit-filled Body of Christ.

The Sinews of Fellowship and the Ministry of the Members

Let us make just one more visit to our friends at Antioch. What do we see as regards the spiritual ministry? There is no minister in office, only members in function. Not a single minister *over* the Church, but various members *in* the Church exercising their gifts. "Now there were," it says, "*in* the Church at Antioch certain prophets and teachers." There was no one claiming prominence, but all were giving Christ the pre-eminence, for it says "they ministered *unto the Lord*". It was not a performance before men but a service unto God. They were free to "prophesy one by one, that all might learn and all be comforted". Not that there was anarchy in ministry but having gifts differing according to the grace given to each they were called to exercise them under the sovereignty of their unseen, yet ever present Head. Thus they were to wait upon their ministry and in honour prefer one another, the spirits of the prophets being subject to the prophets, for God is not the author of confusion but of peace. In the variety of gifts and their exercise is thus evidenced one operating Spirit. In the distinctive services rendered it is clear that one Lord is the object, and in the diverse operations and activity of the Church, it is seen that the same God inspires and energises all. Here the sinews of fellowship have full play, and as a result the whole Church never ceases to be on the move. It is of interest to note the plurality of leading men. Their position is not so much official in character; they are where they are, in the forefront of God's people, because of spiritual growth and capacity. They are emerging, by reason of the constant use of their gifts, to a maturity in the handling of holy things. Then too it is worthy of mention that these prophets and teachers are all men. This is not just fortuitous, nor does it mean that women are not gifted, but both men and women can only serve effectively in the Body of Christ if they keep their appointed place in the order of God, for God has set woman under the leadership of man, and appointed a place to every member in the Body as it hath *pleased* Him. The gifts of all must ever be exercised in that recognition. One other point is that amongst these brethren there was a great diversity not only of gift but of background. Socially, racially and educationally there were great differences. There were black and white, Jew and Gentile, the high and the low, but all were united together in the bands of the Body; in a fellowship of mutual giving and receiving, of caring and sharing, that all might grow up together into Christ.

Now in the course of this ministry and growth, divinely originated expansion took place. This was not the outcome of fleshly religious enthusiasm or the impulse of a zealous few, but something altogether born of the Spirit. The discipline of their service affected both mind and body, for it involved fasting and waiting, as well as speaking and working—they obviously had times when the whole Church was in exercise before God for the revelation of His mind. Their ministry was not cluttered or restricted by a hard and fast weekly routine of stereotyped meetings. They were before God to attend to the voice of the Spirit. Then it was that God moved, declared His choice, and announced a separation to a specific and ordained work. In this the Church was counted on, to rise to its responsibility and give the right hand of fellowship to two of its members in their obedience to the will of God. Their response was expressed in four actions. They renewed their fasting. There was no carnal elation centring on the fact that two missionaries were going forth from *their* church; there was no feasting to give the missionaries a send off—but a prostration of spirit in fasting, that having come to know the mind of the Spirit they might continue in the Spirit's course. Secondly, they prayed. Here was a mighty sinew, and it would bind these two sent ones, to the saints at Antioch, from the outset of the venture until its end. It would reach to Heaven and, through the Saviour there, extend across the seas to Cyprus and over the hills and valleys of Asia Minor. It would touch them in their weakness and perplexity, and when Paul, battered and bruised, lay left for dead, this sinew in the power of the Spirit would lift him as a fellow-member to go on to the finish, when he could not raise himself. Down all the years of his long ministry, through all his letters, especially those written in prison, this sinew, active and powerful, binds him to the saints, and the saints to himself, through Jesus Christ their Lord. Now their prayer is one of committal to God, not of ordination on behalf of God; and they know that the supply of strength for service flows from the same source as salvation—even from the grace of God. In this alone was their mutual trust as they bade them Godspeed. Thirdly, they laid hands on them thus testifying that there was no independent action on the part of the Church or the departing servants of the Lord. They were identified with each other under the leadership of Christ. The Harvest was His and so were the servants, and the Church at Antioch by the laying on of hands identified themselves with Barnabas and Saul, as workers together with Him, by whose authority they had been both called and sent. Finally, they let them go. That is the correct rendering of the words "they sent them away". It means that Antioch could never say, "*We* sent you. You are *our* missionaries, you must do what *we* say." They are not in this sense at the beck and call of the Church. They are sent forth by the Holy Ghost. This is important, also, for the servant to realise, because he then looks not to the church he leaves, but to the Lord who has said, "I will never leave you nor forsake you"—"Lo, I am with you always even unto the end of the age". So with sinews of fellowship binding them all together, though by distance they be sundered far, Barnabas and Saul depart for Seleucia.

As we follow their journey into Cyprus, and later up into Asia Minor, and on to Perga, Antioch-by-Pisidia, Iconium, Lystra, Derbe and back again through these same towns to the church at Antioch, we are conscious of an unseen control upon these men. The atmosphere of the Church from which they set forth is with them all the way. Their work is now not in the local church but beyond it. It is a different operation, but the self-same Spirit is operating still. At each stage of the journey it is the Spirit of God and the Word of God that are always dominant. They are not men working on their own initiative or at their own charges. They are bond-slaves of the Lord that bought them. Men were to take account of them as 'ministers of Christ (the word is "*huperetes*"—"under-rowers") and stewards of the mysteries of God'.* They were not the strategists or programmers of the work, but men, appointed as straightforward serving people† ("*diakonos*") according to the gift of the grace of God. To the man who was less than the least of all saints was this grace given to preach among the Getiles the unsearchable riches of Christ. Only in this recognition could they be used to make all men see what was the fellowship of the mystery which from the beginning of the world had been hid in God. The exercise of apostolic authority was only possible when the apostles continued under the authority of their Lord and Head, and in fellowship with the Spirit who formed the Body and dwelt in every member. As Paul and Barnabas planted the seed of the Word and it was watered with prayer and care, there was a reproduction of saints and

* I Cor. 4, v. 1.   † Eph. 3, v. 7.

churches after the kind of saints and church which they knew at Antioch. In city after city the planting continues, and when in a little while Paul and Barnabas retraced their way through these same centres, they recognised these churches in formation as the Lord's planting and as God s husbandry. Though the apostles had preached, they represented not the achievement of the apostles but the increase of God. Creation, generation and reproduction, all these life processes are His from above. Guided by the Spirit, they strengthened these young believers in a richness of fellow-ship, God, as it were, laying sinews upon them. These sinews were of the same kind that held and strengthened the apostles in their going forth, for we read, "And when they had ordained them elders in every church, and had prayed with fasting, they commended them to the Lord, on whom they had believed." The sinews of fellowship never restrict the work of God. They only facilitate it. They did not attach these young believers and churches to themselves, saying "You are our converts and our sheep." Nor did they settle down in any centre to become a kind of resident pastor or officially recognised minister. Their aim was to teach faithful men who would be able to teach others also. They did not insist, either, on binding these young churches with artificial links to Antioch. They did not saddle them with an alien name such as the Antiochan Mission Church in Lystra. These people in Asia Minor had been given the Word of God. They had been born anew by the Spirit of God; and given an entrance into the Kingdom of God. In Him alone was their salvation, and to Him alone their witness. He was sufficient; and to Him they com-mended them. Thus on returning to the church at Antioch, from whence they had been commended to the grace of God, their whole report was of what *God* had wrought. Gathering the church together, they rehearsed all that their God had done and how *He* had opened the door of faith unto the Gentiles. The glory was ascribed not to the apostles, or to a "mission-ary-minded" Antioch assembly, but to God alone. This was the fellow-ship of the Church functioning in ministry. The essential work had all been done in the unseen realm of the Spirit. The secret of their invincible strength and astounding progress was ever in their links with the Man at God's right hand. Theirs was single-heartedness, individually and cor-porately, towards the Lord Jesus Christ. He was central to all their vision and all their action. As in His personal life on earth, so now in His spiritual body, the Church, all praise and honour were coming home to

God. No wonder the whole Body was full of light. The members were not concerned with making a vain show in the flesh, or boasting in another man's line of things. They did not vaunt a magnificent concern for the heathen or glory in a string of mission stations across the pagan Roman world. On the contrary, they pursued a course of meek submission to the will of God and thus the work of God became effectual. This became more and more evident in later missionary journeys. They were not allowed to speak where they liked, however clamant the need. They were bond-slaves and were obliged to do what their Master told them through His Spirit. Their task was to so minister the Gospel in the appointments of God, that the Gentiles, sanctified by the Holy Ghost, might become an offering acceptable to God. They were so to preach, to warn and to teach, that they might be able to present every man perfect in Christ Jesus. Thus they laboured not in fleshly zeal or in a sentimental passion for the lost, but according to *His* constraining love and power, which worked within them mightily. Thus the labours of these early missionaries issued in something for God and not in reputation for themselves or for "their group." All their activity was characterised by a savour of Christ. They and the local church of their association, moved as workers together with God, and as they so moved, they became together, and in their distinctive ministries, vessels of His praise and sharers of His joy.

The Sinews of Fellowship and the Control of the Members

At first sight as we read these things we may feel that whilst this was all very wonderful, yet surely there had to come a point where the work developed to such an extent that some kind of discipline was necessary, both in the local churches and in the activities of spreading the Gospel in the regions beyond them. That this was so was undoubtedly the case, but it was not to be the occasion of human improvisation but rather of realising the Divine provision for such a contingency. Just as in the human body certain organs come into action as a person matures, so in the Body of Christ the full function of each member, the joints and the bones, only becomes apparent in growth and development. The tragedy is that so often we do not give God time to reveal His own ways of control in the Body but quickly introduce conditions and aids of one kind and another, and sometimes even religious straight-jackets and supporting ecclesiastical trusses, all of which are foreign to the Body and only incapacitate it in its normal functions. The True Body of Christ is always in perfect health. It is incapable of corruption, That is imperative for faith to see. We only have to take away the armour of Saul, and those after God's own heart, like David, will have a chance to operate. It is then the giants begin to fall. What the Body needs is not more paraphernalia, but the chance to sling, in faith, one pebble at the command of God.

As news of the Spirit's work at Antioch and in Asia Minor began to filter back to the believers in Jerusalem, and it was realised that Gentiles were flooding into the fellowship of the Church, many became uneasy. It was clear that this new wine was no longer being contained in the old skins of Judaism but was calling for new skins and actually finding them in unimagined places. At this the prejudices of not a few in Judea and Jerusalem intensified and the old skins began to tighten. Eventually representatives of these conservative and traditional elements came down from Judea to Antioch and began to play havoc in the Church, insisting on the re-introduction of circumcision as a factor needful for salvation. What was to be done? Arbitrarily throw the intruders out of the Church? Take unilateral action and excommunicate them as far as the Church in Antioch was concerned? This would only rupture the sinews of fellowship existing between the saints there, and the saints at Jerusalem. The account, in Acts fifteen, of the gathering at Jerusalem convened to decide upon the tremendous issues involved, is recorded, that down all the history of the Church, we might see how God can control His people if they will but recognise the Head who is over them, and the bonds that bind them. Where matters affecting the very basis of salvation were involved the leaders in Antioch were convinced from the start that such questions must be squarely faced. They therefore decided in fellowship, that Paul and Barnabas should go to Jerusalem to confer with the brethren there, thus preventing schism in the Body. Paul and Barnabas did not embark in any self-willed defence of their position, to have it out with the brethren at the capital. The context shows very clearly that their going was a carefully considered exercise of the believers with whom they were associated in Antioch. Furthermore, certain others were to accompany them, so that right from the beginning all was done from Antioch's side in a spirit of fellowship and godly caution. All along the way to Jerusalem, Paul and Barnabas had wholehearted fellowship with God's people. In places like Phenice and Samaria, they proclaimed the works that the Lord had wrought amongst the Gentiles, and left, as a result, a trail of joy behind them amongst all their brethren. This clearly declares that Paul and Barnabas were moving in the Spirit. They had no bitterness or self-assertiveness in their approach, but recognised their indissoluble links with all believers wherever they came. On arrival, they were received by the Church in an openness of spirit, and we note that far from immediately starting on a doctrinal discussion, they simply told them all that *God* had done with them. It was not what *we* at Antioch believed, or the way *we* at Antioch had expanded, or the kind of outreach that *we* at Antioch had achieved. These men were genuinely God-centred, not Church-centred, and all they had to say testified of the power and grace of God.

At this juncture, the record tells us, "there rose up certain of the sect of the Pharisees which believed, saying, that it was needful to circumcise Gentile believers, and to command them to keep the law of Moses." Now the clash seemed certain. It is important to see that once a sectarian and opposition spirit was manifest, the whole matter was withdrawn from the public Church gathering. It is a mistaken notion to think that all matters of doctrine and practice are to be discussed by the Church as a whole. Beyond a certain point it is essentially the task of the spiritual leadership. There are certain things which babes in Christ cannot receive as yet. There are certain things which ought not to be named amongst the saints. There are elements in a Church which are carnal, and unable to discuss certain issues inherent in a doctrinal exposition or a complex situation, without showing recrimination and bitterness. Failure to recognise this has led to many a company casting its babes to the devil's lions instead of nurturing them in Christ. There is a spiritual care and restraint, which in its exercise is not a lording it over God's heritage, but a true concern for the saints. Unconditional business meetings and "free for all" Bible readings were not a basic feature of the New Testament churches. The care and guidance of spiritual men was essential in all circumstances. Meetings were open, of course, for the exercise of gift, but only unto edification. There is a scriptural warrant for a divinely appointed leadership to silence elements that do not comply with the order of God. This is laid down for us in I Corinthians, fourteen and Titus, one, "God is not the author of confusion, but of peace, as in all churches of the saints." We can never view the church as a democratic institution. It is a living organism, theocratically controlled.

What did the apostles, elders, and the visitors from Antioch do in their private session together? The Authorised Version says "there was much disputing" but this word "disputing" has a content here which is rather different from what we might imagine. It means "joint-seeking". They searched together for the solution of God. The sinews of fellowship were holding firm. The final word of the three leading figures is now set before us. It is a threefold cord and is not easily broken. Each pointed to God, and no other, as the Originator of this inexplicable flow of blessing to the Gentiles through the preaching of the Gospel. None of them expressed a private viewpoint or ground their private axe. Each said, "It is God." Peter speaks from the personal standpoint and gives the *witness of experience*. He says, "It was God who made choice among us. It was God who decreed that by my mouth the Gentiles should hear the word of the Gospel. It was God who bare them witness and gave them the Holy Ghost, even as He did to us." Inherent in these remarks is the thought that it was not Peter himself who undertook this unexpected departure from tradition— but that in spite of himself and in spite of his prejudices—God did it. This was his experience in the matter and now he can only bear witness to the fact and declare, "We believe that through the grace of the Lord Jesus Christ we shall be saved, even as they." To go against that is not a question of opinion, he says, it is to tempt God. Then follows Paul. He gives the *witness of the work*. The interest deepens. They keep silent we are told. They give audience. The hand of God is upon them and as they listen, the wonders and miracles of God's work amongst the Gentiles unfold before them. God has done it and who can refute it? Now the victory is almost won. The gainsayers are silent and James begins to speak. He gives us the *witness of the Word*. There has been a personal testimony and there has been an account of the work. These in themselves might be dismissed by some as too subjective, and too limited to the personal thoughts, feelings and judgements of the persons themselves, to be really valid. Now James brings them all to the Word and shows that all that has been said is in accordance with the Word of God. He answers, Yes it is of God, for God says, through His inspired word given to Simeon, that He will take out a people from the Gentiles for His Name. He says again, quoting from the prophet Amos, that Christ is going to build a dwelling for himself; that He is going to set it up that the residue of men might seek the Lord and all the Gentiles upon whom His Name is called.

This is the word of the Lord, James reminds them, and it is *He* who does all these things. It is *God* who knows all His works from the beginning, "wherefore my sentence is, that we trouble not them, which from among the Gentiles are turned to *God*". There is probably no other portion of Scripture where we can see more clearly how the sinews of fellowship operate in counsel and leadership. All is traced back to the Source and Centre, God Himself. All is related to His purpose and to His Name. The fullest scope of the whole problem is considered—drawing on Peter itinerating in Palestine, Barnabas and Paul operating in Asia Minor and James serving in Jerusalem. The witness of personal experience, the witness of the work at large, and the final authoritative witness of the Word all combine to bring full conviction that this thing is of God. Here is spiritual control by a spiritual leadership. No wonder we now read that it pleased the apostles and elders and the *whole* Church to send chosen men of their company to Antioch, with Paul and Barnabas. As assembled with one accord, they could say, "It seemed good to the Holy Ghost *and* to us." Hence by these means a decision was reached which was in accordance with God's mind and commended itself to every man's conscience.

What a victory for the Spirit! Such then are the principles and perspectives of control. They can be applied in the local church as overseers emerge, and in the work beyond it, especially where workers move in groups or as a team, such as Paul and his company frequently did. It prevents oligarchy—that is independent rule by the official few. It prevents anarchy—that is independent action by individuals, without reference to constituted authority. Personal leading of the Spirit is fully recognised and yet the wisdom of the truly spiritual is marshalled in irresistible strength and commends itself to the spiritual and moral judgement of all present. Here are the safeguards against both tyranny and lawlessness. Here the younger submits to the elder, yet all submit one to another. Here recognition of those who have the rule of the flock of God is encouraged and adventurism on the part of novices restrained. If we examine the writings and activities of the men who took part in this great "joint-seeking" we shall see that Peter, Paul and James, though not infallible as men, nevertheless lived out what they preached. They wielded authority but were obedient to Supreme Authority. They gave commands, and yet they did not lord it over their brethren. They were servants of all men for Jesus' sake. Here is something then very practical, something born of God and altogether sustained by Him. There is no hierarchy—no ecclesiastical parade of power—simply, healthy sinews of fellowship, binding together members of a Body, in which each holds to the Head and has a function to fulfil.

The Sinews of Fellowship and the Care of the Members

One of the earliest insights into the character of the Creator reveals Him to us as the God of care. He comes forth from setting the stars in their courses, to set His plants in the soil. He wanted grass and fruit trees and a garden; an oasis in the chaos that would proclaim His care; and when all is set it almost seems as if the All-sufficient God is at a loss. The record runs, "There was no man to till the ground." He lacked a creature with a heart of care. Then He made him and touched him with the touch of God to understand, to love, to serve. Then He lost him and the thistles grew. A little while and human blood seeped through the cursèd earth. Was that the sting of Cain's transgression, or was it this, that Cain would dare to say, "Am I my brother's keeper?" That on the earth, God's highest creature had now a heart that did not care? Of all the men that lived between the first Adam and the last, only one was spoken of as being after God's own heart. Is it coincidence that the phrase "the sure mercies of David" became a byword? David, the man who cared; the man who would slay a lion or kill a bear for the safety of a lamb. The man who would bring food to his mistrustful brothers or play a tune for a melancholic king. David who could love a Jonathan and beget a friendship that long centuries have not eclipsed; and when all the hardships were forgotten and the battles won, remember lame Mephibosheth, and lift him, dead dog though he was, to the table of the king. Here is the touch of God upon a man. Then comes great David's greater Son. In ages past He shone between the Cherubims but always with a shepherd heart. He comes the Word made flesh, glorious yet gracious, the God of Holiness and yet the God of tenderness. He is the God who cares. In all His ministry He has regard to man in all his need. He brings His healing grace alike to spirit, soul and body. No detail misses Him. He weeps for our sins, He groans for our sadness, He feels the leper's anguish, the beggar's sores, a woman's tears. He it is who bears our griefs and carries our sorrows; and in all our affliction He is afflicted. It is this same Jesus who is Head of the Church today. This same Jesus who pleads at God's right hand. This

same Jesus who shall return again. Meanwhile He has given us His Spirit
to be in us. His love is poured out into our hearts by the Holy Ghost. If
ever our fellowship with Him and with His members is to be known or
shown, then love must be the way.

They told me in the prison that Communists care; that the hungry in
the earth are their concern and the downtrodden, their special burden;
that they are the champions of the exploited classes. I looked at the men
beside me in the cells, each with his heartbreak; most of them ordinary
men whose wives and children knew not where they were. They were
enemies of the people, I was told, like myself, betrayers of the good of all
humanity, reactionaries retarding history, worthy of death but still spared
by the People's Government. Now we must learn to hate. We must covet
the class-consciousness of the workers. Our past was iniquitous, now we
must turn to Marxism and seek a new life and a new China, but nothing
could be built until class-consciousness was awakened and the spirit of
hatred burned so fiercely that every shred of feudalism and imperialism
would be swept away. We were bewildered. "You must tell nothing
outside the prison if you are released," the regulations read. "You must
tell nothing in the prison that you saw outside," they ordered us. "It is
your duty to report on your fellow prisoners," they insisted. These were
the lessons; hatred, secrecy and mutual spying. Such were the hallmarks
of their "new man". I was a Christian, what could I say? "Love your
enemies," Jesus had taught, "bless them that curse you, do good to them
that hate you, and pray for them which despitefully use you and persecute
you; that ye may be the children of your Father which is in Heaven."
When I spoke of my Lord they took me out and did their best to silence
me. They would not have Him to reign over them. At the mention of
His name, blasphemy all but shattered the cell. Meanwhile, outside, the
songs of the revolution gave way to tears, the hopes of the peasants were
drowned in blood, the freedom of the masses was forgotten in the
tyranny of forced labour. Families were torn asunder—the firing squads
took their toll—famine gradually stalked the land and at last the communes
crushed the people in a vice-like grip in the name of progress. But un-
perturbed, Mao Tse Tung still takes the salute upon the Gate of Heavenly
Peace. Do they care? They say they care, but I have no reason to believe
so. Where hatred reigns the heart is turned to stone.

In a world of violence, cruelty, slavery and superstition the Church was born. Into that dark mist of iniquity overshadowing the murky waters of humanity came the Spirit—He was God's dove on the face of the deep and brought forth life out of the chaos. So as the apostolic ministry developed, all over the Roman empire there sprang into being communities of men and women filled with a burning love for God and their fellows. This was unbelievable. It was something never known on earth before. These communities stood out in stark contrast to everything around them; the distinctive, vital feature always being, they loved one another. It was a complete mystery how people, who were of such different stations in life and of such varied background, and even from different nations, could entertain such genuine affection toward each other and indeed show the kindness and tenderness of God towards all men as they did. The love of Christ became suspect as a social disease disrupting pagan society, rebuking its barbarity and self-seeking. It was branded as an alien formenting force. Christians with their new loyalties and new habits were viewed as enemies of the people, and a menace to humanity. Perhaps there is not so much difference after all, in the spirit behind the pagan imperialism of Rome and that behind the pagan Communism of China. Would that our testimony today might be the same as the Church's then!

Let us take just one illustration of how the sinews of fellowship operated in the care of the members in those pracarious and barbarous times. We take for granted today the idea of a welfare state where the strong are compelled to share the burdens of the weak, and the healthy share the expenses of the sick, but in the days of the early Church this was unheard of. Yet under the constraint of the Spirit the believers pioneered in that world of total disregard for suffering, a mutual care of one another and of all men, that all history has not been able to forget.

It first began in the church at Antioch with the prophecy of Agabus. Taught to listen to the voice of the Spirit, this revelation of impending famine in the south called forth an immediate response. In Acts we read that every man according to his ability determined to send relief unto the brethren which dwelt in Judaea, which also they did and sent it . . . This was the first famine relief the world ever knew. It was the Spirit of the God of care who put it in their hearts. If we think phrase by phrase through this statement of what they did we see how deep and thorough it was. They acted individually and responsibly—they gave proportionately and deliberately; and finally they did it effectively. This was the beginning of a great movement of mutual care. As Paul moves through Asia and Europe we get a wonderful sight of the Body of Christ in action and of the sinews of fellowship operating to the care of the members that comprised it.

This first gesture of fellowship was not wasted on the believers in Jerusalem. Perhaps it played its part in smoothing the way during the great joint-seeking of Acts fifteen, for at the close of the session James, Cephas and John who had given to Paul and Barnabas the right hand of fellowship asked them still that they might remember the poor. "This," says Paul, "we were forward to do".*

During his missionary journeys Paul strengthened the links between the saints by telling of others' need and fostering mutual concern between the churches. By the time he comes to his third journey the need is so great that the emphasis becomes inseparable from his message. As he goes through Galatia and Phrygia strengthening the disciples, he tells them of the bitter conditions existing in Jerusalem. The church there was being starved almost out of existence, and the churches of Galatia are confronted with their inescapable responsibility. When he comes to Ephesus he finds time to write to the church at Corinth. He says, "I have told the believers in Galatia to gather gifts for the saints at Jerusalem—now will you do the same? Do not wait till I come but each Lord's Day, lay something aside as God has prospered you, and then when I come, we can arrange for someone to go with me, if possible, to Jerusalem for its safe delivery." In this way the sinews were stengthened. Imagine Paul's delight when he got news back saying that they were going right ahead on the project. Love of the unseen Lord had kindled a love for their unseen brothers and sisters suffering privation in Judaea. This was surely the work of God. Eventually Paul moves on to Troas, and being much concerned that Titus did not meet him as anticipated, presses on into Macedonia. There he opens up his heart to the believers, probably in Philippi, where the saints were much given to communicating with the Lord's servants. He tells them the whole story and says how those in Achaia (chiefly Corinth) have been deeply moved to make a contribution to meet the needs of hungry believers in Jerusalem. As they listen the Spirit works powerfully in the hearts of these Macedonians. The churches of Galatia are giving, the churches of Achaia are giving, then what about themselves? A great love sweeps

* Gal. 12, v. 10.

through them and the whole occasion results in their fresh dedication to the Lord. The pangs of hunger soon become their own. Other members are suffering, and as they think about it they sense their need in their own bodies and yearn for them in their hearts. They have but little themselves but out of their deep poverty their liberality abounds. Shortly afterwards Titus arrives from the south. Paul looks expectantly for news, wondering how the gifts are coming together in Corinth, but he is dumbfounded with disappointment. A whole year has passed. From what he understood they were already on the move then, but to his astonishment Titus tells him that nothing has been forthcoming. Taking up his quill, Paul pens what is our second letter to the Corinthians. "Let me tell you about the churches here in Macedonia," he says. "I told them about your readiness to contribute to the relief of the poor saints at Jerusalem and when they heard it they were quite affected. They were so moved that they gave themselves afresh to the Lord, and then, although poor, made a gift which really I feel was more than they could afford. But now what has happened to you? A whole year has gone by since you talked about giving for this work. Whatever you do, do fulfil your word. Just imagine what it will be if, when I come to you, some of the brethren from here accompany me. What will I look like, when after boasting about your generosity, they find that you have in actual fact contributed nothing at all. I shall look so small, but that is the least of it; what do you think you will look like? See that the gift is ready then. Do not give grudgingly. God loves a cheerful giver. This service of yours will not only help the saints but it will result in thanksgiving to God and stimulate to prayer on your behalf." This is the vein in which he writes to the Corinthians. He softens the rebukes by assuring them of his faith in their intentions. Twice he expresses his confidence in them and ends by saying, that may be after all, it was superfluous to write at all. Thus he appeals to them, and once again we see the sinews of fellowship growing and strengthening between the people of God. In the energy of the Spirit the Christians of Antioch, Galatia, Macedonia and Achaia rise in a common exercise of care to minister to those on the verge of starvation in Jerusalem. Paul himself has gone to all lengths. The churches have given. The sinews hold. Later when writing to the Romans, he can report to them, that "it hath pleased them of Macedonia and Achaia to make a certain contribution to the poor saints which are at Jerusalem". Not only was the task fulfilled but it was counted a pleasure. This was not merely devotion to duty, but devotion to the Lord flowing out in unstinted love to others. If we follow Paul to Jerusalem we see with what zeal and determination he pursues his responsibility of ministering to the saints. If need be, he will seal this gift in his own blood; and in the face of bonds and imprisonment he is able at length to testify within the city walls of the old capital that "now after many years I come bringing alms to my nation". The sum of money must have been considerable even by human standards, but who could measure its worth to God? Here was the life of the Church outpoured in loving sacrifice, the precious evidence of those unseen sinews binding the people of God together across the then known world. This is something of which Communism is wholly ignorant. This is a perspective born out of the love of God, a love which answers to man's need in every age.

When we think of the Spirit's onward march in those early decades, is there anything more we have to say?

CHAPTER XXVII

RED SKY AT DAWN

"It will be foul weather today for the sky is red and lowring."
"Hold fast till I come . . . he that overcometh and keepeth my words to
the end to him will I give power over the nations. And I will give him
the Morning Star."

"AN hour or two through odd copses and once more over the river, this
time by an old timber cantilever bridge, brought us to real nomad
country. One could see the black low tents dotting the undulating grassy
folds and, on the expanse of pasture, herds of sheep and yak roaming afar.
It was well on in the afternoon, and we decided to spend the night with
the nomads. We were given a fierce but warm welcome as the dogs leapt
at us from their stakes and the woolly-haired nomad folk, in their rough
sheepskin gowns, came running out to lead our horses into a suitable
tethering place. We walked into one of the tents where the camp people
had arranged for us to pass the night. Once settled in, we spread out our
bedding on our saddle rugs around the fire, took our fill of some tsamba
and buttered tea, and then chatted away into the twilight. The nomads
were still pottering around for quite a while, but at last we were left in
the silence. I hardly seemed to have been dozing more than a few minutes
when I awoke to see the woman of the tent blowing the fire with some
goatskin bellows. I looked out through the slit above my head. It was still
pitch dark. It must have been something like three o'clock in the morning.
About half-past four we all began to move. There was an exacting day
ahead. John Ting, a Chinese believer and fellow-worker had arranged with
the horsemen to reach Batang by nightfall, which would mean at least
thirteen hours' riding, including the crossing of a 15,000-foot pass. By the
time we had arisen and got some hot tea inside us, it was the dawn. Peering
out through the door of the tent I could see the planet Venus, scintillating
in the pale blue of the morning sky, one dominating point of light above

the steely ridges. In the tent John was folding his bedding and humming the familiar hymn.

> 'He's the lily of the valley, the bright and
> Morning Star.
> He's the fairest of ten thousand to my
> soul.'

It somehow gave a ring to the day."*

Had our eyes that morning scanned a lower horizon we would have glimpsed a dull red glow arising in the eastern sky, an augur of the violent tempest of the red revolution about to break across the roof of the world—but God had filled our eyes with the Morning Star. Thus we broke camp and climbed upward into the dawn and as we reached the summit there was light on the mountain and the far horizons of a distant land where for the most part no human foot had trod . . .

Yet today the valley of the shadow is with us still and all above the sky is red. Not long and the cruel red horse of war will stride forth amongst the nations and the great sword take all peace from off the earth. Soon shall the world reel in convulsions, the sun be darkened and a blood-red moon usurp the heavens. A little while and even the seas will be tinged with carnage for to blood, it says, one-third shall surely change. Then shall the scarlet woman stained with her sins, all red like crimson, ride on the beast and reach forward to her doom. Meanwhile the world and they that dwell therein fill up the goblet of their pleasure with its red, red wine. Seductively it yields its colour in the cup and moves itself aright, but they forget, that at the last, it biteth like a serpent. Red pottage glut's man's vision as hungry from the hunt of life he lifts his petty bowl of present things and lets his birthright go. The sky is red, yet to the Christian, high above the portents of the storm, there shines the Morning Star of God, the promise of the Coming of His Lord.

Give us a bride's heart then, dear Lord, that whether alone, or met together, we might know Thou art enough for our poor souls; and in the triumph of the fellowship to which thy blood has bought us, say with the Spirit—even so Lord Jesus, Come!

* See *When Iron Gates Yield.*